Advance Praise for
A Short Guide to College Writing

"This has to be about the best written book on college writing I have read in years. It has all the essentials one requires in a book, written in a clear and inviting style. I particularly liked the chapters that dealt with analysis, argumentation and research papers."

"I like the selection of materials and examples the best—the authors have used materials from a variety of sources and disciplines, and they are refreshingly free of the trite and overused materials most books use."

Rachana Sachdev
Susquehanna University

"The writing samples are excellent in that they show how a writer moves from the messiness of first drafts to the polished finished draft. Few guides do this well."

"I would tell colleagues that this *Short Guide* is one of the best I have read.... I think it's important to approach writing as a matter of making good choices and this guide does that particularly well."

Chere L. Peguesse
Valdosta State University

"The text is rich with examples selected from a range of disciplines and interests and representing both student and professional writers. The discussion represents the best of what is known about current theories on composition, presented in clear language, and illustrated with the experiences of both student and professional writers."

"This text, though 'short,' is thorough in its discussion of the writing process and of how writers read their writing from an audiences' perspective, an ingredient I'm seeing for the first time here. Prior discussions of this topic have been brief and unsatisfying. I find the chapters on clarity and conciseness helpful; every student will find something to refer to here to aid revision."

Bruce Closser
Andrews University

"It is refreshing to find a rhetoric so clearly targeted to the right level of our students.... Too often rhetorics, in aiming for relevance, aim too low. The hypothetical assignments here are plausible and are nicely expanded as subsequent examples return to them."

Amy Pawl
Washington University

"I am pleased to find a rhetoric that does not dictate particular assignments or order of work. This should make this book more valuable to students in all situations across the country. The quality of thought and writing is good and certainly sincere."

Mary Sauer
Indiana University and Purdue University

"Its sound advice, helpful handbook, and economical size make it possible for students to have a ready reference text adaptable to the pursuit of almost any subject matter without a lot of extra material...."

Von Underwood
Cameron University

Sylvan Barnet was born in Brooklyn, New York, and educated at Erasmus Hall High School, New York University (BA), and Harvard University (MA, PhD). For a while he was a semi-professional magician, but when he found that he could fool all of the people all of the time the work became boring, and so he became a college professor. He taught Composition and English Literature at Tufts University, for thirty years, published scholarly articles on Shakespeare, and is the author and co-author of several books about the art of writing.

Pat Bellanca was born in East Hanover, N.J.; she holds degrees in English from Wellesley College (BA) and Rutgers University (MA, PhD). She teaches in the Expository Writing Program at Harvard College and is Director of Writing Programs at the Harvard Extension School, the university's open-enrollment evening division. Her research interests include Composition Studies and Gothic Fiction, fields that are not unrelated.

Marcia Stubbs was born in Newark, N.J., where she was drum majorette of Weequahic High School's band, and she was educated at Stanford University and the University of Michigan. She has taught at Tufts University, Harvard University, and Wellesley College, where she has directed the Writing Program. In addition to annotations on students' compositions, she has written poems and verse translations, and is the co-author of several books on writing.

A Short Guide
to College Writing

A Short Guide to College Writing

Sylvan Barnet
Tufts University

Pat Bellanca
Harvard University

Marcia Stubbs
Wellesley College

PENGUIN ACADEMICS

Longman

New York   San Francisco   Boston
London   Toronto   Sydney   Tokyo   Singapore   Madrid
Mexico City   Munich   Paris   Cape Town   Hong Kong   Montreal

Senior Vice President/Publisher: Joseph Opiela
Acquisitions Editor: Lynn M. Huddon
Executive Marketing Manager: Carlise Paulson
Production Manager: Denise Phillip
Project Coordination, Text Design, and Electronic Page Makeup:
    Electronic Publishing Services Inc., NYC
Cover Designer/Manager: Nancy Danahy
Cover Illustration/Photo: © PhotoDisc, Inc.
Photo Researcher: Julie Tesser
Manufacturing Buyer: Al Dorsey
Printer and Binder: R.R. Donnelley & Sons Company, Harrisonburg
Cover Printer: Phoenix Color

For permission to use copyrighted material, grateful acknowledgment is made to the copyright holders on p. 370, which are hereby made part of this copyright page.

Library of Congress Cataloging-in-Publication Data

Barnet, Sylvan.
  A short guide to college writing / Sylvan Barnet, Pat Bellanca,
Marcia Stubbs.— 1st ed.
      p. cm.
Includes index.
  ISBN 0-321-09101-9
  1. English language—Rhetoric. 2. Report writing. I.
Bellanca, Pat. II. Stubbs, Marcia. III. Title.
  PE1408 .B4315 2002
  808'.042—dc21

2001050429

Please visit our website at http://www.ablongman.com

ISBN 0-321-09101-9

1 2 3 4 5 6 7 8 9 10—DOH—04 03 02 01

Contents

PART THREE   A WRITER'S HANDBOOK   243

Preface

A Short Guide to College Writing offers students practical advice on writing successful college essays from the beginning of the process to the end. The student, having received a writing assignment, can turn to this book for advice about choosing a topic, developing a thesis, writing an analysis, constructing a paragraph, documenting a source, using a semicolon. The instructor can suggest chapters or passages the student should consult in generating ideas, revising a draft, editing a revision, or preparing a final copy.

We emphasize analysis, argument, and research because skill in these matters is central to college writing—whether the student is writing a short essay for a required first-year composition class, or a longer essay for an art history course, or a term paper for a cultural studies seminar. When students write essays, most of what they write sets forth a thesis and its support, which is to say that their writing advances a point of view, explains ideas, and lets the readers see how the writers arrived at them.

Because they want to be believed, writers must present their ideas and evidence persuasively, and cite and document their sources accurately. *A Short Guide to College Writing* offers practical and accessible advice on all these matters. The book will be useful not only to students in first-year composition courses, but also to students in writing-intensive and Writing Across the Curriculum courses—courses that focus on a particular academic topic. We therefore omit writing assignments and extended readings. When there is too much, the saying goes, something is missing. This book, we hope, offers just enough.

Acknowledgments

We thank the following reviewers for their suggestions: Alan Baragona, Virginia Military Institute; Bruce Closser, Andrews University; Gloria Gitlin, Baylor University; J. Paul Johnson, Winona State University; Mary

M. Juzwik, University of Wisconsin-Madison; Joan Livingston-Weber, Western Illinois University; Craig N. Owens, Indiana University; Amy Pawl, Washington University; Chere L. Peguesse, Valdosta State University; Rachana Sachdev, Susquehanna University; Mary Sauer, Indiana University Purdue University Indianapolis; and Von Underwood, Cameron University.

We are deeply grateful to Frances FitzGerald for giving us permission to reprint portions of her notes and manuscript for *Fire in the Lake*. We also thank Dr. Howard Gotleib, Director of Special Collections at Boston University's Mugar Library, and Sean D. Noël, Public Service and Fiscal Administrator at Special Collections, for their generosity in making those materials available to us.

At Longman, our editor, Lynn Huddon, watched over the project with exemplary care and patiently guided us through the several revisions of the manuscript. At Electronic Publishing Services Inc., Alan Kaplan, our production editor, turned the manuscript into a book: It was a pleasure to work with him. We also thank Diane Kraut and Julie Tesser for securing text and photo permissions respectively; and Nancy Danahy for her work on the cover design.

Finally, we thank the following friends and colleagues for their advice and support: Marilyn Brown, Peter Buck, Patricia A. Cahill, Nora Cameron, Jody Clineff, Michael Curley, Nancy Sommers, Kerry Walk, and Wini Wood.

Sylvan Barnet

Marcia Stubbs

Pat Bellanca

PART ONE

THE WRITING PROCESS

The Balloon of the Mind
Hands, do what you're bid:
Bring the balloon of the mind
That bellies and drags in the wind
Into its narrow shed.

— *William Butler Yeats*

CHAPTER ONE

DEVELOPING IDEAS

> All there is to writing is having ideas. To learn to
> write is to learn to have ideas.
>
> —*Robert Frost*

Starting

How to Write: Writing as a Physical Act

"One takes a piece of paper," William Carlos Williams wrote, "anything, the flat of a shingle, slate, cardboard and with anything handy to the purpose begins to put down the words after the desired expression in mind." Good advice, from a writer who produced novels, plays, articles, book reviews, an autobiography, a voluminous correspondence, and more than twenty-five books of poetry, while raising a family, enjoying a wide circle of friends, and practicing medicine in Rutherford, New Jersey. Not the last word on writing (we have approximately 30,000 of our own to add), but where we would like to begin: "One takes a piece of paper . . . and . . . begins to put down the words. . . ."

Some Ideas About Ideas: Strategies for Invention

When asked to write an essay for a college course, students often have one of two complaints: "I have nothing to say," or "I have the ideas but

I don't know how to express them." When we face a blank page, words and ideas may elude us. We must actively seek them out. Since classical times the term "invention," from the Latin *invenere* ("to come upon," or "to find"), has been used to describe the active search for ideas. Invention includes such activities as asking and answering questions, listing, clustering, and freewriting. In the following pages we'll briefly describe several invention strategies. All of these strategies have one step in common: starting to write by writing.

Asking Questions and Answering Them

One of the first things journalists learn to do in getting a story is to ask six questions:

- who?
- what?
- when?
- where?
- why?
- how?

The questions that journalists ask are appropriate to their task: to report who did what to whom, and so on. Learning to write academic essays is largely learning to ask—and to answer—questions appropriate to academic disciplines.

Asking questions can be a useful strategy early in the writing process, especially for students who feel they don't have much to say about the material they've been asked to write about. That material, most often, will be a text of some kind: a written text (perhaps a treaty, or a judicial opinion, or a speech, or a poem), or some other object of interpretation (a film, painting, music video, even food on a plate). The first step in developing ideas about a text is to look closely at it. Asking questions and answering them is one way to focus your attention; it's also a way to begin finding things to say. Unexpected answers often emerge as soon as we raise a question.

In analyzing a visual text, for example, an art history student might ask and answer certain basic questions:

- When, where, and by whom was the work made?

- Where would the work originally have been seen? (Almost certainly *not* in a museum.)
- What purpose did the work serve?
- In what condition has the work survived?
- For whom was the work made?
- From what materials was it made?

Then, depending on the work, the student might pose more detailed questions. If, say, the work is a photograph (for example, Dorothea Lange's *Migrant Mother*, reprinted below), the following questions might be appropriate:

- What is the focus of the composition?
- What is the apparent distance between the viewer and the subjects?
- What is the mother's facial expression?
- How are the figures arranged?
- What's surprising or strange about the image?
- How might the subject have felt about being photographed?

Dorothea Lange, *Migrant Mother, Nipomo, California,* 1936. Gelatin-silver print. © Corbis.

A student in a sociology seminar writing a review of research on a topic would ask other kinds of questions about each study under review:

- What major question is posed in this study?
- What is its chief method of investigation?
- What mode of observation was employed, and is the mode limited in some way?
- How is the sample of observations defined, and is the sample representative?

A student in a literature class writing an analysis or exposition of a poem (for example, the Yeats poem reprinted on page 1) would ask yet other kinds of questions:

- What is the poem about?
- What does the balloon represent?
- What is the speaker's tone?
- What does his tone reveal about his attitude toward the poem's subject?
- What makes this attitude complicated, tricky to pin down?

Students in all disciplines—art history, social science, and literature are given here only as examples—learn what questions matter by listening to lectures, participating in class discussions, and reading assigned books and articles. The questions differ from discipline to discipline, but the process—of asking and answering the questions that matter—is common to all of them.

Listing   Like asking questions and answering them, **listing** is a way to generate ideas; it can also help you pin down ideas that seem formless or vague. Listing is an especially useful strategy when you are making a comparison—of two figures in a photograph, for example, or two characters in a story, or two positions on an issue. Start writing by listing the similarities, and then list the differences. Or, start writing both lists at once, making brief entries, as they occur to you, in parallel columns.

Listing can help you generate and develop ideas; it can also help you to find a topic to write about. Suppose, for example, you have been assigned to write an essay on a form of popular culture that interests you. You can begin simply by listing some of the first forms of popular culture that occur to you as you think about the subject:

```
Popular Culture
movies, sci-fi, sci-fi movies?
TV movies, detective serials
soap operas (why are they called operas?
  Why soap operas?)
music videos
cop shows--NYPD Blue, Homicide
male/female detectives
the blues
```

But having written "the blues" above, you begin to think of the words to a song:

> When a woman takes the blues
> She tucks her head and cries
> But when a man catches the blues
> He catches a freight and rides

By the time you have written these lyrics out from memory, you have pretty much decided that you'll write on the blues. You're interested in the blues and already know something about them; you have some CDs and tapes at hand; and an idea for an essay is beginning to form:

"He catches a freight and rides . . ."

Why all this talk of traveling? (It's worth remembering that an unanswered question is an essay topic in disguise.) You begin to search your memory, perhaps you play some tapes, maybe take some notes. The blues are full of travel, you find, but of different kinds. You begin, once again, to make a list, to jot down words or phrases:

```
disappointed lover        back to the South
travel to a job           life is a trip
from the South            jail
fantasy travel
```

Your new list provides more than a topic; you are now several steps closer to a draft of an essay that you think you may be able to write, on the meaning of travel in the blues.

Clustering   **Clustering,** though it takes a different visual form, is similar to listing. Sometimes ideas don't seem to line up vertically, one after another. Instead, they seem to form a cluster, with one idea or word related to a group of several others. It may be useful then to start by putting a key word or phrase (let's stay with TRAVEL IN THE BLUES) in a circle in the center of a page, and then jotting down other words as they occur, encircling them and connecting them appropriately. A map or cluster might look like the diagram shown here.

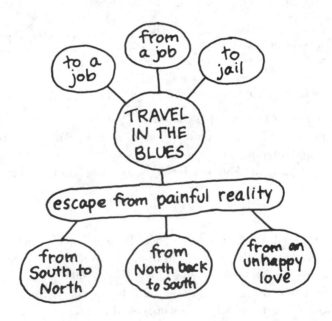

If you start writing by putting down words that occur to you in a schematic way—in a map or cluster—it may help you to visualize the relationship between ideas. The visualization may also prompt still other ideas and the connections between them.

Freewriting   One reason students have trouble getting words down on paper is that they mistakenly believe they must draft, revise, and edit their work simultaneously. In fact, however, these processes are separate, and the attempt to do them all at once can be paralyzing. **Freewriting** can help students who feel that they have ideas, but don't know how to get them on paper, because the strategy enables them to forget the rules for a while and just start writing.

To try freewriting, all you need to do is put your hands on the keyboard or pick up a pen and *start writing*. Forget about crafting the perfect introductory paragraph; don't worry about grammar or spelling or punctuation. If you can't think of the right word, write something close to it, or leave a blank space and move on. If you find yourself going in a direction you hadn't anticipated, keep writing anyway. Maybe there's something worth thinking about down the road—you won't know until you get there. If, for example, you're writing about why you disagree with one argument in the passage, a point on which you agree with the author may occur to you. Fine. Write it down now, while you're thinking of it. You can organize your points of agreement and disagreement later. Even if what you're thinking is something along the lines of "I hate this poem" (or photograph or whatever), put the thought down on paper and keep going. Why do you hate the poem? Is it confusing? Why? Does it appear to say two different things? What are they? Even an apparently unpromising line of thought can produce ideas. But if you reach what appears to be a dead end, simply move on, or start again someplace else. You are writing to discover what you think, and it's a good idea to work as quickly as you can. (Take Satchel Paige's advice: Don't look back; something might be gaining on you.)

Focusing

What to Write About: Subject, Topic, Thesis

So far, we've discussed several strategies for discovering and generating ideas. But to write a successful college essay, it's not enough simply to choose a **subject** and to have ideas about it; the next step is to begin to give those ideas some focus. To do so, you must narrow your area of interest to a **topic** within the subject, a process you may already have begun as you followed one or more of the above invention strategies. And you must state your idea about that topic in the form of a **thesis,** an argument, a *point.*

Finding a Topic   Any assignment requires you to narrow the subject so that you can treat it thoroughly in the allotted space and time. Therefore you write not on political primaries (a subject), but on a specific proposal to abolish them (a topic); not on penguins (a subject), but on the male penguin's role in hatching (a topic). A good general rule in finding a topic is to follow your inclinations: Focus on something about the subject that interests you.

Suppose that for a religion course, your assignment is to read the Book of Ruth in the Hebrew Bible and to write an essay of 500 to 1000 words on it. If you start with a topic like "The Book of Ruth: A Charming Tale," you're in trouble. The topic is much too vague. In writing about it you'll find yourself hopping around from one place in the book to another, and in desperation saying things like "The Book of Ruth is probably one of the most charming tales in all literature," when you haven't read all literature, and couldn't define *charm* precisely, if your life depended on it.

What to do? Focus on something that interested you, or surprised you, or confused you about the book. (If you read the book with pencil in hand, taking some notes, underlining some passages, putting question marks at others, you'll have some good clues to start with.) The book is named after Ruth, but perhaps you find Naomi the more interesting character. If so, you might jot down: "Although the Book of Ruth is named after Ruth, I find the character of Naomi more interesting."

Stuck again? Ask yourself some questions. *Why* do you find her more interesting? To answer that question, reread the book, focusing your attention on all the passages in which Naomi acts or speaks or is spoken of by others. Ruth's actions, you may find, are always clearly motivated by her love for Naomi. But Naomi's actions are more complex, more puzzling. If you're puzzled, trust your feeling—*there is something puzzling there*. *What* motivated Naomi? Convert your question to "Naomi's Motivation" and you have a *topic*.

"Naomi's Motivation" is a topic in literary criticism, but if your special interest is, for example, economics, or sociology, or law, your topic might be one of these:

Economic Motivation in the Book of Ruth

Attitudes toward Intermarriage in the Book of Ruth

The Status of Women in the Book of Ruth

Any one of these topics might be managed in 500 to 1000 words. But remember, you were assigned to write on the Book of Ruth. Suppress the impulse to put everything you know about economics or intermarriage or the-status-of-women-through-the-ages in between two thin slices, an opening sentence and a concluding sentence, on the Book of Ruth.

Let's take another example. Suppose that in a course on Modern Revolutionary Movements you're assigned a research essay on any subject covered by the readings or lectures. You're interested in Mexican history, and after a preliminary search you decide to focus on the Revolution of 1910 or some events leading up to it. Depending on what is available in your library, you might narrow your topic to one of these:

Mexican Bandits—The First Twentieth-Century Revolutionists

The Exploits of Joaquin Murieta and Tiburcio Vasquez—Romantic Legend and Fact

In short, it is not enough to have a subject (the Book of Ruth, revolutions); you must concentrate your vision on a topic, a significant part of the field, just as a landscape painter or photographer selects a portion of the landscape and then focuses on it. Your interests are your most trustworthy guides to the portion of the landscape on which to focus.

Developing a Thesis   As you think about your topic and information relating to it, try to formulate a **tentative thesis.** This *tentative* thesis is a working hypothesis, a proposition to be proved, disproved, or revised in light of information you discover. It ought to be *a statement about which intelligent people might disagree.* Readers won't bother to finish reading an essay if its thesis is an obvious truth; there's no particular reason to argue a point that everyone would agree on.

Your "working thesis," which usually can be stated in a sentence or two, will help you to maintain your focus, to keep in mind the points that you must support with evidence: quotations, facts, statistics, reasons, descriptions, and illustrative anecdotes. But be prepared to modify your working thesis, perhaps more than once, and perhaps substantially. Your first draft might, for example, contain this tentative thesis:

```
Naomi's character is more interesting than Ruth's
because her behavior is more complicated.
```

That tentative thesis might be revised at a later stage:

```
Although Naomi's actions suggest her concern for her
daughter-in-law, they also reveal self-interest.
```

Note that both the working thesis and the revised thesis are *arguable*. One can imagine a reader *dis*agreeing with either statement. "No," such a reader might say, "Ruth's behavior is *not* more complicated than Naomi's." Or: "I disagree—Naomi *is* concerned about her daughter-in-law; she's not self-interested at all." (Presumably this reader will see things differently by the end of the finished essay, if the evidence the writer has presented is convincing, if the arguments are persuasive.)

Once you begin amassing evidence to support your arguments, you may find to your surprise that the evidence supports a different thesis. Your best ideas on your topic may turn out to be radically different from the ideas with which you began. As we pointed out earlier, writing is not simply a way to express ideas you already have, it is also a way to discover new ones.

Although essays based on substantial analysis or research almost always include an explicit thesis sentence in the finished essay, short essays based on personal experience often do not. An essay recounting a writer's experience of racism, for example, or conveying the particular atmosphere of a neighborhood, is likely to have a central idea or focus, a **thesis idea,** rather than a **thesis sentence.** But whether stated or implied, the thesis idea must be developed (explained, supported, or proved) by evidence presented in the body of the essay. The kind of evidence will vary, of course, not only with your topic but also with your audience and purpose.

Developing Ideas

What constitutes evidence, and where does it come from? Writers explain, support, and develop their ideas with material derived from the reading, thinking, note-taking, questioning, and remembering that are part of the writing process from beginning to end. Materials for developing an essay on Naomi's motivation will be passages from the Book of Ruth, quotations that the writer introduces and explains. Similarly, materials for an essay on the blues will be quotations from a thoughtful selection of lyrics. Materials for developing an essay on Dorothea Lange's photograph will include a detailed description of the figures, a discussion of their relation to each other, and perhaps some information about the photographer herself. In all of these instances, in fact, imagining a reader helps a writer develop ideas.

Thinking About Audience and Purpose

Thinking about your audience, about what you want your readers to understand and believe, is central to the revision process, which we discuss in Chapter 2. But thinking about audience and purpose can be helpful at earlier stages of writing too, when you are trying to develop an idea and to work up evidence to support it. If you are uncertain how to begin, or if, on the other hand, you are overwhelmed by the materials you have unearthed and don't know how to sort them out, try asking yourself these questions:

- Who are my readers?
- What do they need to know?
- What do I want them to believe?
- Why should they care about what I have to say?

When you ask, "Who is my reader?" the obvious answer—the teacher who assigned the essay—is, paradoxically, the least helpful. To learn to write well, you'll have to force that fact out of your mind, pretend it isn't true, or you're likely to feel defeated from the beginning. Write instead for someone who understands your material less well than you. Remember: *When you write, you are the teacher.* It's probably easier to assume the role of the teacher if you imagine your reader to be someone in your class, that is, someone intelligent and reasonably well informed who shares some of your interests but who does not happen to be you, and who therefore doesn't see the material in precisely the way you do. That reader can't know your thoughts unless you organize them and explain them clearly and thoroughly.

Writing academic essays usually requires examining and evaluating texts and other evidence beyond your personal experience or previous knowledge. Nevertheless, you still must trust your own ideas. Trusting your own ideas does not, of course, mean being satisfied with the first thought that pops into your head. Rather, it means respecting your ideas enough to examine them thoughtfully; it means testing, refining, and sometimes changing them. But it is always your reading of a text, your conduct of an experiment, your understanding of an issue that your essay attempts to communicate. If it does so, your reader will care— because you've brought new ideas, new insights, to the topic at hand.

Writing the Draft

If you have used one or more of the invention strategies we discuss above, and if you've begun to develop a focus on a topic within your larger subject, you should at this point have some sense of what your essay will be about. Now is the time to start writing the draft. How to begin?

1. Sit down and start writing. If you have the ideas but don't know how to express them, start writing anyway. Resist the temptation to check your e-mail, to make a cup of soup, to call your mother. Now is *not* the time to do your laundry or to make your bed. Sit down and start putting one word after another.

2. Start with something easy. Start anywhere. Start with what comes to mind first. For example, you might start by summarizing the passage you're responding to or by sketching any one of your ideas about it. *Don't think you must start with an introductory paragraph;* you can write an introduction later, once your ideas have become better defined. It doesn't matter where you begin, only that you do begin. Start anywhere, and keep going.

3. Try freewriting. Just write. Pick up your pen, or put your hands on the keyboard, think about the material you've chosen to write about, and write what you're thinking. Don't worry about spelling or punctuation or grammar; don't censor yourself. No one but you will see what you've written. Your goal here is simply to put words on paper; you can evaluate them later.

4. Plan to stop writing. Give yourself a time limit. If you tend to procrastinate, try keeping your first sessions short. Promise yourself that you'll stop working after, say, twenty minutes, and *keep that promise.* If at the start you limit your writing sessions, you accomplish two things. You reduce anxiety: The thought of working at your desk for twenty minutes is not nearly as daunting as the thought of writing four or five pages.

And after twenty minutes you'll have *something* down on paper. You can gradually increase the length of the sessions—to an hour, or three, or whatever is reasonable, given the assignment and your schedule.

5. Revise later. After a few false starts and probably more than one session, your ideas will begin to take form on the page. But at this early stage, don't expect them to appear in final form, beautifully organized and in polished sentences. Ideas rarely exist that way in one's mind. In fact, until we put them into words, ideas are usually only rough impressions or images, not clear thoughts at all. (As E. M. Forster wrote, "How do I know what I think until I see what I say?") Once you do get some ideas down on paper, you can begin to see which ones must be developed or deleted, where connections need to be made, where examples need to be added. At this stage, you may be close to having a first draft. Whether or not you like what you've written, take a rest from it. Do something else: Make your bed, or if you like, just climb into it.

CHAPTER TWO

DRAFTING AND REVISING

> I have never thought of myself as a good writer.
> Anyone who wants reassurance of that should
> read one of my first drafts. But I'm one of the
> world's great revisers.
>
> —*James Michener*

Reading Drafts

In Chapter 1, we focused on how to have ideas and how to get them down
on paper. We suggested that from the start of a project the writer is almost
simultaneously both inventing ideas and refining them. But we also
advised that, particularly at the start, it's best to suspend critical judgment until you have begun to capture your thoughts, however roughly
expressed, on paper. In this chapter, we will focus on ways to improve
and refine rough drafts. First, we want to make what may seem like an
obvious point: To improve the draft you have written, *you must first read
it.* Moreover, you must try to read it objectively and critically.

Imagining Your Audience and Asking Questions

To read your draft objectively, to make sure that you have said what
you intended to say, first put it aside for a day, or at least for a couple
of hours. Then read it through thoughtfully, as if you were not the writer,
but someone reading if for the first time. As you read, try to imagine

the questions such a reader might want or need to ask you to understand what you meant. Then, read your draft again, asking yourself the following questions:

1. Does the draft present an idea? Does it have a focus or make a unified point?

2. Is the idea or are the ideas clearly supported? Is there convincing evidence? Are there sufficient specific details?

3. Is the material effectively organized?

There are many other questions you might ask, and we'll suggest some before we're done. But let's start with these.

1. Does the draft present an idea? Does it have a focus or make a unified point? If, on reading your draft objectively, you find that it doesn't have an idea, a point to develop, then there's probably no reason to tinker with it. It may be best to start again, using the invention techniques we discussed earlier. (Rereading the assignment is probably a good idea too.)

Let's suppose, however, that you do find some interesting material in your draft but that you're not yet sure what it adds up to. The chances are that some extraneous material is getting in your way—some false starts, needless repetition, or interesting but irrelevant information. Some pruning is probably in order.

Picasso said that in painting a picture he advanced by a series of destructions. A story about a sculptor makes a similar point. When asked how he had made such a lifelike image of an elephant from a block of wood, the sculptor answered, "Well, I just knocked off everything that didn't look like elephant." Often, revising a draft begins with similar "destruction." Having identified the main point that you want to pursue, don't be afraid to hack away competing material until you can see that point clearly in its bold outline. Of course you must have a lot of stuff on paper to begin with (at the start, nothing succeeds like excess). But often you must remove some of it before you can see that you have in fact roughly formulated the main point you want to make, and even produced some evidence to support it.

2. Is the idea (or are the ideas) clearly supported? Is there convincing evidence? Are there sufficient specific details? Writers are always reluctant to delete. Students with an assignment to write 500 or 1000 words by a deadline are, understandably, among the most reluctant. But, almost certainly, once you have settled on the focus of your essay, you will be adding material as well as deleting it. It isn't enough simply to state a point; you must also prove or demonstrate it.

If you argue, for example, that smoking should be banned in all public places, including parks and outdoor cafes, you must offer reasons for your position and also meet possible objections with counterarguments; perhaps you will cite some statistics. If you are arguing that in Plato's *Apology* Socrates' definition of truth goes beyond mere correspondence to fact, you will need to summarize relevant passages of the *Apology* and introduce quotations illuminating Socrates' definition. Almost always a draft needs the addition of specific details and examples to support and clarify its generalizations.

3. Is the material effectively organized? As you prune away the irrelevancies and add the specific details and examples that will clarify and strengthen your point, as your draft begins more and more to "look like an elephant," ask yourself if the parts of your draft are arranged in the best order. If you have given two examples, or stated three reasons, with which one is it best to begin? Ask yourself if paragraphs are in a reasonable sequence. Will the relationship of one point to the next be clear to your reader? Does the evidence in each paragraph support point of that paragraph? (The same evidence may be more appropriate to a different paragraph.) Does your opening paragraph provide the reader with a focus? Or, if it performs some other important function, such as getting the reader's attention, does the essay provide the reader with a focus soon enough?

In general, in working on the organization of drafts, follow two rules:

- Put together what belongs together.

- Put yourself in the position of your reader; make it as easy as possible for the reader to follow you.

Peer Review: The Benefits of Having a Real Audience

Occasionally a writing assignment will specify the reader you should address. More often, your reader must be imagined. We usually suggest imagining someone in your class who has not thought about your topic or considered the specific evidence you intend to examine.

In many writing classes, students routinely break up into small groups to read and discuss each other's work. Peer review, as this practice is commonly called, is useful in several ways.

First, peer review gives the writer a real audience, readers who can point to what puzzles or pleases them, who ask questions and make suggestions, who may often disagree (with the writer or with each other), and who frequently, though not willfully, misread. Though writers don't necessarily like everything they hear, reading and discussing their work with others almost always gives them a fresh perspective on their work, and a fresh perspective may stimulate thoughtful revision. (Having your intentions misread, because your writing isn't clear enough, can be particularly stimulating.)

Moreover, when students write drafts that will be commented on, they are doing what professional writers do. Like journalists, scholars, engineers, lawyers—anyone whose work is ordinarily reviewed many times, by friends and spouses, by colleagues, and by editors, before the work is published—students who write drafts for peer review know they will have a chance to discuss their writing with their colleagues (other students) before submitting a final version for evaluation. Writers accustomed to writing for a real audience are able, to some extent, to internalize the demands of a real audience. Even as they work on early drafts, they are sensitive to what needs to be added, or deleted, or clarified. Students who discuss their work with other students derive similar benefits. They are likely to write and revise with more confidence, and more energy.

The writer whose work is being reviewed is not the sole beneficiary. When students regularly serve as readers for each other, they become better readers of their own work, and consequently better revisers. Learning to write is in large measure learning to read.

Peer review in the classroom takes many forms; we'll look in a moment at an example as we trace a student's essay that is revised largely as a result of peer review. But even if peer review is not part of your writing class, you may want to work with a friend or another student in the class, reading each other's drafts.

When you work on your essay with your classmates or your friends, good manners and academic practice require that you thank them for their help, that you **document** their contributions. You can offer a sentence or two of general thanks at the end of the essay—something like this:

> I'd like to thank the members of my peer revision
> group, Rebecca Sharp and Isabella Thorpe, for
> helping me to clarify the main idea of my essay
> and for suggesting ways to edit my sentences.

Or you can thank your peer reviewers for their specific contributions by inserting a footnote or endnote at the end of the sentence that contains an idea or words you wish to acknowledge, and then writing a sentence like this:

> Kevin Doughten drew my attention to the narrator's
> play on words here; I wish to thank him for
> helping me develop this point.

From Assignment to Essay: A Case History

On September 12, Suki Hudson was given the following assignment: Write an essay (roughly 500 words) defining racism or narrating an experience in which you were either the victim or the perpetrator of a racist incident. Your essay should offer a thesis supported by evidence from your experience. Bring a first draft with two copies to class on September 16 for peer review. Revised essay due September 26.

Suki kept no record of her first thoughts and jottings on the topic, but what follows is an early attempt to get something down on paper. Because it was far from the finished essay she would write, not yet even a first draft, we label it a Zero Draft:

Zero Draft. Sept. 13

It was a warm sunny day in the playground. My
three-year-old brother and other children were playing
gaily until one of the boys' mothers interrupted. She
called her son, whispered something, and when he went
back to the playground he excluded my brother from
playing together. I didn't know what to call the
incident, but my heart ached as I watched my little

```
brother enviously looked at the other kids. I
immediately left the playground with him, and the
playground has never been the same since that day.
```

At that point, having reached the end of the anecdote, Suki stopped. What she had written was not yet an essay, and it was far short of the suggested 500 words, but it was a start, which is all she had hoped to accomplish on this first try.

Later she read what she had written, and asked a friend to read it and see if he had any suggestions. It was a frustrating conversation. The friend didn't understand why Suki thought this was a "racist incident." Why did Suki leave the playground? Why hadn't she just asked the boy's mother for an explanation? The questions took her by surprise; she felt annoyed, then miserable. So she changed the subject.

But "the subject" didn't go away. Still later, she wrote the following account of the conversation in her journal:

```
Sept. 13:


    I asked J to read my paper and he thought I was
being paranoid. Why didn't I just ask the boy's
mother what was the matter? But I could not have
even thought of going up to the woman to question
her motives. It was beyond my control if she wanted
to be ignorant and cruel to a different race. (Or
was it really my ignorance to walk away from a
simple explanation?)
```

The following day, looking over what she had written, it occurred to her to try adding the journal entry to the anecdote. Maybe in a concluding paragraph she could explain why what happened in the playground was obviously a racist incident.

Here is the conclusion:

```
Sept. 14


    Most people in modern society don't recognize
the more subtle cases of racism. People feel if they
are not assaulting physically they are not violating
the law, and as long as they are living according to
```

```
the law, racism is not committed. However, the law or
the constitution does not protect the human heart
from getting hurt, and without a doubt the most
critical racist action could be committed by close
friends or their loved ones.
```

But having written that last line Suki was struck by something odd about it. The woman in the playground was not a loved one, nor was she a close friend. Still, it was true that racist acts can be committed by friends, and even if the acts are undramatic, they should be recognized as racist acts. At this point, she thought that she had a thesis for her essay, but she also realized that she had begun to recall a different experience. Starting again, she wrote the following account:

```
     In Korea, I had a very close friend whose father
was Chinese. Although her mother was a Korean woman,
they were treated as foreign people in town, and they
were singled out on many occasions. Her father died
when she was little but everyone in town knew she
was a half Chinese. Her mother ran a Chinese
restaurant, and they lived very quietly. My family
knew her mother well and I was close friends with
the girl and for many years I was the only friend
she ever had. However, as I entered junior high
school my new group of friends didn't approve of her
background, and I drifted away from her. She was a
very quiet, shy person and although I stopped calling
or visiting her, she always remembered me on holidays
to send presents. After graduating from junior high
school she went to Taiwan to live with her
grandparents, whom she had never met. I gathered she
could not stand the isolation any longer at her age.
Many years later I realized how cruel I had been to
her, and I tried to locate her without success.
```

The following day Suki combined the two drafts (hoping to come closer to the 500 words), added a new concluding paragraph, and (rather disgusted with the whole assignment) typed up her first draft to hand in the next day. She photocopied it, as instructed, for peer review in class.

As we said earlier, peer review in the classroom takes many forms. Ordinarily, the instructor distributes some questions to be answered by both the writer and the readers. Typically the writer is asked to speak first, explaining how far along he or she is in writing the essay, and what help readers might give. The writer might also be asked, "What are you most pleased with in your writing so far?"

Readers are then asked to respond. Instructions may vary, depending on the particular assignment, but the questions distributed in Suki's class, shown here, are fairly typical.

Questions for Peer Review   Writing 125R

Read each draft once, quickly. Then read it again, with the following questions in mind:

1. What is the essay's topic? Is it one of the assigned topics, or a variation from it? Does the draft show promise of fulfilling the assignment?
2. Looking at the essay as a whole, what thesis (main idea) is stated or implied? If stated, where is it stated? If implied, try to state it in your own words.
3. Looking at each paragraph separately:
   What is the basic point (the topic sentence or idea)? How does the paragraph relate to the essay's main idea or to the previous paragraph?
   Is each sentence clearly related to the previous sentence?
   Is the paragraph adequately developed? Are there sufficient specific details or examples?
   Is the transition from one paragraph to the next clear?
4. Look again at the introductory paragraph. Does it focus your attention on the main point of the essay? If not, does it effectively serve some other purpose? Does the opening sentence interest you in the essay? Do you want to keep reading?
5. Is the conclusion clear? Is the last sentence satisfying?
6. Does the essay have a title? Is it interesting? Informative?
7. What is the greatest strength of the essay? What is its main weakness?
8. What is the most important piece of advice you would offer on this essay?

First Draft What follows is first the draft Suki gave the two members of her group, and then a summary of the group's discussion. Before reading her draft aloud (the procedure the instructor recommended for this session), Suki explained how she had happened to narrate two experiences and asked which narrative she should keep, or if she could keep both.

First Draft

S. Hudson

Sept. 16

1   It was a warm sunny day in the playground. My three-year-old brother and other children were playing gaily until one of the boys' mothers interrupted. She called her son to whisper something and when he went back to the playground he excluded my brother from playing together. I didn't know what to call the incident, but my heart ached as I watched my little brother enviously looked at other kids. I immediately left the playground with him, and the playground has never been the same since that day.

2   A friend of mine said I was being paranoid. It would have been appropriate to ask the boy's mother what was the matter, or if she had anything to do with the kids excluding my brother from playing. But I could not have even thought of going up to the woman to question her motives. It was beyond my control if she wanted to be ignorant and cruel to a different race, or perhaps my ignorance to walk away from a simple explanation.

3   Most people in modern society recognize only the dramatic instances of racism, and on a daily basis people don't recognize the more subtle cases of racism. People feel if they are not assaulting physically they are not violating the law, and as long as they are living according to the law, the racism is not committed. However, the law or the constitution does not protect the human heart from getting hurt, and without a doubt the most critical

racist action could be committed by close friends or their loved ones.

4   In Korea, I had a very close friend whose father was Chinese. Although her mother was a Korean woman they were treated as foreign people in town, and they were singled out on many occasions. Her father died when she was little, but everyone in town knew she was a half Chinese. Her mother ran a Chinese restaurant, and they lived very quietly. My family knew her mother well and I was close friends with the girl and for many years I was the only friend she ever had. However, as I entered junior high school my new group of friends didn't approve of her background and I drifted away from her. She was a very quiet, shy person, and although I stopped calling or visiting her, she always remembered me on holidays to send presents. After graduating from junior high school she went to Taiwan to live with her grandparents whom she had never met. I gathered she could not stand the isolation any longer at her age. Many years later, I realized how cruel I have been to her, and I tried to locate her without success.

5   She was a victim in a homogeneous society, and had to experience the pain she did not deserve. It is part of human nature to resent the unknown, and sometimes people become racist to cover their fears or ignorance.

Summary of Peer Group Discussion

1. The group immediately understood why the friend (in the second paragraph) had difficulty understanding that the first incident was racist. It might well have been racist, but, they pointed out, Suki had said nothing about the racial mix at the playground. It does become clear by the fourth paragraph that the writer and her brother are Korean, but we don't get this information early enough, and we know nothing of the race of the woman who whispers to her son. Suki had neglected to say—because it was so perfectly obvious to her—that she and her brother were Korean; the mother, the other child, in fact all others in the playground, were white.

2. Suki's readers confirmed her uneasiness about the third paragraph. They found it confusing. (a) Suki had written "people don't recognize the more subtle cases of racism." Did she mean that the mother didn't recognize her action as racist, or that Suki didn't? (b) In the first paragraph Suki had written "I didn't know what to call the incident." But then the second paragraph is contradictory. There she seems to accuse the mother of being "cruel to a different race." (c) And the last sentence of the third paragraph, they agreed, in which Suki writes of racist acts "committed by close friends," did not tie in at all with the first part of the essay, although it did serve to introduce the second anecdote.

3. Her group was enthusiastic, though, about Suki's telling of the two stories and advised her to keep both. Both were accounts of more or less subtle acts of racism. One student thought that they should appear in chronological order: first the Korean story and then the more recent story, set in the playground. But both readers were sure that she could find some way to put them together.

4. They were less sure what the essay's thesis was, or whether it even had one. One student proposed:

> Subtle racist acts can be as destructive as dramatic instances (implied in paragraph 3).

The other proposed combining:

> It is part of human nature to resent the unknown

and

> . . . sometimes people become racist to cover their fears or ignorance (from the final paragraph).

All three members of Suki's group (Suki included) thought that the ideas in the essay were supported by the narratives. But the draft didn't yet hang together: Suki would have to work on the way the separate parts connected.

5. One member of the group then pointed out that the second paragraph could be deleted. The friend mentioned in it (who called Suki "paranoid") had been important to Suki's thinking about her first draft, but served no useful purpose in the draft they were looking at, and other details in that paragraph were murky.

6. On the other hand, the first paragraph probably needed additional details about the setting, the people involved, what each did. How does a three-year-old know he's been excluded from a play group? What happened? What did the other children do? What did he do? And, as the group had seen at once, some details were needed to establish the racist nature of the incident. They also reminded Suki that her essay needed a title.

7. Finally, some small details of grammar. Suki's English is excellent, although English is her second language. But the other two in her group, being native speakers of English, were able to catch the slightly odd diction in

> she always remembered me on holidays to send presents

and the error in

> my heart ached as I watched my little brother enviously looked at other kids.

Suki asked if the past tense was right in

> I realized how cruel I have been to her

and the others supplied:

> I realized how cruel I had been to her

(though they could not explain the difference).

Final Version   Several days later Suki consulted her notes and resumed work on her draft, and by September 25, the night before it was due, she was able to print the final version, which now included a title. (See page 28 for final version:)

Suki Hudson

Ms. Cahill

Writing 125R

September 20, 2001

Two Sides of a Story

1   It was a warm sunny day in the playground. My three-year-old brother and two other small boys were playing together in the sandbox. My brother was very happy, digging in the sand with a shovel one of the other boys had brought, when one of the mothers sitting on a bench across from me called to her son. She bent over and whispered something to him, and he went right over to my brother and pulled the shovel out of his hand. He pushed my brother aside and moved to the other side of the sandbox. The other boy followed him, and they continued to play. My heart ached as I watched my little brother enviously looking at the other kids. I didn't fully understand what had happened. I looked across at the mother, but she turned her head away. Then I picked up my brother and immediately left the playground with him.

2   I thought the woman was extremely rude and cruel, but I didn't think then that she was behaving in a racist way. We had only recently come here from

Korea, and although I had been told that there was much racism in America, I thought that meant that it was hard for some people, like blacks, to find jobs or go to good schools. In some places there were street gangs and violence. But I didn't understand that there could be subtle acts of racism too. I was aware, though, in the playground that my brother and I were the only Koreans, the only nonwhites. When the woman turned her face away from me it felt like a sharp slap, but I was ignorant about her motives. I only guessed that she told her child not to play with my brother, and I knew that the playground was never the same since that day.

3   That incident was several months ago. When I started to think about it again recently, I thought also of another time when I was ignorant of racism.

4   In Korea, I had a very close friend whose father was Chinese. Although her mother was a Korean woman they were treated as foreign people in town, and they were singled out on many occasions. Her father died when she was little, but everyone in town knew she was half Chinese. Her mother ran a Chinese restaurant, and they lived very quietly. My family knew her mother well and I was close friends with

the girl, and for many years I was the only friend
she ever had. However, as I entered junior high
school my new group of friends didn't approve of
her background and I drifted away from her. She was
a very quiet, shy person, and although I stopped
calling or visiting her, she always remembered to
send me presents on holidays. After graduating
from junior high school, she went to Taiwan to live
with her grandparents, whom she had never met. I
gathered she could not stand the isolation any
longer at her age. Many years later, I realized how
cruel I had been to her, and I tried to locate her
without success.

5   She was a victim in a homogeneous society, and
had to experience pain she did not deserve. There was
no law to protect her from that, just as there was
no law to protect my little brother. Perhaps the
woman in the playground did not realize how cruel she
was being. She probably didn't think of herself as a
racist, and maybe she acted the way I did in Korea,
without thinking why. It isn't only the dramatic acts
that are racist, and maybe it isn't only cruel people
who commit racist acts. It is part of human nature
to fear the unknown, and sometimes people become
racist to cover their fears, or ignorance.

Acknowledgments

I would like to thank Ann Weston and Tory Chang
for helping me to develop my main point, and to
organize and edit my essay.

Notes, Drafts, Revisions:
An Historian Revises Her Work

As we face the empty computer screen, we imagine that more experienced writers are efficiently filling up *their* computer screens with lucid sentences, organized paragraphs, brilliant ideas. Not so—or at least, not usually so. For most writers, most of the time, ideas emerge through the revision process; focus, organization, and clarity result from rereading and rewriting. Drafts written by experienced writers can be as messy and apparently unpromising as drafts written by the rest of us.

By way of illustration, we reprint here an excerpt from *Fire in the Lake: The Vietnamese and the Americans in Vietnam*, by the journalist and historian Frances FitzGerald. FitzGerald went to South Vietnam as a reporter in 1966, just a few years after she graduated from college; reports she wrote that year for the *New York Times*, the *Atlantic Monthly*, and other publications were the basis of *Fire in the Lake*, which was published in 1972. In this book, FitzGerald argues in part that cultural differences and racial biases doomed from the start the American mission, the goal of which was to prevent the spread of Communism by supporting South Vietnam in the war against Communist North Vietnam.

In the passage that follows, FitzGerald discusses some of the consequences of American policy in Vietnam, policy that required American officials to aid the Saigon government, which they knew to be corrupt. Following the excerpt, we reprint portions of FitzGerald's drafts of the beginning of the piece. The drafts are typewritten, of course, but because they are, it is possible to trace the writer's revision process, a process that can be obscured by the word processor's cut-and-paste function and delete key. Although the typescript looks very different from word-processed copy, it's worth noting that a writer using a pen or a computer would use FitzGerald's strategies. In the early stages of the draft process, you will see FitzGerald **asking questions and answering them,** and **listing** her ideas. Throughout the process, you will see her **revising her thesis** as she incorporates new ideas and evidence, and eliminates material that isn't relevant to her larger point.

At the end of the chapter, we reprint some advice FitzGerald received on an early version of *Fire in the Lake* from one of her editors.

Franceʃ FitzGeral∂
Prospero's Army[1]

1   The effort of trying to hold reality and the official version of reality together finally took its toll on the Americans in Vietnam. When added to all the other strains of war, it produced an almost intolerable tension that expressed itself not in a criticism of American policy so much as in a fierce resentment against the Vietnamese. The logic of that anger was a simple one, combined of guilt and illusions destroyed. The nature of those illusions was even less apparent to Americans than it had been to the French, but the illusions were nonetheless powerful. At the Senate Foreign Relations Committee hearings in 1965, General Maxwell Taylor, just returned from the ambassadorship in Saigon, said in describing the pacification program: "We have always been able to move in the areas where the security was good enough. But I have often said it is very hard to plant the corn outside the stockade when the Indians are still around. We have to get the Indians farther away in many of the provinces to make good progress." In Vietnam American officers liked to call the area outside GVN[2] control "Indian country." It was a joke, of course, no more than a figure of speech, but it put the Vietnam War into a definite historical and mythological perspective: the

---

[1]Editors' note. The title refers to two characters in Shakespeare's *The Tempest*; Prospero, a duke who was ousted from his dukedom, arrives at an island, where he enslaves Caliban, its only inhabitant other than Ariel, a spirit. Prospero regards Caliban (whose name is a corruption of *cannibal*) as a brute.
[2]Government of South Vietnam; the American-supported Saigon government.

Frances FitzGerald's Department of Defense ID card. From the Frances FitzGerald Collection, Department of Special Collections, Boston University.

Americans were once again embarked upon a heroic and (for them-selves) almost painless conquest of an inferior race. To the Ameri-can settlers the defeat of the Indians had seemed not just a nationalist victory, but an achievement made in the name of humanity—the triumph of light over darkness, of good over evil, and of civilization over brutish nature. Quite unconsciously, the American officers and officials used a similar language to describe their war against the NLF.[3] According to the official rhetoric, the Viet Cong did not live in places, they "infested areas"; to "clean them out" the American forces went on "sweep and clear" opera-tions or moved all the villagers into refugee camps in order to "san-itize the area." Westmoreland spoke of the NLF as "termites." The implications of this language rarely came to consciousness (some of the American field commanders actually admired the Front as a fighting force), but they were nonetheless there. The Americans were white men in Asia, and they could not conceive that they might fail in their enterprise, could not conceive that they could be morally wrong.

2   Beyond all the bureaucratic and strategic interests in the war, it was this "can do" attitude, this sense of righteous mission that had

[3]The National Liberation Front, a South Vietnamese guerrilla organization opposed to the Saigon government.

led the U.S. government deeper and deeper into Vietnam. Moral infallibility, military invincibility—the two went together and were not to be differentiated, not in Vietnam, in any case, where the enemy was not only Communist but small, yellow, and poor. The difficulty was that the "allies" of the United States belonged within almost the same category—the same category with the one term of Communism removed. The distinction—Communist, non-Communist—so obvious in theory, became an elusive one in practice when juxtaposed with the much greater contrast between Americans and Vietnamese.

3   In coming to Vietnam, most American advisers, for instance, expected their "counterparts" to render them their due as members of a more "advanced" society. The expectation was not, after all, unreasonable, since the U.S. government sent them out to advise the Vietnamese. But the advisers tended to see themselves in the roles of teacher and older brother, and when the Vietnamese did not respond to them in the expected manner—when they did not even take their advice—few succeeded in reconstructing the truth of the matter. Few saw that the Vietnamese were not the pupils of the Americans, but people with a very different view of the world and with interests that only occasionally coincided with their own. For those few who succeeded there were an equal number of others [...] who took an extreme parochial view, looking upon the Vietnamese as savages or children with empty heads into which they would pour instruction. Covered with righteous platitudes, theirs was an essentially colonialist vision, born out of the same insecurity and desire for domination that had motivated many of the French. When their "counterparts" did not take their instruction, these advisers treated the Vietnamese like bad pupils, accusing them of corruption or laziness, and attempted to impose authority over them. And when the attempt at coercion failed, they retreated from the Vietnamese entirely, barricading themselves in behind American weapons and American PX[4] goods, behind the assumption of American superiority and the assumption that the Vietnamese were not quite human like themselves.

4   "Don't you realize," exploded one young embassy officer, "don't you realize that everything the Americans do in Vietnam is founded on a hatred of the Vietnamese?" His outburst was shocking, for he,

[4]Post Exchange; located on a military base or installation, a store that serves military personnel.

of all Americans in Vietnam, had managed to preserve a sense of balance. He understood the point of view of the Vietnamese officials as well as the Americans, and because of his own success at reconciling the two, he had believed that the best in both would prevail. Two years earlier he had confidence that the two could find some common ground for cooperation against the NLF. But he, the diplomat *par excellence*, had seen his compatriots turn into spineless bureaucrats and frustrated proconsuls. And into murderers.

5   In 1969 an incident came to the attention of the U.S. Congress that had occurred a year and a half before in the wake of the Tet[5] offensive. On a routine search and destroy operation a company from the American Division had walked into the village of My Lai and without provocation had gunned down three hundred and forty-seven civilians, most of them women and children. A photographer had taken pictures of screaming women, dead babies, and a mass of bodies piled up in a ditch. Even once substantiated, the story seemed incredible to many people. How could American soldiers have committed such an atrocity? The congressional subcommittee investigating the incident wrote much later, "What obviously happened at My Lai was wrong. In fact it was so wrong and so foreign to the normal character and actions of our military forces as to immediately raise a question as to the legal sanity at the time of those men involved." But as teams of psychiatrists were later to show, Lieutenant William Calley and the other men involved were at the time quite as "sane" as the members of the congressional committee who investigated them. The incident was not exceptional to the American war.

6   Young men from the small towns of America, the GIs who came to Vietnam found themselves in a place halfway round the earth among people with whom they could make no human contact. Like an Orwellian army, they knew everything about military tactics, but nothing about where they were or who the enemy was. And they found themselves not attacking fixed positions but walking through the jungle or through villages among small yellow people, as strange and exposed among them as if they were Martians. Their buddies were killed by land mines, sniper fire, and mortar attacks, but the

---

[5]The Tet Offensive, named after the Vienamese Lunar New Year holiday, took place in January 1966; it was a large-scale offensive operation by the NLF during which thirty provincial capitals in the South were attacked.

enemy remained invisible, not only in the jungle but among the people of the villages—an almost metaphysical enemy who inflicted upon them heat, boredom, terror, and death, and gave them nothing to show for it—no territory taken, no visible sign of progress except the bodies of small yellow men. And they passed around stories: you couldn't trust anyone in this country, not the laundresses or the prostitutes or the boys of six years old. The enemy would not stand up and fight, but he had agents everywhere, among the villagers, even among the ARVN[6] officers. The Vietnamese soldiers were lazy and the officials corrupt—they were all out to get you one way or another. They were "gooks," after all. Just look how they lived in the shacks and the filth; they'd steal the watch off your arm.

7   And the stories of combat were embellished: about how the enemy attacked Alpha Company one night and hundreds of them were killed, but they kept on coming in "human waves," screaming like banshees. It didn't matter how many you killed because they were fanatics who didn't know the value of human life. In boot camp or in the barracks late at night, an experienced sergeant would tell about how the VC[7] killed women and children and tortured their prisoners, cutting off the ears of their victims, or their genitals. And how the ARVN soldiers did the same when their American advisers weren't around.

8   There was terror in these stories, but also a kind of release, since if the Vietnamese did not act like human beings, then they did not have to be treated as such. All the laws of civilization were suspended. "And when you shot someone you didn't think you were shooting at a human. They were a gook or a Commie and it was okay, 'cause, like, they [the American officers] would tell you they'd do it to you if they had the chance." The expressiveness of the soldiers' language made even more explicit the fact that these stories were largely fantasies—and fantasies of exactly the same sort that the Americans had created about the Indians and Prospero about Caliban. Like the French soldiers before them, GIs mentally stripped the Vietnamese of their humanity in order to deliver themselves of their own guilty desires. The war brought out their latent sadism, as perhaps all wars between races (and particularly guerrilla wars) have brought it out of all armies. The Americans were no different—that was the shock.

---

[6]Army of the Republic of South Vietnam; the American-supported South Vietnamese Army.
[7]Viet Cong; Communist guerrillas.

FitzGerald's Notes and Drafts

"Prospero's Army" is focused, lucid, persuasive. Each paragraph develops an aspect of the central idea of the passage and is carefully linked to the paragraphs that precede and follow it. The eight paragraphs are packed with information, with vivid quotations from the American officials, with careful analysis of the language those officials used to talk about the Vietnamese and of the stories American soldiers told about them.

Pre-draft Notes FitzGerald's early jottings and drafts look very different from the finished piece of writing. In her **pre-draft notes** [A]

[A] Pre-draft Notes

```
        Just report here
        Sense of superorority (show this rather than analyse --
    can include MaxwellTaylor) And like early settlers -- sense
    of moral superiority as well as technological. (Here the military
    briefer and Pike.)
            Above -- technological and money superiority that makes
    them completely insensitive to the requirements of the situation.
    Thus Kahn, Mang Thit, etc.
        They think what is wanted is better life -- not realizing that
    VC program is almost entirely political -- power to the people
    (not to sansl Americans and bourg middle-men)
    Wisfulfillment
        All the way from lowest prov rep to Johnson (look what
    Clifford says about reading the reports) The system is slanted
    that way, from the begin ing by "progress reports" -- by
    measurement of input rather than the whole situation. That is
    what Komer speaks of
    a. how it happens
    b. what are aims?
    c. What becomes of Americans in Vietnam so long exposed to the
    contraditiction betweeen aims (apparantly being reached) and
    reality.
            American policy as a projection of own values -- has nothing
    to do with the Vietnamese, but what they have been brought
    up believing about themselves. They cannot see the harshness
    of the political conflict -- expect VC to come in when business
    is good, when democracy in place. They do not realize that to
    do this requires fundamental change. Confusion is that they
    speak of "rev" and they do not mean it any more than "rev
    new soap".
```

she seems almost to be talking to herself, reminding herself of what to do and when to do it ("just report here"; "show this rather than analyse") and asking the questions she'll begin to answer in the draft: "What are aims?"; "What becomes of Americans in Vietnam so long exposed to the contraditiction [*sic*] between aims (apparently being reached) and reality." It's worth noting how this question, the central idea of the piece ("What becomes of Americans in Vietnam so long exposed to the contraditiction [*sic*] between aims… and reality"), evolves as FitzGerald revises. It becomes, in the first sentence of the published version,

> The effort of trying to hold reality and the official version of reality together finally took its toll on the Americans in Vietnam,

a much more precise and concise version of the sentence that appears in a **later draft** [D] which we reprint on page 41:

> Though the fiction of "progress" and "reform" could have continued forever, the burden of supporting it was considerable, particularly for those Americans who had to deal with the daily reality.

In a **working outline** [B], this central idea is stated at the top of the page in the rather abstract (even vague) phrase.

Working Outline   In the working outline, FitzGerald moves the discussion of "moral superiority" from place to place; the sequence of ideas corresponds only partly to the final order in which they appear. Ideas sketched in this outline—the similarity between the "early settlers" of the American frontier and the Americans in Vietnam, for example—become central to the revision. Other ideas (about technology, for example) are deleted as FitzGerald refines her focus.

In the notes above and in subsequent drafts, FitzGerald appears to be writing quickly and freely: She abbreviates words, leaves sentences unfinished, and is unconcerned with spelling and punctuation. It's clear that her purpose is simply to get her ideas into words on paper. She refines and develops some of those ideas in subsequent drafts; she drops others completely as she sharpens her focus.

Early Draft   One of FitzGerald's goals in this piece of writing, as she says in her notes, is to provide a "definite historical context" for American

[B] Working Outline

3.

The reaction of people caught between reality and illusion
a. Take on side of Saigon govt agst interests of the Americans
b. Hatred

the metaphor of the Indians — put the war in a definite historical context.

Treatment of Viets in country as noble savages)

(revision) Also sense of moral superiority — mil briefar and Pike. Directed agst the enemy — but also by a kind logic, agst other Viets. Homaths (by many)

For the soldiers — very simple — they had come to find Comms only to find that all Viets are "gooks". This is the end of the logic of Rusk.

For the civilians and others — more complicated. They had come expecting a relationship — if not commander, then older brother — only to find that the Viets do not reciprocate. They do not obey and they have no interest in becoming Americans. Therefore frustration and hatred.

Result is that no one in the country speaks out against the inhumanity — against the violation of all the Genva Treaty.

Here again, as with the French, the psychology of terror — feeling that what the other side does is obscene. They are filthy savages and therefore it does not matter what is done to them. (same as with the Indians)
The tortures
The My Lai and other massacres
The soldiers carrying around obscen picture

But more than that — the systematic killing and harassment of civilian population as outlined by Westmoreland.

(Above This a. of taking side with Saigon is should come before invicibility — attempt to reconcile their own desires with the reality. A part of the involvement. Reason that they cannot see that they are doing is myth of invincibility.

For soldiers — contact supposedly only with the enemy. For civilians, vv. But those are the wateforis rather than soldier and civilian.

Moral superiority — the logic is that what they do is bad because it is on purpose, whereas all our killiings are 'scientific' or due to techno accident. Or n the last usart (Pike) by mistake. And this is clearly not true.

attitudes toward the Vietnamese. In her **early draft** [C], FitzGerald's idea about "historical context" begins to develop. She begins invoking ideas about the frontier and about the "early settlers." She refers to "noble savages," and then changes her mind and crosses out the sentence in which this term appears. Between the lines, near the middle of the page, she writes the phrase "Indian country?" In the margins are other notes as well, notes she seems to have written to herself on rereading the draft: "Enlarge"; "could expand and improve"; "What he is really doing is colonialist."

[C] Early Draft

[handwritten annotations throughout the draft]

Go into a sense of superiority.

making progress in the war could, perhaps, go on forever, it the effort
of supporting ti took its toll on the Americans, particularly on those in
the lower ranks who had to deal with the day-to-day reality. The conflict
between thezi their expectations and the reality produced in soldiers and
civilians alike an intense resentment — a resentment not against the
American command but against the Vetnamese. The logic was a simple one
or the war policy *For the GIs*
for the GIs. They had come to Vietnam (so they had been told by Dean Rusk among
others) to defend out valiant Free World Allies against the totalitarian
Cimmunists

The logic was a simple one: America is the greatest country on earth and
therefore it must be our Vietnamese 'allies' who are causing all the trouble
abd preventing us from winning this war. For the civilians and advisors the
often
logic was confirmed by their personal experiences with their counterparts.
These Americans had come to Vietnam with certain expectations of their
"counterparts", or rather, of their relationship to them. They had seen
themselves in the role of older brother, or teacher — they had expected the
Vietnamese to render them their due as x members of a more "advanced" society.
They had expected gratitude for their efforts, and when they had got neither
gratitude nor "cooperation" or obedeience, they had failed to reconstruct the
Vietnamese point of view. They had failed to see that the Vietnamese were
not "noble savages" empty of ideas and For some the deception was even
more pronounced, for they For the men like the Marine colonel with his
would find
carpentry sets, the deception would be all the more pronounced, for they
had looked upon the Vietnamese Vietnam as a blank page and the Vietnamese
as pupils with empty heads waiting for their know how" and their democratic
principles to be poured in. When the Vietnamese showed them that they were
not How could one explain that the Vietnamese were not puils but, people
with a very differenct view of the world and interests that only occasionally

From the Frances FitzGerald Collection, Department of Special Collections, Boston University.

Later Draft   FitzGerald begins expanding on these ideas about the frontier, Indians, and colonialism in later drafts [D] and [E]. The first excerpt, [D], begins to develop the analogy hinted at in the early draft [C], the parallel between Americans in Vietnam and settlers on the frontier. FitzGerald develops the analogy further—with quotations and

[D] Later Draft

> Though the fiction of "progress" and "reform" could have continued
> burden   took its toll
> forever, the effort of supporting it was considerable, particularly for those
>
> Americans who had to deal with the daily reality. ~~mtxthmxxxx~~. When added to
>
> all the other pressures of the war and of working with the Vietnamese
>
> it ~~maxxiadxixz~~ it produced an almost intolerable tension that expressed
>   often   nerortic behavior   often in
> itself sometimes in internal battles, sometimes in a fierce resentmmnt of
>
> the Vietnamese   some times in anger against the Vietnamese.
>
> The logic of that anger was a simple one: the United States is ghe greates
>
> country on earth and therefore it must be out allies who are creating all
>   (The apparant truth of the statement häad all the innter
> the difficulties (but it had   complexities force behind it.
>
> ..historical or mythological perspective: the Americans were once again
>
> setting out on a heroci nut for them almost painless conquest of an inferior
>
> face. The defeat of the indidians had seemed not just a nationalist victory
>
> but an achievement made in the name of the whole human race — the triumph
>   of
> of light over darkness, of good over evil and a step s.xixtaxyzxfor civilization
>   raw
> over nature. ~~Axxwhitexmenxdxmxixyzixez~~ Though the parallel analogy was
>
> rarely came to consciousness, it was nonetheless there. As white men in Asia,
>
> the Americans did not conceive they could fail in their enterprise, did not
>
> conceive they could be wrong. Moral infallibility, military invicibility —
>
> the two went together and had not to be reconciled — not in VN in any case,
>
> where the enemy was not only Communist but small, yellow and poor. And behind
>   sense of a
> (Above. Behind all the ~~diplxmxxix~~ it was this "can do" attitude, this sunse
> righteous mission   further and further
> of superiority that led the US government into the war   (Perhaps here notd
>
> on CIA man —feflecting opinion in the country

From the Frances FitzGerald Collection, Department of Special Collections, Boston University.

specific evidence—in the second excerpt, [E], where she begins to consider the implications of the language Americans in Saigon used to describe the Viet Cong. She'll combine these two passages in a subsequent draft of the piece. This draft, in the meantime, is still several steps from the version FitzGerald submitted to her publishers, but it has begun to look like a focused piece of writing.

The revision process for FitzGerald was hard work—for both the author and her editors. At one point during the early stages of writing the draft, one of her editors wrote to her in frustration:

> So far in our working together on this book, I have suggested that you keep working and regard the completed material as first-draft only. I now

[E] Later Draft

```
Xrevisionist movies showing the Indians as brave and noble people,
        merely
thaz Hollywood had transcribed -- and quite accurately -- what
the frontiersmen had thought of the Indians at the time: that
thye were 'sazagzs  dirty savages, tricky and untrustworthy
pagan sagages. The defeat of the Indians was seen not just as
a nationalist victory (the way the Vietnamese had regarde their
defeat of the Chinese) but an schtexe triumph of light over
               good
darkness, of virtue over evil and step towards the provress of
the whole human race. Quite cons unconsciously -- for their
remakrs often showed no real hostility -- the Americans soldiers
and officials adopted the same kind of rhetoric in speaking of
the Viet Cong. The Viet Cong "infested areas", etc....clear
operations  The image of America as a disingectant  for germ-
ridden feces.(Also trickery -- they would not "stand up and fight"
they were cowardly
For the Americans as well as the French, the Vietnam war was
"la sale guerre".) And they were bound to win. Moral infallibility,
military invicibility -- the two had not to be distinguished, --
not in Vietnam, in any case, where the enemy was not only
Communist, but small, poor and yellow. (later, irony for GIs)
```

From the Frances FitzGerald Collection, Department of Special Collections, Boston University.

begin to see I was wrong. The present material is *pre* first draft; it has not yet got to the point where an editor can do anything with it. It is so rough, so lacking in clarity, that all we can do is throw up our hands. Frankie, you have to solve the problem of articulating the Vietnam problem, both in the organization and the style of your book. I think you have a lot of work to do before solving it. If you believe you should keep forging ahead before you solve it, simply to cover the area you want the book eventually to cover, by all means do so; but when that is done, I am afraid you have another task ahead of you that is at least as daunting.

Fire in the Lake went on to win the Bancroft Prize for History, the National Book Award, and the Pulitzer Prize.

CHAPTER THREE

SHAPING PARAGRAPHS

Paragraph Form and Substance

It is commonly said that a good paragraph is

- *unified* (it makes one point, or it indicates where one unit of a topic begins and ends);

- *organized* (the point or unit is developed according to some pattern); and

- *coherent* (the pattern of development, sentence by sentence, is clear to the reader).

In this chapter, we will say these things too. But first we feel obliged to issue this warning: You can learn to write a unified, organized, coherent paragraph that no one in his or her right mind would choose to read. Here is an example:

    Charles Darwin's great accomplishments in the
field of natural science resulted from many
factors. While innate qualities and
characteristics played a large part in leading him
to his discoveries, various environmental
circumstances and events were decisive factors as
well. Darwin himself considered his voyage on the
Beagle the most decisive event of his life,
precisely because this was to him an educational

```
experience similar to if not more valuable than
that of college, in that it determined his whole
career and taught him of the world as well.
```

Notice that the paragraph is unified, organized, and coherent. It has a **topic sentence** (the first sentence, which briefly states the main idea of the paragraph). It uses **transitional devices** ("while," "as well," "Darwin himself") and, as is often helpful, it **repeats key words.** But notice also that it is wordy, vague, and inflated ("in the field of," "many factors," "qualities and characteristics," "circumstances and events," "precisely because," "educational experience," "similar to if not more valuable than"). It is, in short, thin and boring. To whom does it teach what?

Consider, by contrast, these paragraphs from another essay on Darwin:

> Charles Darwin's youth was unmarked by signs of genius. Born in 1809 into the well-to-do Darwin and Wedgwood clans (his mother was a Wedgwood, and Darwin himself was to marry another), he led a secure and carefree childhood, happy with his family, indifferent to books, responsive to nature. The son and grandson of impressively successful physicians, he eventually tried medical training himself, but found the studies dull and surgery (before anesthesia) too ghastly even to watch. So, for want of anything better, he followed the advice of his awesome father (6'2", 336 pounds, domineering in temperament) and studied for the ministry, taking his B.A. at Christ's College, Cambridge, in 1831.
>
> Then a remarkable turn of events saved Darwin from a country parsonage. His science teacher at Cambridge, John Stevens Henslow, arranged for Darwin the invitation to be naturalist on H.M.S. *Beagle* during a long voyage of exploration. Despite his father's initial reluctance, Darwin got the position, and at the end of 1831 left England for a five-year voyage around the globe that turned out to be not only a crucial experience for Darwin himself, but a passage of consequence for the whole world.
>
> —*Philip Appleman*

Notice how full of life these paragraphs are, compared to the paragraph that begins by asserting that "Charles Darwin's great accomplishments in the field of natural science resulted from many factors." These far more interesting paragraphs are filled with specific details, facts, and names that combine to convey ideas. We finish reading them with a sense of having learned something worth knowing, from someone fully engaged not only with the topic, but also with conveying it to someone else.

The one indispensable quality of a good paragraph is **substance.** A paragraph may define a term, describe a person or a place, make a comparison, tell an anecdote, summarize an opinion, draw a conclusion; it may do almost anything provided that it holds the readers' attention by telling them something they want or need to know, or are reminded of with pleasure.

But even a substantial paragraph does not guarantee that you'll hold the attention of your readers, because readers, like writers, are often lazy and impatient. If readers find that they must work too hard to understand you, if they are confused by what you write, they can and will stop reading. The art of writing is in large part the art of keeping your readers' goodwill while you teach them what you want them to learn. Now, experienced writers can usually tell what makes a satisfactory unit, and their paragraphs do not always exactly follow the principles we are going to suggest. But we think that if you follow these principles you will develop a sense of paragraphing. Or, to put it another way, you will improve your sense of how to develop an idea.

The Shape of a Paragraph

First, an obvious point: The shape of a paragraph—the way in which its idea is set forth—will largely depend not only on the content but also on the position of the paragraph in the essay. To take the first point first: The content of a paragraph explaining something may move from cause to effect, or from effect to cause; the content of a paragraph arguing a point may move from evidence to conclusion, or from conclusion to evidence. But the position of the paragraph, its place in the essay as a whole, will also determine its shape. An opening paragraph will in one way or another lead into the topic (its main point may therefore come at the end). A middle paragraph should follow easily from the preceding paragraph, and it should also lead into the next paragraph—so a middle paragraph might begin with a transitional sentence (a sentence that begins with a "Furthermore" or a "Nevertheless") and announce its main point in the second sentence. Or even in its last sentence. We will discuss such matters in detail in the following pages. But here we can say that when you revise a draft, you want to make certain not only that each paragraph in clear in itself but also that it fits neatly into your essay.

Paragraph Unity: Topic Sentences, Topic Ideas

The idea developed in each paragraph often appears, briefly stated, as a **topic sentence.** Topic sentences are most useful, and are therefore especially common, in paragraphs that offer arguments; they are much less useful, and therefore less common, in narrative and descriptive paragraphs.

The topic sentence usually is the first sentence in the paragraph—or the second, if the first sentence is transitional—because writers usually want their readers to know from the start where the paragraph is going. Sometimes, though, you may not wish to forecast what is to come; you may prefer to put your topic sentence at the end of the paragraph, summarizing the points that earlier sentences have made, or drawing a generalization based on the earlier details. Even if you do not include a topic sentence anywhere in the paragraph, the paragraph should have a topic idea, an idea that holds the sentences together.

Examples of Topic Sentences at Beginning and at End, and of Topic Ideas

1. The following paragraph, from an essay in which a professor of physiology compares Darwin and Freud, begins with a topic sentence.

> To begin with, Darwin and Freud were both multifaceted geniuses with many talents in common. Both were great observers, attuned to perceiving in familiar phenomena a significance that had escaped almost everyone else. Searching with insatiable curiosity for underlying explanations, both did far more than discover new facts or solve circumscribed problems, such as the structure of DNA: they synthesized knowledge from a wide range of fields and created new conceptual frameworks, large parts of which are still accepted today. Both were prolific writers and forceful communicators who eventually converted many or most of their contemporaries to their positions.
>
> —*Jared Diamond*

The first sentence announces the topic the rest of the paragraph will develop, the talents Darwin and Freud had in common. Each sentence that follows this topic sentence develops or amplifies it by considering one of the talents the two men shared. The second sentence concerns their powers of observation. The third sentence concerns their curiosity about "underlying explanations" and their ability to create "new conceptual frameworks."

Note also the logical order of subtopics in the paragraph: The discussion moves from *observation,* to *analysis* and *synthesis,* to *communication.*

2. The next paragraph has its topic sentence at the end:

> If we try to recall Boris Karloff's face as the monster in the film of *Frankenstein* (1931), most of us probably think of the seams holding the pieces together, and if we cannot recall other details we assume that the face evokes horror. But when we actually look at a picture of the face rather than recall a memory of it, we are perhaps chiefly impressed by the high, steep forehead (a feature often associated with intelligence), by the darkness surrounding the eyes (often associated with physical or spiritual weariness), and by the gaunt cheeks and the thin lips slightly turned down at the corners (associated with deprivation or restraint). The monster's face is of course in some ways shocking, but probably our chief impression as we look at it is that this is not the face of one who causes suffering but of one who himself is heroically undergoing suffering.
>
> —*Sylvia Rodriguez*

When the topic sentence is at the end, the paragraph usually develops from the particular to the general, the topic sentence serving to generalize or summarize the information that precedes it. Such a topic sentence can be especially effective in presenting an argument: The reader hears, considers, and accepts the evidence before the argument is explicitly stated, and if the evidence has been effectively presented the reader willingly accepts the conclusion.

3. The next paragraph has no topic sentence:

> A few years ago when you mentioned Walt Disney at a respectable party— or anyway this is how it was in California, where I was then—the standard response was a headshake and a groan. Intellectuals spoke of how he butchered the classics—from *Pinocchio* to *Winnie the Pooh,* how his wildlife pictures were sadistic and coy, how the World's Fair sculptures of hippopotamuses were a national if not international disgrace. A few crazies disagreed, and since crazies are always the people to watch, it began to be admitted that the early Pluto movies had a considerable measure of *je ne sais quoi,* that the background animation in *Snow White* was "quite extraordinary," that *Fantasia* did indeed have *one* great sequence (then it became two; now everyone says three, though there's fierce disagreement on exactly which three).
>
> —*John Gardner*

The topic here is, roughly, "Intellectuals used to scorn Disney, but recently they have been praising him." Such a sentence could easily begin the paragraph, but it is not necessary because even without it the reader has no difficulty following the discussion. The first two sentences talk about Disney's earlier reputation; then the sentence about the "crazies" introduces the contrary view and the rest of the paragraph illustrates the growing popularity of this contrary view. The paragraph develops its point so clearly and consistently (it is essentially a narrative, in chronological order) that the reader, unlike the reader of a complex analytic paragraph, does not need the help of a topic sentence either at the beginning, to prepare for what follows, or at the end, to pull the whole together.

Unifying Ideas into Paragraphs

Although we emphasize **unity** in paragraphs, don't assume that every development or refinement or alteration of your thought requires a new paragraph. Such an assumption would lead to an essay consisting entirely of one-sentence paragraphs. A good paragraph may, for instance,

- ask a question *and* answer it, or
- describe an effect *and* then explain the cause, or
- set forth details *and* then offer a generalization.

Indeed, if the question or the effect or the details can be set forth in a sentence or two, and the answer or the cause or the generalization can be set forth in a sentence or two, the two halves of the topic should be pulled together into a single paragraph. Only if, for example, the question is long and complex and the answer equally long or longer, will you need two or more paragraphs.

Let's consider three paragraphs from an essay on ballooning. In the essay from which the following paragraphs are taken, the writer has already explained that ballooning was born in late eighteenth-century France and that almost from its start there were two types of balloons, gas and hot air. Notice that in the paragraphs printed below the first is on gas, the second is chiefly on hot air (but it helpfully makes comparisons with gas), and the third is on the length of flights of both gas and hot-air balloons. In other words, each paragraph is about one thing—gas balloons, hot-air balloons, length of flight—but each paragraph also builds on what the reader has learned in the previous paragraphs. That the third paragraph is about the flights of gas *and* of hot-air balloons does not mean that it lacks unity; it is a unified discussion of flight lengths.

> Gas balloons swim around in air like a sleeping fish in water, because they weigh about the same as the fluid they're in. A good, big, trans-Atlantic balloon will have 2,000 pounds of vehicle, including gas bag and pilot, taking up about 30 cubic feet (as big as a refrigerator), plus 300 pounds of a "nothing" stuff called helium, which fills 30,000 cubic feet (as big as three houses). Air to fill this 30,000 cubic feet would also weigh 2,300 pounds, so the balloon system averages the same as air, floating in it as part of the wind.
>
> Hot-air balloons use the same size bag filled with hot air instead of helium, kept hot by a boot-sized blowtorch riding just over the pilot's head. Hot air is light, but not as light as helium, so you can't carry as much equipment in a hot-air balloon. You also can't fly as long or as far. Helium will carry a balloon for days (three and a half days is the record), until a lot of gas has leaked out. But a hot-air balloon cools down in minutes, like a house as soon as its heat source runs out of fuel; and today's best fuel (heat for weight), propane, lasts only several hours.
>
> A good hot-air flight goes a hundred miles, yet the gas record is 1,897 miles, set by a German in 1914 with the junk (by today's standards) they had then. Unmanned scientific gas balloons have flown half a million miles, staying up more than a year. Japan bombed Oregon in World War II with balloons. Two hot-air balloonists, Tracy Barnes and Malcolm Forbes, have made what they called transcontinental flights, but each was the sum of dozens of end-to-end hops, trailed by pick-up trucks, like throwing a frisbee from Hollywood to Atlantic City.
>
> —*David Royce*

Because Royce's paragraphs are unified, the reader is able to proceed from point to point without stumbling and without confusion. By contrast, the following paragraph, from a book on athletic coaching, lacks unity, and the effect is disconcerting.

> Leadership qualities are a prerequisite for achievement in coaching. A leader is one who is respected for what he says and does, and who is admired by his team. The coach gains respect by giving respect, and by possessing knowledge and skills associated with the sport. There are many "successful" coaches who are domineering, forceful leaders, gaining power more through fear and even hate than through respect. These military-type men are primarily from the old school of thought, and many younger coaches are achieving their goals through more humanistic approaches.

Something is wrong here. The first half of the paragraph tells us that "a leader is one who is respected for what he says and does," but the second half of the paragraph contradicts that assertion, telling us that "many" leaders hold their position "more through fear and even hate than through respect." The trouble is *not* that the writer is talking about two kinds of leaders; a moment ago we saw that a writer can in one paragraph talk about two kinds of balloons. The trouble here is that we need a unifying idea if these two points are to be given in one paragraph. The idea might be: There are two kinds of leaders, those who are respected and those who are feared. This idea might be developed along these lines:

> Leadership qualities are a prerequisite for achievement in coaching, but these qualities can be of two radically different kinds. One kind of leader is respected and admired by his team for what he says and does. The coach gains respect by giving respect, and by possessing knowledge and skills associated with the sport. The other kind of coach is a domineering, forceful leader, gaining power more through fear than through respect. These military-type men are primarily from the old school of thought, whereas most of the younger coaches achieve their goals through the more humane approaches of the first type.

Organization in Paragraphs

A paragraph needs more than a unified point; it needs a reasonable **organization** or sequence. Exactly how the parts of a paragraph will fit together depends on what the paragraph is doing.

1. If it is *describing* a place, it may move from a general view to the significant details—or from immediately striking details to some less obvious but perhaps more important ones. It may move from near to far, or from far to near, or from the past to the present.

2. If it is *explaining*, it may move from cause to effect, or from effect to cause, or from past to present; or it may offer an example.

3. If it is *arguing*, it may move from evidence to conclusion, or from a conclusion to supporting evidence; or it may offer one piece of evidence, for instance an anecdote that illustrates the argument.

4. If it is *narrating*, it will likely move chronologically.

5. If a paragraph is *classifying* (dividing a subject into its parts), it may begin by enumerating the parts and go on to study each, perhaps in climactic order. Here is an example from a student essay on masks:

The chief reasons people wear masks are these: to have fun, to protect themselves, to disguise themselves, and to achieve a new identity. At Halloween, children wear masks for fun; they may, of course, also think they are disguising themselves, but chiefly their motive is to experience the joy of saying "boo" to someone. As for protection, soldiers wore masks in ancient times against swords and battle-axes, in more recent times against poison gas. Masked bank robbers illustrate the third reason, disguise, and though of course this disguise is a sort of protection, a robber's reason for wearing a mask is fairly distinct from a soldier's. All of these reasons so far are easily understood, but we may have more trouble grasping the reason that people use masks in order to achieve a new identity. In some religious rituals, masks may be worn to frighten away evil spirits, or they may be disguises so that the evil spirits will not know who the wearer is. But most religious masks are worn with the idea that the wearer achieves a new identity, a union with supernatural powers, and thus in effect the wearer becomes—really becomes, not merely pretends to be—a new person.

Notice that the first sentence offers four reasons for wearing masks. The rest of the paragraph amplifies these reasons, one by one, and in the order indicated in the first sentence. Since the writer regards the last reason as the most interesting and the most difficult to grasp, she discusses it at the greatest length, giving it about as much space as she gives to the first three reasons altogether.

The way in which a paragraph is organized, then, will depend on the writer's purpose. Almost always, one purpose is to make something clear to a reader, which means that the writer must present information in an orderly way. Among the common methods of organizing a paragraph, and keeping things clear, are the following:

1. General to particular (topic sentence usually at the beginning)

2. Particular to general (topic sentence usually at the end)

3. Enumeration of parts or details or reasons (probably in climactic order)

4. Question and answer

5. Cause and effect

6. Comparison and contrast

7. Analogy

8. Chronology

9. Spatial order (e.g., near to far, or right to left)

The only rule that can cover all paragraphs is this: Readers must never feel that they are wandering in a maze as they follow the writer to the end of the paragraph.

Coherence in Paragraphs

In addition to having a unified point and a reasonable organization, a good paragraph is **coherent;** that is, the connections between ideas in the paragraph are clear. Coherence can often be achieved by inserting the right transitional words or by taking care to repeat key words.

Transitions

Richard Wagner, commenting on his work as a composer of operas, said "The art of composition is the art of transition," for his art moved from note to note, measure to measure, scene to scene. **Transitions** establish connections between ideas; they alert readers to what will follow. Here are some of the most common transitional words and phrases.

1. **amplification or likeness:** similarly, likewise, and, also, again, second, third, in addition, furthermore, moreover, finally

2. **emphasis:** chiefly, equally, indeed, even more important

3. **contrast or concession:** but, on the contrary, on the other hand, by contrast, of course, however, still, doubtless, no doubt, nevertheless, granted that, conversely, although, admittedly

4. **example:** for example, for instance, as an example, specifically, consider as an illustration, that is, such as, like

5. **consequence or cause and effect:** thus, so, then, it follows, as a result, therefore, hence

6. **restatement:** in short, that is, in effect, in other words

7. **place:** in the foreground, further back, in the distance

8. **time:** afterward, next, then, as soon as, later, until, when, finally, last, at last

9. **conclusion:** finally, therefore, thus, to sum up

Consider the following paragraph:

> Folklorists are just beginning to look at Africa. A great quantity of folklore materials has been gathered from African countries in the past century and published by missionaries, travelers, administrators, linguists, and anthropologists incidentally to their main pursuits. No fieldworker has devoted himself exclusively or even largely to the recording and analysis of folklore materials, according to a committee of the African Studies Association reporting in 1966 on the state of research in the African arts. Yet Africa is the continent supreme for traditional cultures that nurture folklore. Why this neglect?
>
> —*Richard M. Dorson*

The reader gets the point, but the second sentence seems to contradict the first: The first sentence tells us that folklorists are just beginning to look at Africa, but the next tells us that lots of folklore has been collected. An "although" between these sentences would clarify the author's point, especially if the third sentence were hooked on to the second, thus:

> Folklorists are just beginning to look at Africa. Although a great quantity of folklore materials has been gathered from African countries in the past century by missionaries, travelers, administrators, linguists, and anthropologists incidentally to their main pursuits, no fieldworker has devoted himself...

But this revision gives us an uncomfortably long second sentence. Further revision would help. The real point of the original passage, though it is smothered, is that *although* many people have incidentally collected folklore materials in Africa, *professional* folklorists have not been active there. The contrast ought to be sharpened:

> Folklorists are just beginning to look at Africa. True, missionaries, travelers, administrators, linguists, and anthropologists have collected a quantity of folklore materials incidentally to their main pursuits, but folklorists have lagged behind. No fieldworker . . .

In this revision the words that clarify are the small but important words "true" and "but." The original paragraph is like a jigsaw puzzle that's missing some tiny but necessary pieces.

Repetition

Coherence is also achieved through the **repetition** of key words. When you repeat words or phrases, or when you provide clear substitutes, such as pronouns and demonstrative adjectives, you are helping the reader to keep step with your developing thoughts. Grammatical constructions too can be repeated, the repetitions or parallels linking the sentences or ideas.

In the following example, notice how the repetitions provide continuity.

> In the movement from the miraculous prose of Toni Morrison to the screen, the story of *Beloved* has lost some of its breadth, complexity, and imaginative range. But its central messages—historical and human—have been sustained and, in some ways, enhanced by the gifts of the innovative Jonathan Demme and his associates and by the talent and commitment of the actors. We see in the film the wounds of slavery, inflicted and then self-inflicted through resistance—or, rather, we see the memories of these wounds as they still disturb the free. We see the resources of an African-American community for defining those wounds, for quarreling about them, and for healing them. The story of trauma and recovery is distinctive, but it is told so as to invite others in, into the haunted house at 124 Bluestone and into Baby Sugg's clearing in the woods.
>
> *—Natalie Zemon Davis*

Notice not only the exact repetitions ("wounds," "we see," "them") but also the slight variations, such as "inflicted," and "self-inflicted"; and the parallel construction of the last phrases of the last sentence ("into the haunted house [...] into Baby Sugg's clearing"), which brings a sense of closure to the paragraph.

Linking Paragraphs Together

Since each paragraph in an essay generally develops a single idea, a single, new aspect of the main point of the essay, as one paragraph follows another, readers should feel they are getting somewhere, smoothly and without stumbling. As you move from one paragraph to the next, from one step in the development of your main idea to the next, you probably can keep your readers with you if you link the beginning of each new paragraph to the end of the paragraph that precedes it. Often a single transitional word (such as those listed on page 52–53) will suffice; sometimes repeating key terms will help connect a sequence of paragraphs together and make your essay, as many writers put it, "flow."

Consider the movement of ideas in the following essay written in response to an assignment that asked students to analyze a family photograph.

Cheryl Lee

Writing 125

Ms. Medina

April 1, 2001

The Story Behind the Gestures

1   At the close of my graduation ceremony, my entire family gathered together to immortalize the special moment on film. No one escaped the flash of my mother's camera because she was determined to document every minute of the occasion at every possible angle. My mother made sure that she took pictures of me with my hat on, with my hat off, holding the bouquet, sitting, standing, and in countless other positions. By the time this family picture was taken, my smile was intact, frozen on my face. This is not to say that my smile was anything less than genuine, for it truly was a smile of thankfulness and joy. It is just that after

posing for so many pictures, what initially began as a spontaneous reaction became a frozen expression.

2   The viewer should, however, consider not so much the frozen expressions of those in the photograph, but rather the fact that the picture is posed. A posed picture supposedly shows only what the people in the picture want the viewer to see--in this case, their happiness. But ironically the photograph reveals much more about its subjects than the viewer first imagines. The photograph speaks of relationships and personalities. It speaks about the more intimate details that first seem invisible but that become undeniable through the study of gestures.

3   In the photograph, the most prominent and symbolic of gestures is the use and position of the arms. Both my father and mother place an arm around me and in turn around each other. Their encircling arms, however, do more than just show affection; they unify the three figures into a close huddle that leads the viewer's eye directly to them as opposed to the background or the periphery. The slightly bended arms that rest at their sides act as arrows that not only reinforce the three figures as the focal point but also exclude the fourth figure, my brother, from sharing the spotlight. Unlike the other members of

Cheryl Lee, *The Story Behind the Gestures: A Family Photograph.* Reprinted by permission of the author, Cheryl Lee Rim.

the family whose arms and hands are intertwined, Edwin stands with both hands down in front of him, latching onto no one. The lack of physical contact between the huddled figures and Edwin is again emphasized as he positions himself away from the viewer's eye as he stands in the periphery.

4   Edwin's position in the photograph is indicative of him as a person, for he always seems to isolate himself from the spotlight, from being the center of attention. Thus, it is his decision to escape public scrutiny, not the force of my parents' arms that drives him to the side. His quiet, humble nature directs him away from even being the focal point of a picture and leads him towards establishing his own

individuality and independence in privacy. His long
hair and his "hand-me-down" clothes are all an
expression of his simply being himself. The reason
behind his physical independence is the emotional
independence that he already possesses at the age of
sixteen. He stands alone because he can stand alone.

5   While Edwin stands apart from the other three
figures, I stand enclosed and protected. The lock of
arms as well as the bouquet restrain me; they
dissuade me from breaking away in favor of
independence. Although my mother wants me to achieve
the same kind of independence that Edwin has
achieved, she works to delay the time when I actually
will move away to the periphery. Perhaps my being the
only daughter, the only other female in the family,
has something to do with my mother's desire to keep
me close and dependent as long as possible. Her arm
reaches out with bouquet in hand as if to shield me
from the world's unpleasantness. Even though my
father also holds onto me with an encircling arm, it
is my mother's firm grip that alone persuades me to
stay within the boundary of their protective arms.

6   Her grip, which proves more powerful than my
father's hold, restrains not only me but also my
father. In the picture, he falls victim to the same

outstretched hand, the same touch of the bouquet. Yet this time, my mother's bouquet does more than just restrain; it seems to push my father back "into line" or into his so-called place. The picture illustrates this exertion of influence well, for my mother in real life does indeed assume the role of the dominant figure. Although my father remains the head of the household in title, it is my mother around whom the household revolves; she oversees the insignificant details as well as the major ones. But my father doesn't mind at all. Like me, he also enjoys the protection her restraining arm offers. It is because of our mutual dependence on my mother that my father and I seem to draw closer. This dependence in turn strengthens both of our relationships with my mother.

7   At the time the picture was taken, I seriously doubt that my mother realized the significance of her position in the picture or the import of her gestures. All of us in fact seem too blinded by the festivity of the occasion to realize that this photograph would show more than just a happy family at a daughter's graduation. The family photograph would inevitably become a telling portrait of each member of the family. It would, in a sense, leave us vulnerable to the speculative eyes of the viewer, who

in carefully examining the photograph would recognize
the secrets hidden in each frozen expression.

A few observations on these paragraphs may be useful. First, notice that each paragraph in the sequence examines a different aspect of the photograph and introduces a new point into the discussion. The first paragraph gives background information (the photograph was taken at Lee's graduation); the second paragraph states the writer's point—that studying the gestures of her family members enables us to understand their "personalities and relationships." Each succeeding paragraph treats one of these gestures (paragraph 2, for example, considers the encircling arms) or one of the personalities or relationships. Paragraph 4 focuses on the writer's brother Edwin; paragraph 5 focuses on Lee's relationship to her mother; paragraph 6 focuses on her mother and father. We might think that symmetry requires that each family member get a single paragraph, but given the complexity of their relationships to each other, and given the mother's dominance in the family, it makes sense that things don't break down so neatly and that Lee devotes two paragraphs to her mother.

Second, notice how Lee makes the essay cohere. Although she uses some transitional words ("however" at the beginning of the second paragraph; "while" at the beginning of the fifth paragraph), she establishes coherence in this essay primarily by repeating the key terms of her discussion. The first sentence of each new paragraph picks up a word or phrase from the last sentence of the paragraph preceding it. The phrase "frozen expressions" links the end of the first paragraph to the beginning of the second; "gesture" links the second paragraph to the third; "position" links the third to the fourth; "stand" links the fourth to the fifth; and so on. These links are hardly noticeable on a first reading, but because Lee uses transitions and repetition effectively, the writing flows, and the reader never stumbles.

Paragraph Length

Although a paragraph can contain any number of sentences, two is probably too few, and ten might be too many. It is not a matter, however, of counting sentences; paragraphs are coherent blocks, substantial units of your essay, and the spaces between them are brief resting places allowing the reader to take in what you have said. One double-spaced, word-processed page of writing (approximately 250 words) is about as much as the reader can take before requiring a slight break. On the other hand, a single page with half a dozen paragraphs is probably faulty because the reader is too often interrupted with needless pauses and because the page has too few *developed* ideas: An assertion is made, and then another, and another. These assertions are unconvincing because they are not supported with detail.

The Use and Abuse of Short Paragraphs

A short paragraph can be effective when it summarizes a highly detailed previous paragraph or group of paragraphs, or when it serves as a transition between two complicated paragraphs, but unless you are sure that the reader needs a break, avoid thin paragraphs. A paragraph that is nothing but a transition can usually be altered into a transitional phrase or clause or sentence that starts the next paragraph. But of course there are times when a short paragraph is exactly right. Notice the effect of the two-sentence paragraph between two longer paragraphs:

> After I returned to prison, I took a long look at myself and, for the first time in my life, admitted that I was wrong, that I had gone astray—astray not so much from the white man's law as from being human, civilized—for I could not approve the act of rape. Even though I had some insight into my own motivations, I did not feel justified. I lost my self-respect. My pride as a man dissolved and my whole fragile moral structure seemed to collapse, completely shattered.
>
> That is why I started to write. To save myself.
>
> I realized that no one could save me but myself. The prison authorities were both uninterested and unable to help me. I had to seek out the truth and unravel the snarled web of my motivations. I had to find out who I am and what I want to be, what type of man I should be, and what I could do to become the best of which I was capable. I understood that what had happened to me had also happened to countless other blacks and it would happen to many, many more.
>
> *—Eldridge Cleaver*

If the content of the second paragraph were less momentous, it would hardly merit a paragraph. Here the brevity contributes to the enormous impact; those two simple sentences, set off by themselves, seem equal in weight, so to speak, to the longer paragraphs that precede and follow. They are the hinges on which the door turns.

When used for emphasis, short paragraphs can be effective.

Often, though, short paragraphs (like the one directly above) leave readers feeling unsatisfied, even annoyed. Consider these two consecutive paragraphs from a draft of a student's essay on Leonardo's *Mona Lisa*.

```
     Leonardo's "Mona Lisa," painted about 1502,
has caused many people to wonder about the lady's
expression. Different viewers see different things.
     The explanation of the puzzle is chiefly in
the mysterious expression that Leonardo conveys.
The mouth and the eyes are especially important.
```

Sometimes you can improve a sequence of short paragraphs merely by joining one paragraph to the next. But unsatisfactory short paragraphs usually cannot be repaired so simply: The source of the problem is usually not that sentences have been needlessly separated from each other, but that generalizations have not been supported by details, or that claims haven't been supported by evidence. Here is the student's revision, strengthening the two thin paragraphs of the draft.

Leonardo da Vinci, *Mona Lisa.* © Alinari/Art Resource.

Leonardo's "Mona Lisa," painted about 1502, has caused many people to wonder about the lady's expression. Doubtless she is remarkably lifelike but exactly what experience of life, what mood, does she reveal? Is she sad, or gently mocking, or uncertain or self-satisfied, or lost in daydreams? Why are we never satisfied when we try to name her emotion?

Part of the uncertainty may of course be due to the subject as a whole. What can we make out of the combination of this smiling woman and that utterly unpopulated landscape? But surely a large part of the explanation lies in the way that Leonardo painted the face's two most expressive features, the eyes and the mouth. He slightly obscured the corners of these, so that we cannot precisely characterize them: although on one viewing we may see them one way, on another viewing we may see them slightly differently. If today we think she looks detached, tomorrow we may think she looks slightly threatening.

This revision is not simply a padded version of the earlier paragraphs; it is a necessary clarification of them, for without the details the generalizations mean almost nothing to a reader.

Introductory Paragraphs

As the poet Byron said, at the beginning of a long part of a long poem, "Nothing so difficult as a beginning." Almost all writers find that the first paragraphs in their drafts are false starts. As we suggest in Chapter 1, we think you shouldn't worry too much about the opening paragraph of your draft; you'll almost surely want to revise your opening later anyway.

When writing a first draft you merely need something to break the ice. But in your finished paper the opening cannot be mere throat-clearing. The opening should be interesting. Among the commonest *un*interesting openings are:

1. A dictionary definition ("Webster says . . .")
2. A restatement of your title. The title is (let's assume) "Anarchism and the Marx Brothers," and the first sentence says, "This essay will

study the anarchic acts of the Marx Brothers." True, the sentence announces the topic of the essay, but it gives no information about the topic beyond what the title already offers, and it provides no information about you either—that is, no sense of your response to the topic, such as might be present in, say, "The Marx Brothers are funny, but one often has the feeling that under the fun the violence has serious implications."

3. A broad generalization, such as "Ever since the beginning of time, human beings have been violent." Again, such a sentence may be fine if it helps you to start drafting, but it should not remain in your final version: It's dull—and it tells your readers almost nothing about the essay they're about to read. (Our example, after all, could begin anything from an analysis of *Gladiator* to a term paper on Bosnia.) To put it another way, the ever-since-the-beginning-of-time opening lacks substance—and if your opening lacks substance, it will not matter what you say next. You've already lost your reader's attention.

What is left? What *is* a good way for a final version to begin? Your introductory paragraph will be at least moderately interesting if it gives information, and it will be pleasing if the information provides focus; that is, if it lets the reader know exactly what your topic is, and where you will be going. Remember, when you write, *you* are the teacher; it won't do to begin,

```
George Orwell says he shot the elephant because . . .
```

We need some information, identifying the text you are writing about:

```
George Orwell, in "Shooting an Elephant," says he
shot the elephant because . . .
```

Even better is,

```
In "Shooting an Elephant," George Orwell sets
forth his reflections on his service as a
policeman in Burma. He suggests that he once shot
an elephant because . . . but his final paragraph
suggests that we must look for additional reasons.
```

Why is this opening better? Because it begins to suggest why the essay is worth reading. It points to a contradiction in the Orwell piece, a problem worth examining: Orwell says one thing, but that thing may not be entirely true.

Compare, for example, the opening sentences from three essays written by students on Anne Moody's *Coming of Age in Mississippi*. The book is the autobiography of an African-American woman, covering her early years with her sharecropper parents, her schooling, and finally her work in the civil rights movement.

```
The environment that surrounds a person from an
early age tends to be a major factor in
determining their character.
```

This is an all-purpose sentence that serves no specific purpose well; it could conceivably begin an essay on almost any topic: a study of the moral development of children, an analysis of the film *Erin Brockovitch*, a biography of Napoleon. Notice also the faulty reference of the pronoun (the plural "their" refers to the singular "a person"), the weaseling of "tends to be a major factor," and the vagueness of "early age" and "environment" and "character." These all warn us that the writer will waste our time.

```
It is unfortunate but true that racial or
color prejudice shows itself early in the life
of a child.
```

Less pretentious than the first example, but it labors the obvious, sounds annoyingly preachy, and still doesn't say much about the topic at hand.

```
Anne Moody's autobiography, Coming of Age in
Mississippi, vividly illustrates how she
discovered her identity as an African-American.
```

Surely this is the best of the three openings. Informative and focused, it identifies the book's theme and method, and it offers an evaluation. The essayist has been considerate of her readers. If we are interested in women's autobiographies or life in the South, we will read on. If we aren't, we are grateful to her for letting us off the bus at the first stop.

Let's look now not simply at an opening sentence but at an entire first paragraph, the opening paragraph of an analytic essay. Notice how the student provides the reader with the necessary information about the book she is discussing (the diary of a man whose son is brain-damaged) and also focuses the reader's attention on the essay's topic (the quality that distinguishes this diary from others).

> Josh Greenfeld's diary, <u>A Place for Noah</u>, records the attempts of a smart, thoughtful man to reconcile himself to his son's autism, a severe mental and physical disorder. Most diaries function as havens for secret thoughts, and Greenfeld's diary does frequently supply a voice to his darkest fears about who will ultimately care for Noah. It provides, too, an intimate glimpse of a family striving to remain a coherent unit despite their tragedy. But beyond affording such urgent and personal revelations, <u>A Place for Noah</u>, in chronicling the isolation of the Greenfelds, reveals how inadequate and ineffectual our medical and educational systems are in responding to families victimized by catastrophic illness.

This example is engaging, in part because it indicates why a reader might be interested in reading the essay it begins: Greenfeld's book is more than just a diary; it also explores the consquences of a problem—catastrophic illness—that can affect anyone.

Of course you can provide interest and focus by other, more indirect means, among them the following:

- A quotation
- An anecdote or other short narrative
- An interesting fact (a statistic, for instance, showing the reader that you know something about your topic)
- A definition of an important term—but not merely one derived from a dictionary
- A question—but an interesting one, such as "Why do we call some words obscene?"
- A glance at a view different from your own
- An assertion that a problem exists

Many excellent opening paragraphs do not use any of these devices, and you need not use any of them if they feel forced. But in your reading you may observe that these devices are used widely. Here is an example of the second device, **an anecdote** that makes an effective, indeed an unnerving, introduction to an essay on aging.

> There is an old American folk tale about a wooden bowl. It seems that Grandmother, with her trembling hands, was guilty of occasionally breaking a dish. Her daughter angrily gave her a wooden bowl, and told her that she must eat out of it from now on. The young granddaughter, observing this, asked her mother why Grandmother must eat from a wooden bowl when the rest of the family was given china plates. "Because she is old!" answered her mother. The child thought for a moment and then told her mother, "You must save the wooden bowl when Grandma dies." Her mother asked why, and the child replied, "For when you are old."
>
> —*Sharon R. Curtin*

The third strategy, **an interesting detail,** shows the reader that you know something about your topic and that you are worth reading. We have already seen (page 44) a rather quiet example of this device, in a paragraph about Charles Darwin, which began "Charles Darwin's youth was unmarked by signs of genius." Here is a more obvious example, from a student essay on blue jeans:

```
That blue jeans or denims are not found only in
Texas is not surprising if we recall that jeans are
named for Genoa (Gene), where the cloth was first
made, and that denim is cloth de Nîmes, that is,
from Nîmes, a city in France.
```

(Such information is to be had by spending about thirty seconds with a dictionary.)

The fourth strategy, **a definition,** is fairly common in analytic essays; the essayist first clears the ground by specifying the topic. Here is the beginning of a student's essay on bilingual education.

```
    Let's begin by defining "bilingual education."
As commonly used today, the term does not mean
teaching students a language other than English
(almost everyone would agree that foreign-language
instruction should be available, and that it is
desirable for Americans to be fluent not only in
```

English but also in some other language); nor does
"bilingual education" mean offering courses in
English as a second language to students whose
native language is, for example, Chinese, or
Spanish or Navajo or Aleut. (Again, almost everyone
would agree that such instruction should be offered
where economically possible.) Rather, it means
offering instruction in such courses as
mathematics, history, and science <u>in the student's</u>
<u>native language</u>, while also offering courses in
English as a second language. Programs vary in
details, but the idea is that the non-native
speaker should be spared the trauma of total
immersion in English until he or she has completed
several years of studying English as a second
language. During this period, instruction in other
subjects is given in the student's native language.

—Tina Bakka

The fifth strategy, **a question,** is briefly illustrated by the opening paragraph of an essay about whether it is sometimes permissible for doctors to lie to their patients.

Should doctors ever lie to benefit their patients—to speed recovery or to conceal the approach of death? In medicine as in law, government, and other lines of work, the requirements of honesty often seem dwarfed by greater needs: the need to shelter from brutal news or to uphold a promise of secrecy; to expose corruption or to promote the public interest.

—*Sissela Bok*

The sixth strategy, **a glance at the opposition,** is especially effective if the opposing view is well established, but while you state it, you should manage to convey your distrust of it. Here is an example:

One often hears, correctly, that there is a world food crisis, and one almost as often hears that not enough food is produced to feed the world's entire population. The wealthier countries, it is said, jeopardize their own chances for survival when they attempt to subsidize all of the poorer countries in which the masses are starving. Often the life-boat analogy is offered: There is room in the boat for only X people, and to take in $X + 1$ is to overload the boat and to invite the destruction of all. But is it true that the world cannot and does not produce enough food to save the whole population from starving?

—*V. Nagarajan*

The seventh strategy, **the assertion that a problem exists,** is common in essays that make proposals. The following example is the first paragraph of a grant proposal written by biomedical engineers seeking government funding for their research project, a new method for treating liver cancer. Notice that the paragraph does not offer the authors' proposal; it simply points out that there is an unsolved problem, and the reader infers that the proposal will offer the solution.

Liver cancer, especially metastatic colorectal cancer, is a significant and increasing health concern. In the United States, half of the 157,000 new cases of colorectal cancer will develop metastases in the liver. These metastases will lead to over 17,000 deaths annually. And while not as significant a health risk as colorectal metastasis, hepatocellular carcinoma is being diagnosed with increasing frequency. The current standard of practice for treating liver cancer is surgical resection, but only 10% of patients are eligible for this procedure. (Circumstances limiting eligibility include the tumor location, the number of lobes affected by the cancer, the patient's general poor health, and cirrhosis.) Further, less than 20% of those patients who undergo resection survive for three years without recurrence. Transplantation is an alternative to resection, but this technique is not appropriate for metastatic disease or for larger cancers, and the shortage of liver grafts limits the usefulness of this technique. Systemic chemotherapy has been shown to have a therapeutic effect on metastases, but it has also been shown to have no effect on long-term survival rates.

—*Michael Curley and Patrick Hamilton*

Clearly, there is no one way to write an opening paragraph, but we want to add that you cannot go wrong in beginning your essay—especially if it's an analytic essay written for a course in the humanities—with a paragraph that includes **a statement of your thesis.** A common version of this kind of paragraph:

- offers some background (if you're writing about a novel, for example, you'll give the author and title as well as relevant information about the novel's plot);

- suggests the problem the essay will address (in the paragraph below, the problem is implied: In *Frankenstein* similar characters meet very different fates; how can we account for the difference?); and

- ends with a sentence that states the main point, or thesis, of the essay.

    In <u>Frankenstein</u>, Mary Shelley frames the
novel with narratives of two similar characters
who meet markedly different fates. Frankenstein,
the medical researcher, and Walton, the explorer,
are both passionately determined to push forward
the boundaries of human knowledge. But while Walton's ambition to explore unknown regions of the
earth is directed by reason and purpose, Frankenstein's ambition to create life is unfocussed and
misguided. This difference in the nature of their
ambitions determines their fates. Walton's controlled ambition leads him to abandon his goal
in order to save the lives of his crew members.
When we last see him, he is heading toward home
and safety. Frankenstein's unchecked ambition
leads to his own death and the self-destruction
of his creature.

Concluding Paragraphs

Concluding paragraphs, like opening paragraphs, are especially difficult if only because they are so conspicuous. Fortunately, you are not
always obliged to write one. Descriptive essays, for example, may end
merely with a final paragraph, not with a paragraph that draws a conclusion. In an expository essay explaining a process or mechanism you
may simply stop when you have finished.

But if you do have to write a concluding paragraph, say something interesting. It is not of the slightest interest to say "Thus we see
..." and then echo your title and first paragraph. There is some justification for a summary at the end of a long essay because the reader
may have half forgotten some of the ideas presented thirty pages earlier, but an essay that can easily be held in the mind needs something
more. A good concluding paragraph rounds out the previous discus-

sion. Such a paragraph may offer a few sentences that summarize (without the obviousness of "We may now summarize"); but it will probably also draw an inference that has not previously been expressed. To draw such an inference is not to introduce an entirely new idea—the end of an essay is hardly the place for that. Rather it is to see the previous material in a fresh perspective, to take the discussion perhaps one step further.

Because all writers have to find out what they think about any given topic, and have to find the strategies appropriate for presenting these thoughts to a particular audience, we hesitate to offer a do-it-yourself kit for final paragraphs, but the following simple devices often work:

- End with a quotation, especially a quotation that amplifies or varies a quotation used in the opening paragraph.

- End with some idea or detail from the beginning of the essay and thus bring it full circle.

- End with a new (but related) point, one that takes your discussion a step further.

- End with an allusion, say to a historical or mythological figure or event, putting your topic in a larger framework.

- End with a glance at the readers—not with a demand that they mount the barricades, but with a suggestion that the next move is theirs.

If you adopt any of these devices, do so quietly; the aim is not to write a grand finale, but to complete or round out a discussion.

Here are the beginning and the end of an essay on change in Emily Dickinson's poetry. (We reprint the beginning as well as the end of the essay to illustrate the first two suggestions above.) Note the way the writer begins the last paragraph with a quotation that amplifies the opening paragraph's point about Dickinson's troubled response to change in the opening paragraphs; note also that the word "palsy," found in the opening paragraph, appears again in the last paragraph.

Emily Dickinson's life knew little change of the conventional sort. As her sister-in-law Susan

wrote in an 1886 obituary, "Miss Emily Dickinson
of Amherst,"

> The death of Miss Emily Dickinson, daughter
> of the late Edward Dickinson, at Amherst on
> Saturday, makes another sad inroad on the
> small circle so long occupying the old
> family mansion. It was for a long
> generation overlooked by death, and one
> passing in and out of there thought of old-
> fashioned times, when parents and children
> grew up and passed maturity together, in
> lives of singular uneventfulness, unmarked
> by sad or joyous crises.

Dickinson lived in the same house all her years but
the one she spent at seminary; she never married;
she never worked. Yet in spite of this permanence--
or because of it--change seemed to fascinate her
and to inspire much of her poetry. She says as much
in a June 1862 letter to her mentor T. W. Higgin-
son, whom she tells that when "a sudden light on
Orchards, or a new fashion in the wind trouble my
attention," she feels a "palsy" that "the Verses
just relieve" (Selected 174). Indeed Dickinson is
probably best known for her many verses on the most
troubling of all changes: "Because I could not stop
for Death / He kindly stopped for me." Yet changes-
-deaths, seasonal changes, shifts in the quality of
light (as at sunset or sunrise)--both trouble and
charm Dickinson. A remark from a letter of April
1873 to her cousins Louise and Frances Norcross
reveals the dichotomy in her attitude. . . .

Now for the final paragraph:

> "Poetry is what Dickinson did to her doubts and
> incomprehension," writes critic David Porter (328),
> and she surely felt doubt about things she knew
> or feared would change. "Because I could not say
> it--I fixed it in the Verse--for you to read--when
> your thought wavers," she wrote in an 1862 letter to
> Samuel Bowles (Selected 170). Dickinson wrote about

change to give it the kind of order she understood, to control it and to fix it and so relieve her "palsy." To this extent, poetry for her must have had an immortal quality, like the wine of Indian Summer, and writing it must have been an ultimate act of faith.

All essayists will have to find their own ways of ending each essay; the five strategies we have suggested are common but they are not for you if you don't find them useful. And so, rather than ending this section with rules about how to end essays, we suggest how not to end them: Don't merely summarize, don't say "in conclusion," don't introduce a totally new point, and don't apologize.

CHECKLIST FOR REVISING PARAGRAPHS

✔ Does the paragraph *say* anything? Does it have substance? (See pp. 43–45.)

✔ Does the paragraph have a topic sentence? If so, is it in the best place? If the paragraph doesn't have a topic sentence, might one improve the paragraph? Or does it have a clear topic idea? (See pp. 46–48.)

✔ If the paragraph is an opening paragraph, is it interesting enough to attract and to hold a reader's attention? (See pp. 63–70) If it is a later paragraph, does it easily evolve out of the previous paragraph, and lead into the next paragraph? (See pp. 54–60.)

✔ Does the paragraph contain some principle of development, for instance from cause to effect, or from general to particular? What is the purpose of the paragraph, and does the paragraph fulfill the purpose? (See pp. 50–52.)

✔ Does each sentence clearly follow from the preceding sentence? Have you provided transitional words or cues to guide your reader? Would it be useful to repeat certain key words, for clarity? (See pp. 52–54.)

✔ Is the closing paragraph effective, and not an unnecessary restatement of the obvious? (See pp. 71–73.)

CHAPTER FOUR

REVISING FOR CONCISENESS

Excess is the common substitute for energy.
—*Marianne Moore*

Writers who want to keep the attention and confidence of their audience revise for conciseness. The general rule is to say everything relevant in as few words as possible. The conclusion of the Supreme Court's decision in *Brown v. the Board of Education of Topeka*, for example—"Separate educational facilities are inherently unequal"—says it all in six words.

The writers of the following sentences talk too much; they bore us because they don't make every word count.

        There are two pine trees which grow behind
    this house.
        On his left shoulder is a small figure
    standing. He is about the size of the doctor's
    head.
        The judge is seated behind the bench and he
    is wearing a judicial robe.

Compare those three sentences with these revisions:

        Two pine trees grow behind this house.
        On his left shoulder stands a small figure,
    about the size of the doctor's head.
        The judge, wearing a robe, sits behind
    the bench.

The time to begin revising for conciseness is when you think you have an acceptable draft in hand—something that pretty much covers your topic and comes reasonably close to saying what you believe about it. As you go over it, study each sentence to see what can be deleted without loss of meaning. Read each paragraph, preferably aloud, to see if each sentence supports the topic sentence or idea and clarifies the point you are making. Leave in the concrete details and examples that support your ideas, but cut out all the deadwood that chokes them:

- extra words
- empty or pretentious phrases
- weak qualifiers
- redundancies
- negative constructions
- wordy uses of the verb *to be*
- other extra verbs and verb phrases.

Instant Prose

Here are some examples of Instant Prose from students' essays:

```
Frequently a chapter title in a book reveals
to the reader the main point that the author
desires to bring out during the course of
the chapter.
```

We could try revising this, cutting the twenty-seven words down to seven:

```
A chapter's title often reveals its thesis.
```

But why bother? Unless the title is an exception, is the point worth making?

```
The two poems are basically similar in many ways,
yet they have their significant differences.
```

True, all poems are both similar to and different from other poems. Start over with your next sentence, perhaps something like: "The two poems, superficially similar in rough paraphrase, are strikingly different in diction."

> Although the essay is simple in plot, the theme encompasses many vital concepts of emotional makeup.
>
> Following a transcendental vein, the nostalgia in the poem takes on a spiritual quality.
>
> Cassell only presents a particular situation concerning the issue, and with clear descriptions and a certain style sets up an interesting article.

Unadulterated Instant Prose. Not even the writers of these sentences now know what they mean.

Writing Instant Prose is an acquired habit, like smoking cigarettes; fortunately it's easier to kick. It often begins in high school, sometimes earlier, when the victim is assigned a ten-page paper, or is told that a paragraph *must* contain at least three sentences, or that a thesis is stated in the introduction to an essay, elaborated in the body, and repeated in the conclusion. If the instructions appear arbitrary, and the student is bored or intimidated by them, the response is likely to be meaningless and mechanical.

Such students have forgotten the true purpose of writing—the discovery and communication of ideas, attitudes, and judgments. They concentrate instead on the word count: stuffing sentences, padding paragraphs, repeating points, and adding flourishes. Rewarded by a satisfactory grade, they repeat the performance, and in time, through practice, develop some fluency in spilling out words without thought or commitment, and almost without effort. Such students may enter college feeling somehow inauthentic, perhaps even aware that they don't really mean what they write—a sure symptom of habitual use of, or addiction to, Instant Prose.

How to Avoid Instant Prose

1. Trust yourself. Writing Instant Prose is not only a habit; it's also a form of alienation. If you habitually use Instant Prose, you probably don't think of what you write as your own but as something you produce on demand for someone else, most likely that unreasonable authority, the teacher, whose mysterious whims and insatiable appetite for words must somehow be satisfied. Breaking the habit begins with recognizing it. It means learning to respect your ideas and experiences, and determining that when you write, you'll write what you mean. This involves taking some risks, of course; habits offer some security or they would have no grip on us. Moreover, we all have moments when we doubt that our ideas are worth taking seriously. Keep writing honestly anyway. The self-doubts will pass; accomplishing something—writing one clear sentence—can help make them pass.

2. Learn to recognize Instant Prose Additives when they crop up in your writing, and in what you read. And you *will* find them in what you read—in textbooks and in academic journals, notoriously.

Here's an example from a recent book on contemporary theater:

> One of the principal and most persistent sources of error that tends to bedevil a considerable proportion of contemporary literary analysis is the assumption that the writer's creative process is a wholly conscious and purposive type of activity.

Notice all the extra stuff in the sentence: "principal and most persistent," "tends to bedevil," "considerable proportion," "type of activity." Cleared of deadwood the sentence might read:

> The assumption that the writer's creative process is wholly conscious bedevils much contemporary criticism.

3. Acquire two things: a new habit, Revising for Conciseness; and what Isaac Singer calls "the writer's best friend," a wastebasket.

Extra Words and Empty Words

Cross out extra words; replace vague, empty, or pretentious words and phrases with specific and direct language. Notice how, in the examples provided, the following words crop up: "significant," "situation," "involving," "effect." These words have legitimate uses, but are often no more than Instant Prose Additives. Cross them out whenever you can. Similar words to watch out for: *aspect, basically, facet, factor, fundamental, manner, nature, type, ultimate, utilization, viable, virtually, vital.* If they make your writing sound good, don't hesitate—cross them out at once.

Wordy

However, it must be remembered that Ruth's marriage could have positive effects on Naomi's situation.

Concise

Ruth's marriage, however, will also provide security for Naomi.

In the revision, the unnecessary "it must be remembered that" has been struck out. For the vague words "positive effects" and "situation," specific words have been substituted. The revision, though briefer, says more.

Wordy

In high school, where I had the opportunity for three years of working with the student government, I realized how significantly a person's enthusiasm could be destroyed merely by the attitudes of his superiors.

Concise

In high school, during three years on the student council, I saw students' enthusiasm destroyed by insecure teachers and cynical administrators.

Again, the revised sentence gives more information in fewer words. How?

Wordy

It creates a better motivation of learning when students can design their own programs involving education. This way students' interests can be focused on.

Concise

Motivation improves when students design their own programs, focused on their own interests.

Weak Intensifiers

Words like *very, quite, rather, completely, definitely,* and *so* can usually be struck from a sentence without loss. Paradoxically, sentences are often more emphatic without intensifiers. Try reading the following sentences both with and without the bracketed words:

At that time I was [very] idealistic.

We found the proposal [quite] feasible.

The scene was [extremely] typical.

The death scene is [truly] grotesque.

Always avoid using intensifiers with *unique*. Either something is unique—the only one of its kind—or it is not. It can't be very, quite, so, pretty, or fairly unique.

Circumlocutions

Roundabout or long-winded ways of saying things weaken your prose and tire your reader. Notice how each circumlocution in the first column is matched by a concise expression in the second.

I came to the realization that	I realized that
She is of the opinion that	She thinks that
The quotation is supportive of	The quotation supports
Concerning the matter of	About
During the course of	During
For the period of a week	For a week
In the event that	If
In the process of	During, while
Regardless of the fact that	Although
Due to the fact that	Because
For the simple reason that	Because
The fact that	That
Inasmuch as	Since
If the case was such that	If
It is often the case that	Often
In all cases	Always
I made contact with	I called, saw, phoned, wrote
At that point in time	Then
At this point in time	Now

Now revise this sentence:

These movies have a large degree of popularity for the simple reason that they give the viewers insight in many cases.

Wordy Beginnings

Vague words and phrases sometimes clog the beginnings of sentences. They're like elaborate windups before the pitch.

Wordy

By analyzing carefully the last lines in this stanza, you find the connections between the loose ends of the poem.

Concise

The last lines of the stanza connect the loose ends of the poem.

Wordy

What the cartoonist is illustrating and trying to get across is the greed of the oil producers.

Concise

The cartoon illustrates the greed of the oil producers.

Wordy

In the last stanza is the conclusion (as usual) and it tells of the termination of the dance.

Concise

The last stanza concludes with the end of the dance.

Wordy

In opposition to the situation of the younger son is that of the elder who remained in his father's house, working hard and handling his inheritance wisely.

Concise

The elder son, by contrast, remained in his father's house, worked hard, and handled his inheritance wisely.

Notice that when the deadwood is cleared from the beginning of the sentence, the subject appears early, and the main verb appears close to it:

The last lines . . . connect . . . .

The cartoon illustrates . . . .

The last stanza concludes . . . .

The elder son . . . remained . . . .

Locating the right noun for the subject, and the right verb for the predicate, is the key to revising sentences with wordy beginnings.

Empty Conclusions

Often a sentence that begins well has an empty conclusion. The words go on but the sentence seems to stand still; if it's not revised, it requires another sentence to explain it.

Empty

"Those Winter Sundays" is composed so that a reader can feel what the poet was saying.

(How is it composed? What is he saying?)

Concise

"Those Winter Sundays" describes the speaker's anger as a child, and his remorse as an adult.

Empty

In both Orwell's and Baldwin's essays the feeling of white supremacy is very important.

(Why is white supremacy important?)

Concise

Both Orwell and Baldwin trace the insidious consequences of white supremacy.

Wordy Uses of the Verbs To Be, To Have, and To Make

Notice that in the preceding unrevised sentences a form of the verb *to be* introduces the empty conclusion: "*was* saying," "*is* very important." In each revision, the right verb added and generated substance. In the following sentences, substitutions for the verb *to be* both invigorate and shorten otherwise substantial sentences. (The wordy expressions are italicized, and so are the revisions.)

Wordy

The scene *is taking place* at night, in front of the capitol building.

Concise

The scene *takes place* at night, in front of the capitol building.

Wordy

In this shoeshining and early rising *there are indications* of church attendance.

Concise

The early rising and shoeshining *indicate* church attendance.

Wordy

The words "flashing," "rushing," "plunging," and "tossing" *are suggestive of* excitement.

Concise

The words "flashing," "rushing," "plunging," and "tossing" *suggest* excitement.

The rule is, whenever you can, replace a form of the verb *to be* with a stronger verb.

To Be	Strong Verb
and a participle ("is taking")	takes
and a noun ("are indications")	indicate
and an adjective ("are suggestive")	suggest

Wordy

The Friar *has knowledge* that Juliet is alive.

Concise

The Friar *knows* that Juliet is alive.

Wordy

The stanzas *make a vivid contrast* between Heaven and Hell.

Concise

The stanzas *vividly contrast* Heaven and Hell.

Like all rules, this one has exceptions. We don't list them here; you'll discover them by listening to your sentences.

Redundancy

Redundancy refers to unnecessary repetition in the expression of ideas. "Future plans," after all, are only plans, and "to glide smoothly" or "to scurry rapidly" is only to glide or to scurry. Unlike repetition, which often provides emphasis or coherence (for example, "government of the people, by the people, for the people"), redundancy can always be eliminated.

Redundant

Any student could randomly sit anywhere. (If the students could sit anywhere, the seating was random.)

Concise

Students could sit anywhere.
Students chose their seats at random.

Redundant

I have no justification with which to excuse myself.

Concise

I can't justify my action.

Redundant

In the orthodox Cuban culture, the surface of the female role seemed degrading. (Perhaps this sentence means what it says. More probably "surface" and "seemed" are redundant.)

Concise

In the orthodox Cuban culture, the female role seemed degrading.
In the orthodox Cuban culture, the female role was superficially degrading.

Redundant

In "Araby" the boy feels alienated emotionally from his family.

Concise

In "Araby" the boy feels alienated from his family.

What words can be crossed out of the following phrases?

  a. throughout the entire article

  b. her attitude of indifference

  c. a conservative type suit

  d. his own personal opinion

  e. elements common to both of them

  f. emotions and feelings

  g. shared together

  h. alleged suspect

Many phrases in common use are redundant. For example, there is no need to write "blare noisily," since the meaning of the adverb "noisily" is already in the verb "blare." Watch for phrases like these when you revise:

round in shape	resulting effect
tall in stature	prove conclusively
must necessarily	connected together
basic fundamentals	very unique
true fact	very universal
free gift	the reason why is because

Negative Constructions

Negative constructions are often wordy and sometimes pretentious.

Wordy

Housing for married students is *not unworthy of* consideration.

Concise

Housing for married students is worth considering.

Better

The trustees should earmark funds for married students' housing. (Probably what the author meant.)

"See what I mean? You're never sure just where you stand with them." © The
New Yorker Collection 1971 Al Rossi from Cartoonbank.com. All Rights Reserved.

The Golden Rule of writing is "Write for others as you would have
them write for you," not "Write for others in a manner not unreason-
ably dissimilar to the manner in which you would have them write
for you."

Extra Sentences, Extra Clauses: Subordination

Sentences are sometimes wordy because ideas are given more elaborate
grammatical constructions than they need. In revising, one can often
reduce these constructions. Two sentences, for example, may be reduced
to one, or a clause may be reduced to a phrase.

Wordy

The Book of Ruth was probably written in the fifth century B.C. It was a
time when women were considered the property of men.

Concise

The Book of Ruth was probably written in the fifth century B.C., when
women were considered the property of men.

Wordy

The first group was the largest. This group was seated in the center of the dining hall.

Concise

The first group, the largest, was seated in the center of the dining hall.

Who, Which, That

Watch for clauses beginning with *who, which,* and *that.*

Wordy

George Orwell is the pen name of Eric Blair, *who was* an English writer.

Concise

George Orwell is the pen name of Eric Blair, an English writer.

Wordy

They are seated at a table *which* is covered with a patched and tattered cloth.

Concise

They are seated at a table covered with a patched and tattered cloth.

Wordy

There is one feature *that is* grossly out of proportion.

Concise

One feature is grossly out of proportion.

It Is, This Is, There Are

Also watch for sentences and clauses beginning with *it is, this is, there are* (again, wordy uses of the verb *to be*). These expressions often lead to a *which* or a *that*, but even when they don't they may be wordy.

Wordy

This is a quotation from Black Elk's autobiography *which* discloses his prophetic powers.

Concise

This quotation from Black Elk's autobiography discloses his prophetic powers.

Wordy

It is frequently considered *that Hamlet* is Shakespeare's most puzzling play.

Concise

Hamlet is frequently considered Shakespeare's most puzzling play.

Wordy

In Notman's photograph of Buffalo Bill and Sitting Bull *there are* definite contrasts between the two figures.

Concise

Notman's photograph of Buffalo Bill and Sitting Bull contrasts the two figures.

(For further discussion of *which* clauses, see also Chapter 11, "Usage," page 295.)

Some Concluding Remarks About Conciseness

We spoke earlier about how students learn to write Instant Prose and acquire other wordy habits—by writing what they think the teacher has asked for. We haven't forgotten that instructors assign papers of a certain length in college too. But the length given is not an arbitrary limit that must be reached—the instructor who asks for a ten-page paper is probably trying to tell you that it's likely to take you ten pages to develop your ideas on the topic at hand. Such, apparently, was the intention of William Randolph Hearst, the newspaper publisher, who cabled an astronomer, "Is there life on Mars? Cable reply 1000 words." The astronomer's reply was, "Nobody knows," repeated 500 times.

What do you do when you've been asked to produce a ten-page paper and after diligent writing and revising you find you've said everything relevant to your topic in seven and a half pages? Our advice is, hand it in. We can't remember ever counting the words or pages of a substantial, interesting essay; we assume that our colleagues elsewhere are equally reasonable and equally overworked. If we're wrong, tell us about it—in writing, and in the fewest possible words.

CHECKLIST FOR REVISING FOR CONCISENESS

✔ Does every word count? Can any words or phrases be cut without loss of meaning?

✔ Are there any empty or pretentious words such as *situation, factor, virtually, significant,* and *utilize?* (See pp. 77–78.)

✔ Do intensifiers such as *very, truly,* and *rather* weaken your sentences? (See pp. 78–79.)

✔ Are there any roundabout or long-winded locutions? Do you say, for example, *at that point in time* when you mean *then,* or *for the simple reason that* when you mean *because?* (See pp. 79, 83.)

✔ Do sentences get off to a fast start? Can you cut any sentences that open with "it is...that"? (See pp. 80–81.)

✔ Can you replace forms of the verbs *to be, to have,* and *to make* with precise and active verbs? (See pp. 81–82.)

✔ Are there any redundancies or negative constructions? (See pp. 83–85.)

✔ Can any sentences be combined using subordination? (See pp. 85–86.)

CHAPTER FIVE

REVISING FOR CLARITY

Here's to plain speaking and clear
understanding.
—*Sidney Greenstreet, in* The Maltese Falcon

Clarity

First, read the following two examples:

We have seen new realities created by the advance of physics. But this
chain of creation can be traced back far beyond the starting point of
physics. One of the most primitive concepts is that of an object. The concepts of a tree, a horse, any material body, are creations gained on the
basis of experience, though the impressions from which they arise are
primitive in comparison with the world of physical phenomena. A cat
teasing a mouse also creates, by thought, its own primitive reality. The
fact that the cat reacts in a similar way toward any mouse it meets shows
that it forms concepts and theories which are its guide through its own
world of sense impressions.

—*Albert Einstein and Leopold Infeld*

Skills constitute the manipulative techniques of human goal attainment
and control in relation to the physical world, so far as artifacts or
machines especially designed as tools do not yet supplement them. Truly

human skills are guided by organized and codified *knowledge* of both the things to be manipulated and the human capacities that are used to manipulate them. Such knowledge is an aspect of cultural-level symbolic processes, and, like other aspects to be discussed presently, requires the capacities of the human central nervous system, particularly the brain. This organic system is clearly essential to all of the symbolic processes; as we well know, the human brain is far superior to the brain of any other species.

—*Talcott Parsons*

Why is the first passage easier to understand than the second?

Both passages discuss the relationship between the brain and the physical world it attempts to understand. The first passage, by Einstein and Infeld, is, if anything, more complex both in what it asserts and in what it suggests than the second, by Parsons. Both passages explain that the brain organizes sense impressions. But Einstein and Infeld further explain that the history of physics can be understood as an extension of the simplest sort of organization, such as we all make in distinguishing a tree from a horse, or such as even a cat makes in teasing a mouse. Parsons only promises that "other aspects" will "be discussed presently." How many of us are eager for those next pages?

Good writing is clear, not because it presents simple ideas, but because it presents ideas in the simplest form the subject permits. A clear analysis doesn't falsely reduce a complex problem to a simple one; it breaks it down into its simple, comprehensible parts and discusses them, one by one. A clear paragraph explains one of these parts coherently, and in language as simple and as particular as the reader's understanding requires and the context allows. Where Parsons writes of "organized and codified *knowledge* of... the things to be manipulated," Einstein and Infeld write simply of the concept of an object. And even "object," a simple but general word, is further clarified by the specific, familiar examples, "tree" and "horse." Parsons writes of "the manipulative techniques of... goal attainment and control in relation to the physical world, so far as artifacts or machines especially designed as tools do not yet supplement them." Einstein and Infeld show us a cat teasing a mouse.

Notice also the clear organization of Einstein and Infeld's paragraph. The first sentence, clearly transitional, refers to the advance of physics traced in the preceding pages. The next sentence, introduced by "But," reverses our direction: We are now going to look not at an advance, but at primitive beginnings. And the following sentences, to the end of the paragraph, fulfill that promise. We move back to primitive human concepts, clarified by examples, and finally to the still more primitive example of the cat. Parson's paragraph is also organized, but the route is much more difficult to follow.

Why do people write obscurely? It's difficult to write clearly.[1] Authorities may be obscure not because they want to tax you with unnecessary difficulties, but because they don't know how to avoid such difficulties. If you have ever tried to install a computer upgrade by following the "easy instructions," you know that the simplest kind of expository writing, giving instructions, can foil the writers most eager for your goodwill (that is, those who want you to use their products). Few instructions, unfortunately, are as unambiguous as "Go to jail. Go directly to jail. Do not pass Go. Do not collect $200."

You can, though, learn to write clearly, by learning to recognize common sources of obscurity in writing and by consciously revising your own work. We offer, to begin with, three general rules:

1. Use the simplest, most exact, most specific language your subject allows.

2. Put together what belongs together, in the essay, in the paragraph, and in the sentence.

3. Keep your reader in mind, particularly when you revise.

Now for more specific advice, and examples—the cats and mice of revising for clarity.

Clarity and Exactness: Using the Right Word

Denotation

Be sure the word you choose has the right explicit meaning, or *denotation.* Did you mean sarcastic or ironic? Fatalistic or pessimistic? Disinterested or uninterested? Biannual or semiannual? Enforce or reinforce? Use or usage? If you're not sure, check the dictionary. You'll find some

---

[1] Our first draft of this sentence read "Writing clearly is difficult." Can you see why we changed it?

of the most commonly misused words discussed in Chapter 11, "Usage," pages 272–99. Here are examples of a few others.

1. Daru faces a dilemma between his humane feelings and his conceptions of justice. (Strictly speaking, a dilemma requires a choice between two equally unattractive alternatives. "Conflict" would be a better word here.)

2. However, as time dragged on, exercising seemed to lose its charisma. (What is charisma? Why is it inexact here?)

3. When I run, I don't allow myself to stop until I have reached my destiny. (What is the difference between *destiny* and *goal?*)

Connotation

Be sure the word you choose has the right *connotation* (association, implication). As Mark Twain said, the difference between the right word and the almost right word is the difference between lightning and the lightning bug.

"I'm not quite clear on this, Fulton. Are you moaning about your prerequisites, your requisites, or perquisites?" © The New Yorker Collection 1976 Mischa Richter from Cartoonbank.com. All Rights Reserved.

1. Boston politics has always upheld the reputation of being especially crooked. ("Upheld" inappropriately suggests that Boston has proudly maintained its reputation. "Has always had" would be appropriate here, but pale. "Deserved" would, in this context, be ironic, implying—accurately—the writer's scorn.)

2. This book, unlike many other novels, lacks tedious descriptive passages. ("Lacks" implies a deficiency. How would you revise the sentence?)

3. New Orleans, notorious for its good jazz and good food . . . . (Is "notorious" the word here? or "famous"?)

4. Sunday, Feb. 9. Another lingering day at Wellesley. (In this entry from a student's journal, "lingering" strikes us as right. What does "lingering" imply about Sundays at Wellesley that "long" would not?)

Because words have connotations, most writing—even when it pretends to be objective—conveys attitudes as well as facts. Consider, for example, this passage by Jessica Mitford, describing part of the procedure used for embalming:

> A long, hollow needle attached to a tube . . . is jabbed into the abdomen, poked around the entrails and chest cavity, the contents of which are pumped out... .

Here, as almost always, the writer's *purpose* in large measure determines the choice of words. Probably the sentence accurately describes part of the procedure, but it also, of course, records Mitford's contempt for the procedure. Suppose she wanted to be more respectful—suppose, for example, she were an undertaker writing an explanatory pamphlet. Instead of the needle being "jabbed" it would be "inserted," and instead of being "poked around the entrails" it would be "guided around the viscera," and the contents would not be "pumped out" but would be "drained." Mitford's words would be the wrong words for an undertaker explaining embalming to apprentices or to the general public, but, given her purpose, they are exactly the right ones because they clearly convey her attitude.

Notice, too, that many words have social, political, or sexist overtones. What is implied by the distinction? Consider the differences in *connotation* in each of the following series:

1. underdeveloped nations, developing nations, emerging nations
2. preference, bias, prejudice

3. upbringing, conditioning, brainwashing

4. intelligence gathering, espionage, spying

5. antiabortion, pro-life; pro-abortion, pro-choice

Avoiding Sexist Language

Traditionally, the male pronouns *he* and *his* have been used to refer to both men and women: "A historian must consider the context of *his* source." But contemporary writers avoid the generic use of male pronouns, because such usage is sexist (our example excludes women historians from the discussion), and because it can be misleading and unclear (the example may suggest that there are no women historians, or that women historians do something different from the men). Common remedies include:

- Using both male and female pronouns: "A historian must consider the context of *his* or *her* source."

- Substituting the plural form: "*Historians* must consider the context of *their* source."

- Eliminating the pronoun: "Historians must consider a source's context."

Note: Writers and speakers sometimes attempt to correct sexist language by using a plural pronoun with a singular subject: "A *historian* must consider *their* source's context." But this approach produces ungrammatical sentences: The pronoun doesn't agree with its antecedent. (For more on agreement, see pages 115–117.) Writers also sometimes use such constructions as "his/her," "him/her," or "s/he": "A historian must consider his/her source." While not incorrect, we think that this approach produces ugly sentences, and we recommend that you use one of the three remedies above.

Likewise, avoid using "man" and "mankind" generically:

"Man's need for approval . . . ."

Substitute gender-neutral terms for gender-specific terms whenever possible—unless, of course, your sentence refers specifically to one gender. The sentence above could thus be revised:

"Humanity's need for approval . . . ."
"Our need for approval . . . ."

Here are more examples of gender-specific or sexist terms, with possible replacements:

Sexist term	Gender-neutral term
chairman	chairperson, chair, head
manpower	personnel
layman	layperson
stewardess	flight attendant
freshman	first-year student
mailman	mail carrier
poetess	poet

Quotation Marks as Apologies

When you have used words with exact meanings (denotations) and appropriate associations (connotations) for your purpose, don't apologize for them by putting quotation marks around them. If the words *copped a plea*, *ripped off*, or *kids* suit your purpose better than *plea-bargained*,

stolen, or *children*, use them. If they are inappropriate, don't put them in quotation marks; find the right words.

Being Specific

In writing descriptions, catch the richness, complexity, and uniqueness of things. Suppose, for example, you are describing a scene from your child-hood, a setting you loved. There was, in particular, a certain tree... and you write: "Near the water there was a big tree that was rather impressive." Most of us would produce something like that sentence. Here is the sentence Ernesto Galarza wrote in *Barrio Boy:*

> On the edge of the pond, at the far side, there was an enormous walnut tree, standing like an open umbrella whose ribs extended halfway across the still water of the pool.

We probably could not have come up with the metaphor of the umbrella because we wouldn't have seen the similarity. (As Aristotle observed, the gift for making metaphors distinguishes the poet from the rest of us.) But we can all train ourselves to be accurate observers and reporters. For "the water" (general) we can specify "pond"; for "near" we can say how near, "on the edge of the pond," and add the specific location, "at the far side"; for "tree" we can give the species, "walnut tree"; and for "big" we can provide a picture, its branches "extended halfway across" the pond: It was, in fact, "enormous."

Galarza does not need to add limply, as we did, that the tree "was rather impressive." The tree he describes *is* impressive. That he accurately remembered it persuades us that he was impressed, without his having to tell us he was. For writing descriptions, a good general rule is: Show, don't tell.

Be as specific as you can be in all forms of exposition too. Take the time, when you revise, to find the exact word to replace vague phrases or clichés. In the following examples we have to guess or invent what the writer means.

Vague
The clown's part in *Othello* is very small.

Specific
The clown appears in only two scenes in *Othello*.

The clown in *Othello* speaks only thirty lines. (Notice the substitution of the verb "appears" or "speaks" for the frequently debilitating "is." And in place of the weak intensifier "very" we have specific details to tell us how small the role is.)

Vague

He feels uncomfortable at the whole situation. (Many feelings are uncomfortable. Which one does he feel? What's the situation?)

Specific

He feels guilty for having distrusted his father.

Vague cliché

Then she criticized students for living in an ivory tower. (Did she criticize them for being detached or for being secluded? For social irresponsibility or studiousness?)

Specific

Then she criticized students for being socially irresponsible.

Using Examples

In addition to exact words and specific details, illustrative examples make for clear writing. Einstein and Infeld, in the passage quoted on page 89, use as an example of a primitive concept a cat teasing not only its first mouse, but also "any mouse it meets." Here is another passage from *Barrio Boy*; like the paragraph from Einstein and Infeld, this paragraph clarifies and develops its topic through examples:

In Jalco people spoke in two languages—Spanish and with gestures. These signs were made with the face or hands or a combination of both. If you bent one arm and tapped the elbow with the other hand, it meant "He is stingy." When you sawed one arm across the other you were saying that someone you knew played the fiddle terribly. To say that a man was a tippler you made a set of cow's horns with the little finger and the thumb of one hand, bending the three middle fingers to the palm and pointing the thumb at your mouth. And if you wanted to indicate, without saying so for the sake of politeness, that a mutual acquaintance was daffy, you tapped three times on your forehead with your middle finger.

—*Ernesto Galarza*

Now look at a student's paragraph, here printed in the left column, from an essay whose thesis is that rage can be a useful mechanism for effecting change. Then compare the left-hand paragraph with the same paragraph, revised, at the right. Note the specific ways, sentence by sentence, the student revised for clarity.

In my high school we had little say in the learning processes that were used. The subjects that we were required to take were irrelevant. One had to take them to earn enough points to graduate. Some of the teachers were sympathetic to our problem. They would tell us about when they were young, how they tried to oppose their school system. But when they were young it was a long time ago, for most of them. The principal would call assemblies to speak on the subject. They were entitled "The Value of an Education" or "Get a Good Education to Have a Bright Future." The titles were not inviting. They had nothing to do with our plight. Most students never

In my high school we had little say about our curriculum. We were required, for example, to choose either American or European History to earn enough points for graduation. We wanted, but were at first refused, the option of Black History. Some of our teachers were sympathetic with us; one told me about her fight opposing the penmanship course required in her school. Nor was the principal totally indifferent-- he called assemblies. I remember one talk he gave called "The Value of an Education in Today's World," and another, "Get a Good Education to Have a Bright Future." I don't recall hearing about a Black History course in

came to any
agreements with the
principal because
most of his thoughts
and views seemed old
and outdated.

either talk. Once,
he invited a group
of us to meet with
him in his office,
but we didn't reach
any agreement. He
solemnly showed us
an American History
text (not the one we
used) that had a
whole chapter
devoted to Black
History.

Jargon and Technical Language

Most dictionaries give three meanings for *jargon:* technical language, meaningless language, and inflated or pretentious language.

The members of almost every profession or trade—indeed, almost all people who share any specialized interest—use the jargon of their field. And this is certainly true of members of academic disciplines. In fact, learning a new discipline involves learning a new vocabulary, a new set of technical terms. Art historians talk of *cubism, iconography,* and *formalism;* Freudians talk of *cathect, libido,* and the *oral phase;* film critics and theorists talk of *anamorphic lenses, optical printers,* and *silent speed.*

Properly used, technical language communicates information concisely and clearly, and it can create a comfortable bond between speakers, or between the writer and the reader.

For example, in the following sentences, concerned with twentieth-century art from a museum publication, the writer reasonably assumes that her readers—most likely people who are interested in and knowledgeable about art—will be able to make sense of such technical terms as "biomorphic," "calligraphic," "gesture," and "Abstract Expressionism":

> In Willem de Kooning's biomorphic black enamel drawing . . . , drawn for a member of the Julliard String Quartet, the artist has abandoned the idea of a central organizing form. Black calligraphic shapes whip across the surface of the paper. There is a sense of gesture, an essential feature of Abstract Expressionism.

Untitled, 1949. Willem de Kooning, American (b. 1904). Black enamel. Sophie M.
Friedman Fund. Courtesy Museum of Fine Arts, Boston. Reproduced with permission. © 2001 Museum
of Fine Arts, Boston. All Rights Reserved. © 2001 Willem de Kooning Revocable Trust/Artists Rights
Society (ARS), New York.

On the other hand, jargon sometimes *is* inflated and pretentious. Con-
sider, for example, the following sentence by an art historian writing on
American Indian baskets made for whites in the early twentieth cen-
tury. (The sentence comes from an essay reprinted in *Unpacking Culture:
Art and Commodity in Colonial and Postcolonial Worlds,* ed. Ruth B.
Phillips and Christopher B. Steiner [Berkeley and Los Angeles: U of
California P, 1999]):

> Native curios were privileged in bourgeois parlor decoration as
> metonymic representations of the premodern, their significations
> enhanced by hand-made production and utilitarian function, two aspects
> of the premodern also valorized in the contemporary American Arts and
> Crafts Movement. (148)

This sentence does communicate information to specialists. In fact,
much academic prose sounds an awful lot like the quoted sentence. Nevertheless, we believe that such language doesn't communicate clearly and
efficiently. One problem with the sentence is that the level of abstrac-
tion is very high. Unlike the term "biomorphic," which means "evok-
ing images of biological organisms," or the term "calligraphic," which
here describes figures that recall the curves and loops of handwriting, the

DILBERT reprinted by permission of United Feature Syndicate, Inc.

terms "premodern," "significations," and "valorized" don't call to mind specific, concrete things. The other problem with such language is that it is inflated, or more complicated than it needs to be. Consider the following paraphrase of the sentence on baskets:

> Middle-class whites valued native curios and displayed them in their parlors. Because these objects were handmade and because they had been used in daily life, they stood for a pre-industrial world, a world celebrated also in the contemporary American Arts and Crafts Movement.

In general, it's best to use plain English—or, at least, the plainest English possible. After all, in an essay you wouldn't speak of a "preliminary overall strategizing concept" when "plan" would do. Don't use abstract, inflated language simply in order to sound impressive. On the other hand, do use the specialized terms of your field if you have come to know what they mean, and if they are the best way to make your point, and if you are fairly confident that your imagined reader is familiar with them. If it's your hunch that your reader does not know the terms, you'll have to define them.

Clichés

Clichés (literally, in French, molds from which type is cast) are trite expressions, mechanically reproduced. Since they are available without thought they are great Instant Prose Additives (see pages 75–77). Writers who use them are usually surprised to be criticized: They find the phrases attractive, and may even think them exact. (Phrases become clichés precisely because they have wide appeal and therefore wide use.) But clichés, by their very nature, cannot communicate the uniqueness of your thoughts. Furthermore, because they come instantly to mind, they tend to block the specific detail or exact expression that will let the reader know what precisely is in your mind. In revising, when you strike out a cliché, you force yourself to do the work of writing clearly. The following example is full of clichés:

> Finally, the long awaited day arrived. Up bright and early . . . . She peered at me with suspicion; then a faint smile crossed her face.

Other examples:

first and foremost	time honored
the acid test	bustled to and fro
fatal flaw	short but sweet
budding genius	few and far between
slowly but surely	D-day arrived
little did I know	sigh of relief
the big moment	last but not least

In attempting to avoid clichés, however, don't go to the other extreme of wildly original, super-vivid writing—"'Well then, say something to her,' he roared, his whole countenance gnarled in rage." It's better to write, "he said." (Anyone who intends to write dialogue should memorize Ring Lardner's intentionally funny line, "'Shut up!' he explained.")

Metaphors and Mixed Metaphors

Ordinary speech abounds with metaphors. We speak or write of the foot of a mountain, the germ of an idea, the root of a problem. Metaphors so deeply embedded in the language that they no longer evoke pictures in our minds are called *dead metaphors*. Ordinarily, they offer us, as writers, no problems: We need neither seek them nor avoid them; they are

"You're right as rain. It's the dawn of history, and there are no clichés as yet. I'll drink to that. © The New Yorker Collection 1972 J. B. Handelsman from Cartoonbank.com. All Rights Reserved.

simply there. (Notice, for example, "embedded" two sentences back.) Such metaphors become problems, however, when we unwittingly call them back to life. Howard Nemerov observes: "That these metaphors may be not dead but only sleeping, or that they may arise from the grave and walk in our sentences, is something that has troubled everyone who has ever tried to write plain expository prose."

Dead metaphors are most likely to haunt us when they are embodied in clichés. Since we use clichés without attention to what they literally say or point to, we are unlikely to be aware of the dead metaphors buried in them. But when we attach one cliché to another, we may raise the metaphors from the grave. The result is likely to be a mixed metaphor; the effect is almost always absurd.

Water seeks its own level whichever way you want to slice it.

Traditional liberal education has run out of gas and educational soup kitchens are moving into the vacuum.

The low ebb has been reached and hopefully it's turned the corner.

Her energy, drained through a stream of red tape, led only to closed doors.

As comedian Joe E. Lewis observed, "Show me a man who builds castles in the air and I'll show you a crazy architect."

Fresh metaphors, on the other hand, imaginatively combine accurate observations. They are not prefabricated ideas; they are a means of discovering or inventing new ideas. They enlarge thought and enliven prose. Here are two examples from students' journals:

```
    I have some sort of sporadic restlessness
in me, like the pen on a polygraph machine. It
moves along in curves, then suddenly shoots up,
blowing a bubble in my throat, making my chest
taut, forcing me to move around. It becomes
almost unbearable and then suddenly it will
plunge, leaving something that feels like a smooth
orange wave.
    Time is like wrapping papers. It wraps
memories, decorates them with sentiment. No matter
(almost) what's inside, it's remembered as a
beautiful piece of past time. That's why I even
miss my high school years, which were filled with
tiredness, boredom, confusion.
```

And here is a passage from an essay in which a student analyzes the style of a story he found boring:

```
Every sentence yawns, stretches, shifts from side
to side, and then quietly dozes off.
```

Experiment with metaphors, let them surface in the early drafts of your essays and in your journals, and by all means, introduce original and accurate comparisons in your essays. But leave the mixed metaphors to politicians and comedians.

Euphemisms

Euphemisms are words substituted for other words thought to be offensive. In deodorant advertisements there are no armpits, only *underarms*, which may *perspire*, but not sweat, and even then they don't smell. A parent reading a report card is likely to learn not that his child got an F in conduct, but that she "experiences difficulty exercising self-control:

(a) verbally (b) physically." And where do old people go? To Sun City, "a retirement community for senior citizens."

We do not advise you to write or speak discourteously; we do advise you, though, to use euphemisms sparingly, when tact recommends them. It's customary in a condolence letter to avoid the word *death*, and, depending both on your own feelings and those of the bereaved, you may wish to follow that custom. But there's no reason on earth to write "Hamlet passes on." You should be aware, moreover, that some people find euphemisms themselves offensive. Margaret Kuhn, for instance, argues that the word *old* is preferable to *senior*. "Old," she says "is the right word. ... I think we should wear our gray hair, wrinkles, and crumbling joints as badges of distinction. After all, we worked damn hard to get them."

In revising, replace needless euphemisms with plain words.

Passive or Active Voice?

Verbs appear in either the active or passive voice. In the active voice, the subject acts on the object: "I wrote the review." ("I" is the subject.) In the passive voice, the subject receives the action: "The review was written by me." (Here, "the review" is the subject.) In general prefer the active voice. The passive voice is often vague and sentences using it are needlessly wordy.

Consider the following passage, the opening paragraph of an analytic essay on the classical aspects of a library at a women's college:

> A person walking by Margaret Clapp Library (1908–1913) is struck by its classical design. The symmetry of the façade is established by the regularly spaced columns of the Ionic order on the first story of the building and by pilasters on the second level. In the center of the lower tier are two bronze doors: On the left door a relief is seen, depicting Sapientia (Wisdom), and on the right is seen the image of Caritas (Charity). The Greco-Roman tradition is furthered by the two bronze statues on either side of the entrance. On the left is Vesta (goddess of the hearth) and on the right Minerva (goodess of wisdom). Through the use of classical architecture and Greco-Roman images, an image is conveyed—one which Wellesley College hopes to create in its women.

Although the paragraph is richly informative, it is sluggish, chiefly because the writer keeps using the passive voice: "A person . . . is struck by"; "symmetry is established by"; "a relief is seen"; "on the right is seen"; "tradition is furthered by"; "an image is conveyed."

Converting some or all of these expressions into the active voice will greatly improve the passage:

Revised

The most striking feature of the Margaret Clapp Library, is its classical design. Regularly spaced columns of the Ionic order on the first story, and pilasters on the second, establish the symmetry of the façade. In the center of the lower tier are two bronze doors: On the left door a relief depicts Sapientia (Wisdom), and on the right Caritas (Charity). A bronze statue on each side of the entrance (Vesta, goddess of the hearth, on the left, and Minerva, goddess of wisdom, on the right) furthers the Greco-Roman tradition. Wellesley College hopes, through the use of classical architecture and Greco-Roman sculpture, to inspire in its students particular ideals.

When is the passive voice appropriate? The passive is appropriate when (1) the doer is obvious ("Bush was elected president in 2000"), or (2) the doer is unknown ("The picture was stolen between midnight and 1:00 A.M."), or (3) the doer is unimportant ("Unexposed film should be kept in a light-proof container").

In revising, consider each sentence in which you have used the passive voice. If the passive suits your meaning, retain it; if it obscures your meaning, change it. More often than not, the passive voice obscures meaning.

Passive Voice

The revolver given Daru by the gendarme *is left* in the desk drawer. (Left by whom? The passive voice here obscures the point.)

Active Voice

Daru leaves the gendarme's revolver in the desk drawer.

Passive Voice

Daru serves tea and the Arab *is offered* some. (Confusing shift from the active voice "serves" to the passive voice "is offered.")

Active Voice

Daru serves tea and *offers* the Arab some.

"*And remember—no more subjunctives where the correct mood is indicative.*"

Finally, avoid what has been called the Academic Passive: "In this essay it has been argued that . . ." This cumbersome form used to be common in academic writing (to convey scientific objectivity) but "I have argued" is usually preferable to such stuffiness.

The Writer's "I"

It is seldom necessary in writing an essay (even on a personal experience) to repeat "I think that" or "in my opinion." Your reader knows that what you write is your opinion. Nor is it necessary, if you've done your job well, to apologize. "After reading the story over several times I'm not really sure what it is about, but . . ." Write about something you are reasonably sure of. Occasionally, though, when there is a real problem in the text, for example the probable date of the Book of Ruth, it is not only permissible to disclose doubts and to reveal tentative conclusions; it may be necessary to do so.

Note also that there is no reason to avoid the pronoun *I* when you are in fact writing about yourself. Attempts to avoid *I* ("this writer," "we," expressions in the passive voice such as "it has been said above" and "it was seen") are noticeably awkward and distracting. And sometimes you may want to focus on your subjective response to a topic in order to clarify a point. The following opening paragraph of a movie review provides an example:

> I take the chance of writing about Bergman's *Persona* so long after its showing because this seems to me a movie there's no hurry about. It will be with us a long time, just as it has been on my mind for a long time. Right now, when I am perhaps still under its spell, it seems to me Bergman's masterpiece, but I can't imagine ever thinking it less than one of the great movies. This of course is opinion; what I know for certain is that *Persona* is also one of the most difficult movies I will ever see; and I am afraid that in this case there is a direct connection between difficulty and value. It isn't only that *Persona* is no harder than it has to be; its peculiar haunting power, its spell, and its value come directly from the fact that it's so hard to get a firm grasp on.

> —*Robert Garis*

Students who have been taught not to begin sentences with *I* often produce sentences that are eerily passive even when the verbs are in the active voice. For example:

1. Two reasons are important to my active participation in dance.
2. The name of the program that I enrolled in is the Health Careers Summer Program.
3. An eager curiosity overcame my previous feeling of fear to make me feel better.

But doesn't it make more sense to say:

1. I dance for two reasons.

2. I enrolled in the Health Careers Summer Program.

3. My curiosity aroused, I was no longer afraid.

A good rule: **Make the agent of the action the subject of the sentence.**

Clarity and Coherence

Writing a coherent essay is hard work; it requires mastery of a subject and skill in presenting it; it always takes a lot of time. Writing a coherent paragraph often takes more fussing and patching than you expect, but once you have the hang of it, it's relatively easy and pleasant. Writing a coherent sentence requires only that you stay awake until you get to the end of it.

We all do nod off sometimes, even over our own prose. But if you make it a practice to read your work over several times, at least once aloud, you give yourself a chance to spot the incoherent sentence before your reader does, and to revise it. Once you see that a sentence is incoherent, it's usually easy to recast it.

Cats Are Dogs

Looking at a picture of a woman, a man once said to the painter Henri Matisse, "That woman's arm is too long." "That's not a woman," Matisse replied, "it's a painting."

In some sentences a form of the verb *to be* mistakenly asserts that one thing is in a class with another. Is a picture a woman? Are cats dogs? Students did write the following sentences:

Incoherent
X. J. Kennedy's poem "Nothing in Heaven Functions as It Ought" is a contrast between Heaven and Hell. (As soon as you ask yourself the question "Is a poem a contrast?" you have, by bringing the two words close together, isolated the problem. A poem may be a sonnet, an epic, an ode—but not a contrast. The writer was trying to say what the poem *does*, not what it *is*.)

Coherent
X. J. Kennedy's poem "Nothing in Heaven Functions as It Ought" contrasts Heaven and Hell.

Incoherent

Besides, he tells himself, a matchmaker is an old Jewish custom. (Is a matchmaker a custom?)

Coherent

Besides, he tells himself, consulting a matchmaker is an old Jewish custom.

Incoherent

Ruth's devotion to Naomi is rewarded by marrying Boaz. (Does devotion marry Boaz?)

Coherent

Ruth's marriage to Boaz rewards her devotion to Naomi.

Incoherent

He demonstrates many human frailties, such as the influence of others' opinions upon one's actions. (Is influence a frailty? How might this sentence be revised?)

Items in a Series

If you were given a shopping list that mentioned apples, fruit, and pears, you would be puzzled and possibly irritated by the inclusion of "fruit." Don't puzzle or irritate your reader with a **false series** of this sort. Analyze sentences containing items in a series to be sure that the items are of the same order of generality. For example:

False series

His job exposed him to the "dirty work" of the British and to the evils of imperialism. ("The 'dirty work' of the British" is a *specific* example of the more *general* "evils of imperialism." The false series makes the sentence incoherent.)

Revised

His job, by exposing him to the "dirty work" of the British, brought him to understand the evils of imperialism.

In the following sentence, which item in the series makes the sentence incoherent?

Why should one man, no matter how important, be exempt from investigation, arrest, trial, and law-enforcing tactics?

Modifiers

A modifier should appear close to the word it modifies (that is, describes or qualifies). Three kinds of faulty modifiers are common: misplaced, squinting, and dangling.

Misplaced Modifiers   If the modifier seems to modify the wrong word, it is called *misplaced.* Misplaced modifiers are often unintentionally funny. The judo parlor that advertised "For $20 learn basic methods of protecting yourself from an experienced instructor" probably attracted more amused readers than paying customers.

Misplaced
Orwell shot the elephant under pressured circumstances. (Orwell was under pressure, not the elephant. Put the modifier near what it modifies.)

Revised
Orwell, under pressure, shot the elephant.

Misplaced
Orwell lost his individual right to protect the elephant as part of the imperialistic system. (The elephant was not part of the system; Orwell was.)

Revised
As part of the imperialistic system, Orwell lost his right to protect the elephant.

Misplaced
Amos Wilder has been called back to teach at the Divinity School after ten years retirement due to a colleague's illness. (Did Wilder retire for ten years because a colleague was ill? Revise the sentence.)

Revise the following:

1. Sitting Bull and William Cody stand side by side, each supporting a rifle placed between them with one hand.

2. Complete with footnotes the author has provided her readers with some background information.

Sometimes other parts of sentences are misplaced:

Misplaced
We learn from the examples of our parents who we are. (The sentence appears to say we are our parents.)

Revised
We learn who we are from the examples of our parents.

Misplaced
It is up to the students to revise the scheme, not the administrators. (We all know you can't revise administrators. Revise the sentence.)

Squinting Modifiers   If the modifier is ambiguous, that is, if it can be applied equally to more than one term, it is sometimes called a *squinting modifier:* It seems to look forward, and it seems to look backward.

Squinting
Being with Jennifer more and more enrages me. (Is the writer spending more time with Jennifer, or is she more enraged? Probably more enraged.)

Revised
Being with Jennifer enrages me more and more.

Squinting
Writing clearly is difficult. (Is this sentence about "writing" or about "writing clearly"?)

Revised
It is clearly difficult to write.

Revised
It is difficult to write clearly.

Squinting
Students only may use this elevator. (Does "only" modify students? If so, no one else may use the elevator. Or does it modify elevator? If so, students may use no other elevator.)

Revised

Only students may use this elevator.

Students may use only this elevator.

Note: The word *only* often squints, seeming to look in two directions. In general, put *only* immediately before the word or phrase it modifies. Often it appears too early in the sentence. (See "Usage," page 290.)

Dangling Modifiers   If the term being modified appears nowhere in the sentence, a modifier is called *dangling*.

Dangling

Being small, his ear scraped against the belt when his father stumbled. (The writer meant that the boy was small, not the ear. But the boy is not in the sentence.)

Revised

Because the boy was small, his ear scraped against the belt when his father stumbled.

Being small, the boy scraped his ear against the belt when his father stumbled.

Dangling

A meticulously organized person, his suitcase could be tucked under an airplane seat. (How would you revise the sentence?)

The general rule: **When you revise sentences, put together what belongs together.**

Reference of Pronouns

A pronoun is used in place of a noun. Because the noun usually precedes the pronoun, the noun to which the pronoun refers is called the *antecedent* (Latin: "going before"). For example:

antecedent   pronoun

When *Sheriff Johnson* was on a horse, *he* was a big man.

But the pronoun can also precede the noun:

pronoun   noun

When *he* was on a horse, *Sheriff Johnson* was a big man.

The word *antecedent* can be used here too. In short, the antecedent is the word or group of words referred to by a pronoun.

Whenever possible, make sure that a pronoun has a clear reference. Sometimes it isn't possible: *It* is commonly used with an unspecified reference, as in "It's hot today," and "Hurry up please, it's time"; and there can be no reference for interrogative pronouns: "What's bothering you?" and "Who's on first?" But otherwise always be sure that you've made clear what noun the pronoun is standing for.

Vague Reference of Pronouns

Vague

Apparently, they fight physically and it can become rather brutal. ("It" doubtless refers to "fight," but "fight" in this sentence is the verb, not an antecedent noun.)

Clear

Their fights are apparently physical, and sometimes brutal.

Vague

I was born in Colón, the second largest city in the Republic of Panama. Despite this, Colón is still an undeveloped town. ("This" has no specific antecedent. It appears to refer to the writer's having been born in Colón.)

Clear

Although Colón, where I was born, is the second largest city in Panama, it remains undeveloped. (On *this*, see also "Usage," page 295.)

Shift in Pronouns   This common error is easily corrected.

1. In many instances the child was expected to follow the profession of your father. (Expected to follow the profession of whose father, "yours" or "his"?)

2. Having a tutor, you can get constant personal encouragement and advice that will help me budget my time. (If "you" have a tutor, will that help "me"?)

Ambiguous Reference of Pronouns   A pronoun normally refers to the first appropriate noun or pronoun preceding it. Same-sex pronouns and nouns, like dogs, often get into scraps.

Ambiguous

Her mother died when she was eighteen. (Who was eighteen, the mother or the daughter?)

Clear

Her mother died when Mabel was eighteen.
Her mother died at the age of eighteen. (Note the absence of ambiguity in "His mother died when he was eighteen.")

Ambiguous

Daru learns that he must take an Arab to jail against his will. (Both Daru and the Arab are male. The writer of the sentence meant that Daru learns he must act against his will.)

Clear

Daru learns that he must, against his will, take an Arab to jail.

The general rule: **Put together what belongs together.**

Agreement

Noun and Pronoun   Everyone knows that a singular noun requires a singular pronoun, and a plural noun requires a plural pronoun, but writers sometimes slip.

Faulty

singular   plural
A *dog* can easily tell if people are afraid of *them*.

Correct

singular   singular
A *dog* can easily tell if people are afraid of *it*.

Faulty

singular   plural
Every student feels that Wellesley expects *them* to do their best.

Correct

singular   singular
Every student feels that Wellesley expects *her* to do her best.

Each, everybody, nobody, no one, and *none* are especially troublesome. See the entries on these words in Chapter 11, "Usage."

Subject and Verb   A singular subject requires a singular verb, a plural subject a plural verb.

Faulty

      plural   singular

Horror *films* bring to light a subconscious fear and *shows* a character who succeeds in coping with it.

Correct

      plural   plural

Horror films bring to light a subconscious fear and *show* a character who succeeds in coping with it.

The student who wrote "shows" instead of "show" thought that the subject of the verb was "fear," but the subject really is "Horror films," a plural.

Faulty

The manager, as well as the pitcher and the catcher, were fined.

Correct

The manager, as well as the pitcher and the catcher, was fined.

If the sentence had been "The manager and the pitcher . . . ," the subject would have been plural and the required verb would be *were:*

The manager and the pitcher were fined.

But in the sentence as it was given, "as well as" (like *in addition to, with,* and *together with*) does *not* add a subject to a subject and thereby make a plural subject. "As well as" merely indicates that what is said about the manager applies to the pitcher and the catcher.

Three Additional Points

1. A **collective noun**—that is, a noun that is singular in form but that denotes a collection of individuals, such as *mob, audience, jury*— normally takes a *singular* verb:

Correct

The mob is at the gate.

Correct

An audience of children *is* easily bored. (The subject is "an audience," *not* "children.")

Correct

The jury is seated.

But when the emphasis is on the individuals within the group—for instance when you are calling attention to a division within the group—you can use a plural verb:

The jury disagree.

Still, because this sounds a bit odd, it is probably better to recast the sentence:

The jurors disagree.

2. Sometimes a sentence that is grammatically correct may nevertheless sound awkward:

One of its most noticeable features is the lounges.

Because the subject is "one"—*not* "features"—the verb must be singular, "is," but "is" sounds odd when it precedes the plural "lounges." The solution: **Revise the sentence.**

Among the most noticeable features are the lounges.

3. When a singular and a plural subject are joined by *or, either… or,* or *neither… nor,* use a verb that agrees in number with the subject closest to the verb. Examples:

Correct

Either the teacher *or the students are* mistaken.

Correct

Either the students *or the teacher is* mistaken.

The first version uses "are" because the verb is nearer to "students" (plural) than to "teacher" (singular); the second uses "is" because the verb is nearer to "teacher" than to "students."

Repetition and Variation

1. Don't be afraid to repeat a word if it is the best word. The following paragraph repeats "joyful," "book," "moments," and "in its"; notice also "joyful" and "joy." Repetition, a device necessary for continuity and clarity, holds the paragraph together.

> *The Brothers Karamozov* is a joyful book. Readers who know what it is about may find this an intolerably whimsical statement. It does have moments of joy, but they are only moments; the rest is greed, lust, squalor, unredeemed suffering, and sometimes terrifying darkness. But the book is joyful in another sense: in its energy and curiosity, in its formal inventiveness, in the mastery of its writing. And therefore, finally, in its vision.
> —*Richard Pevear*

2. Use pronouns, when their reference is clear, as substitutes for nouns. Notice Pevear's use of pronouns; notice also that in the second and third sentences, he substitutes "it" for "book," and then uses "the book" again in the fourth sentence. Substitutions that neither confuse nor distract keep a paragraph from becoming dull.

3. Do not, however, confuse the substitutions we have just spoken of with the fault called Elegant Variation. A groundless fear of repetition sometimes leads students to write first, for example, of "Dostoevesky," then of "the writer," then of "our author." Such variations strike the reader as silly. They can, moreover, be confusing because they can suggest that the student is referring to different writers.

4. But don't repeat a word if it is being used in two different senses.

Confusing
My theme focuses on the theme of the book. (The first "theme" means "essay"; the second means "underlying idea" or "motif.")

Clear
My essay focuses on the theme of the book.

Confusing
Caesar's character is complex. The comic characters, however, are simple. (The first "character" means "personality"; the second means "persons" or "figures in the play.")

Clear

Caesar is complex; the comic characters, however, are simple.

5. Finally, eliminate words repeated unnecessarily. Use of words like *surely, in all probability, it is noteworthy* may become habitual. If they don't help your reader to follow your thoughts, they are Instant Prose Additives. Cross them out.

In general, when you revise, decide if a word should be repeated, varied, or eliminated by testing sentences and paragraphs for both sound and sense.

Clarity and Sentence Structure: Parallelism

Use parallels to clarify relationships. Few of us are likely to compose such deathless parallels as "I came, I saw, I conquered," or "of the people, by the people, for the people," but we can see to it that coordinate expressions correspond in their grammatical form. Consider the following sentence and the revision:

Awkward

He liked drawing and to paint.

Parallel

He liked to draw and to paint.
He liked drawing and painting.

In the first version, "drawing" (a gerund) and "to paint" (an infinitive) are not grammatically parallel. The difference in grammatical form blurs the writer's point that there is a similarity between the two activities; the resulting sentence is fuzzy and awkward.

In the following examples, the parallel construction is printed in italic type.

Awkward

The dormitory rules needed revision, a smoking area was a necessity, and a generally more active role for the school in social affairs were all significant to her.

Parallel

She recommended that the school *revise* its dormitory rules, *provide* a smoking area, and *organize* more social activities.

Awkward

Most Chinese parents disapprove of interracial dating or they just do not permit it.

Parallel

Most Chinese parents *disapprove* of interracial dating, and many *forbid* it.

In parallel constructions, be sure to check the consistency of articles, prepositions, and conjunctions. For example, "He wrote papers on a play by Shakespeare, a novel by Dickens, and a story by Oates," *not* "He wrote papers on a play by Shakespeare, a novel of Dickens, and a story by Oates." The shift from "by" to "of" and back to "by" serves no purpose and is merely distracting.

To sum up:

A pupil once asked Arthur Schnabel (the noted pianist) whether it was better to play in time or to play as one feels; his characteristic mordant reply was another question: "Why not feel in time?"

—*David Hamilton*

CHECKLIST FOR REVISING FOR CLARITY

✔ Is word choice precise and specific? While writing the draft, did you feel that a particular word was close to what you meant, but not quite right? If so, replace that word with the *right* word. (See pp. 91–94.)

✔ Do you offer concrete examples where necessary? (See pp. 96–99.)

✔ Are technical terms used appropriately and helpfully? Can any jargon be replaced with plain English? (See pp. 99–101.)

✔ Does your prose include any dead or mixed metaphors, or clichés? (See pp. 102–04.)

✔ Have you put together what belongs together? Do modifiers appear close to, and refer clearly to, the words they modify? (See pp. 111–13.)

✔ Have you eliminated sexist language? Have you replaced such words as "mankind" and "poetess" with gender-neutral terms, and eliminated the generic "he," "him," and "his"?(See pp. 94–95.)

✔ Have you replaced passive verbs with active verbs where appropriate? (See pp. 105–07.)

✔ Do pronouns have clear references, and do they agree in number with the nouns to which they refer? (See pp. 113–16.)

✔ Does the structure of your sentence reflect the structure of your thought? Are parallel ideas in parallel constructions? (See pp. 119–20.)

CHAPTER SIX

WRITING WITH STYLE

> The friends that have it I do wrong
> When ever I remake a song,
> Should know what issue is at stake:
> It is myself that I remake.
>
> —*William Butler Yeats*

Academic Styles, Academic Audiences

When you write an essay for a course, you are learning how people working in that academic discipline express themselves. To communicate with other people in the discipline, you must adapt your voice to the conventions of the discipline and to the audience's expectations about writing within that discipline. Some disciplines (literature, for example) frown on passive verbs. But in lab reports in the sciences passive verbs are often acceptable, in part because they help focus the reader's attention on the experiment rather than on the person who conducted it, and thereby help to establish authority.

To make matters even more complicated, the conventions are changing, and they vary to some degree from class to class, and instructor to instructor. For example, one literature instructor might accept an essay containing the word "we" (as in "we see here the author's fascination with landscape"); another might object to its use, arguing that the "we" falsely implies that all readers—regardless of race, class, gender, and so on—read all texts in the same way.

These differences frustrate some students. To these students, writing an essay becomes a game of figuring out What the Instructor Wants. (For what it's worth, such students can frustrate instructors a bit too.) It may help both students and instructors to keep in mind that there isn't one *right* style—and that the differences among styles aren't a matter of arbitrary and inscrutable personal taste, but rather a matter of disciplinary convention, and (to some degree) theoretical approach.

It is impossible to list here all the different conventions you'll encounter in college. You don't need to learn them all anyway. You simply need to be alert to the ways in which people talk to each other in the disciplines within which you're writing, and do your best to follow the conventions you observe. We illustrate a few of these differences below.

Here is the first paragraph of an article from a recent issue of the *Cambridge Journal of Economics.*

> In this paper I shall develop a framework which may be used to examine several alternative theories of the rate of interest. The four most widely accepted approaches are the Neoclassical Loanable Funds, Keynes's Liquidity Preference, Neoclassical Synthesis ISLM, and Basil Moore's Horizontalist (or endogenous money). I will use the framework developed here to present a fifth: an integration of liquidity preference theory with an endogenous money approach. I first briefly set forth the primary alternative approaches, then develop an analytical framework based on an asset or stock approach and use it to discuss several theories of the interest rate: those advanced by Keynes, by Moore, by neoclassical theory and the monetarists, by Kregel, and by Tobin. Finally, I shall use the framework to reconcile liquidity preference theory with an endogenous money approach.
>
> —*L. Randall Wray*

Note the use of the pronoun "I," the direct statement of what the writer will do ("In this paper I shall develop a framework . . ."); and the listing of the steps of his procedure ("I first briefly set forth," and so on). A literary critic would be unlikely to present his or her ideas so methodically, as the next example suggests.

Here is the first paragraph of a chapter from a recent study of Bram Stoker's *Dracula*, in which a literary critic analyzes the novel in its social and political context.

"In obedience to the law as it then stood, he was buried in the centre of a *quadrivium*, or conflux of four roads (in this case four streets), with a stake driven through his heart. And over him drives for ever the uproar of unresting London!" No, not *Dracula* (1897), but the closing lines of a much earlier nineteenth-century work, Thomas De Quincey's bleakly ironic essay "On Murder Considered as One of the Fine Arts" (1854). De Quincey is describing how in 1812 the London populace dealt with the body of one of its prize exhibits, a particularly grisly serial killer who had escaped the gallows by hanging himself in his cell in the dead of night. Yet it is difficult for us to read this gleefully chilling passage today without thinking of Bram Stoker's classic vampire novel. The quirky Christian symbolism, the mandatory staking down of the monster to keep it from roaming abroad, the sense of busily self-absorbed London unaware of its proximity to a murderous presence that haunts its most densely populated byways: together these features seem virtually to define a basic iconography for the vampire Gothic as it achieved canonical status in *Dracula*.

—*David Glover*

Note the absence of the pronoun "I" and the presence of the pronoun "we." Note also the playfulness of the style (the reference to a "gleefully chilling passage" and the "staking down of the monster"), the specificity of the language, and the variety in punctuation and sentence structure.

Finally, here is the opening paragraph of a chemistry student's study of the enzyme calf alkaline phosphatase.

```
Enzymes, protein molecules that catalyze
reactions, are crucial for many biochemical
reactions. This research project studies the
actions of the enzyme calf alkaline phosphatase on
the substrate p-nitrophenyl phosphate. The focus
of this research project is the relation of
alkaline phosphatase denaturation to temperature.
Heat denaturation has been well documented in
major biology and chemistry texts, but few
```

textbooks mention how extreme cold affects enzyme
structure and function. This study will examine
how alkaline phosphatase responds to both high and
low temperatures.

-Hilary Suzawa

Note the absence of personal pronouns (the *"research project* studies"),
the orderly and careful presentation of information (including the brief
definition of the word "enzymes" in the first sentence), and the clear
statement of purpose. (You might compare this writer's first sentence with
Glover's—deliberately misleading—opening.)

Defining Style

As we suggest above, style in academic writing is partly a matter of disciplinary conventions. But style also reflects the individual writer's mind,
his or her values and sensibility. Style is not simply a flower here and
some gilding there; it pervades the whole work. Van Gogh's style, or Walt
Disney's, let us say, consists in part of features recurring throughout a single work and from one work to the next: angular or curved lines, hard
or soft edges, strong or gentle contrasts, and so on. Pictures of a seated
woman by each of the two artists are utterly different, and if we have seen
a few works by each, we can readily identify who did which one. Artists
leave their fingerprints, so to speak, all over their work. Writers leave
their voiceprints.

Although the word *style* comes from the Latin *stilus* and originally
refered to a Roman writing instrument, even in Roman times *stilus* had
acquired a figurative sense, referring not only to the instrument but also
to the writer's choice of words and arrangement of words into sentences.
But is it simply the choice and arrangement of words we comment on
when we speak of a writer's style, or are we also commenting on the
writer's mind? Don't we feel that a piece of writing, whether it's on Civil
War photographs or on genetics and intelligence, is also about the writer?
The writing, after all, sets forth the writer's views of his or her topic. It
sets forth perceptions and responses to something the writer has thought
about. The writer has, from the start, from the choice of a topic, revealed
that he or she found it worth thinking about. The essay, in attempting
to persuade us to think as the writer does, reveals not only how and what

the writer thinks, but also what he or she values. As E. B. White puts it, "no writer long remains incognito."

When we write about things "out there," our writing always reveals the form and likeness of our minds, just as every work of art reveals the creator as well as the ostensible subject. A portrait painting, for example, is not only about the sitter, it is also about the artist's perceptions of the sitter; hence the saying that every portrait is a self-portrait. Even photographs are as much about the photographer as they are about the subject. Richard Avedon said of his portraits of famous people, "They are all pictures of me, of the way I feel about the people I photograph." A student's essay similarly, if it is truly written, is not exclusively about "*La Causa* and the New Chicana"; it is also about her perceptions and responses to both racism and sexism.

Style and Tone

Suppose we take a page of handwriting, or even a signature. We need not believe that graphology is an exact science to believe that the shape of the ink-lines on paper (apart from the meaning of the words) often tells us something about the writer. We look at a large, ornate signature, and we sense that the writer is confident; we look at a tiny signature written with the finest of pens, and we wonder why anyone is so self-effacing.

More surely than handwriting, the writer's style reveals, among other things, his or her attitude toward the self, toward the reader, and toward the subject. The writer's attitudes are reflected in what is usually called *tone.* It is difficult to separate style from tone but we can try. Most discussions of style concentrate on what might be thought of as ornament: figurative language ("a sea of troubles"), inversion ("A leader he is not"), repetition and parallelism ("government of the people, by the people, for the people"), balance and antithesis ("It was the best of times, it was the worst of times"). Indeed, for centuries style has been called "the dress of thought," implying that the thought is something separate from the expression; the thought, in this view, is dressed up in stylistic devices. But in most of the writing that we read with interest and pleasure, the stylistic devices are not ornamental but integral. When we talk about wit, sincerity, tentativeness, self-assurance, aggressiveness, objectivity, and so forth, we can say we are talking about style, but we should recognize that style now is not a matter of ornamental devices that dress up some idea,

but part of the idea itself. And "the idea itself" includes the writer's unified yet appropriately varied tone of voice.

To take a brief example: The famous English translation of Caesar's
report of a victory,

> I came, I saw, I conquered,

might be paraphrased thus:

> After getting to the scene of the battle, I studied the situation. Then I
> devised a strategy that won the battle.

But this paraphrase loses much of Caesar's message; the brevity and the
parallelism of the famous version, as well as the alliteration (came, con
quered), convey tight-lipped self-assurance—convey, that is, the tone that
reveals Caesar to us. And this tone is a large part of Caesar's message.
Caesar is really telling us not only about what he did, but also about what
sort of person he is. He is perceptive, decisive, and effective. The three
actions, Caesar in effect tells us, are (for a man like Caesar) one. (The
Latin original is even more tight-lipped and more unified by alliteration: *veni, vidi, vici.*)

Let's look now at a longer sentence, the opening sentence of Lewis
Thomas's essay "On Natural Death":

> There are so many new books about dying that there are now special
> shelves set aside for them in bookstores, along with the health, diet and
> home-repair paperbacks and the sex manuals.

This sentence could have ended where the comma is placed: The words
after "bookstores" are, it might seem, not important. One can scarcely
argue that by specifying some kinds of "special shelves" Thomas clarifies an otherwise difficult or obscure concept. What, then, do these additional words do? They tell us nothing about death and almost nothing
about bookshops, but they tell us a great deal about Thomas's *attitude*
toward the new books on death. He suggests that such books are fad-
dish and perhaps (like "the sex manuals") vulgar. After all, if he had
merely wanted to call up a fairly concrete image of a well-stocked book-
store, he could have said "along with books on politics and the environment," or some such thing. His next sentence runs:

Some of them are so packed with detailed information and step-by-step instructions for performing the function you'd think this was a new sort of skill which all of us are now required to learn.

Why "you'd think" instead of, say, "one might believe"? Thomas uses a colloquial form, and a very simple verb, because he wants to convey to us his commonsense, homely, down-to-earth view that these books are a bit pretentious—a pretentiousness conveyed in his use of the words "performing the function," words that might come from the books themselves. In short, when we read Thomas's paragraph we are learning as much about Thomas as we are about books on dying. We are hearing a voice, perceiving an attitude, and we want to keep reading, not only because we are interested in death but also because Thomas has managed to make us interested in Thomas, a thoughtful but unpretentious fellow.

Now listen to a short paragraph from John Szarkowski's *Looking at Photographs.* Szarkowski is writing about one of Alexander Gardner's photographs of a dead Confederate sharpshooter.

Among the pictures that Gardner made himself is the one reproduced here. Like many Civil War photographs, it showed that the dead of both sides looked very much the same. The pictures of earlier wars had not made this clear.

© Bettman/Corbis.

Try, in a word or two, to characterize the tone (the attitude, as we sense it in the inflection of the voice) of the first sentence. Next, the tone of the second, and then of the third. Suppose the second and third sentences had been written thus:

> It showed that the dead of both sides looked very much the same. This is made clear in Civil War photographs, but not in pictures of earlier wars.

How has the tone changed? What word can you find to characterize the tone of the whole, as Szarkowski wrote it?

Finally, a longer passage by the same writer. After you read it, try to articulate the resemblances between this and the other—qualities that allow us to speak of the writer's tone.

> There are several possible explanations for the fact that women have been more important to photography than their numbers alone would warrant. One explanation might be the fact that photography has never had licensing laws or trade unions, by means of which women might have been effectively discriminated against. A second reason might be the fact that the specialized technical preparation for photography need not be enormously demanding, so that the medium has been open to those unable to spend long years in formal study. A third possible reason could be that women have a greater natural talent for photography than men do. Discretion (or cowardice) suggests that this hypothesis is best not pursued, since a freely speculative exploration of it might take unpredictable and indefensible lines. One might for example consider the idea that the art of photography is in its nature receptive, or passive, thus suggesting that women are also.

Acquiring Style

In the preceding pages we said that your writing reveals not only where you stand (your thesis) and how you think (the structure of your argument), but also who you are and how you take yourself (your tone). To follow our argument to its limit, we might say that everything in this book—including rules on the comma (where you breathe) is about style. We do. What more is there to say?

Clarity and Texture

First, a distinction Aristotle makes between two parts of style: that which gives clarity, and that which gives texture. Exact words, concrete illustrations of abstractions, conventional punctuation, and so forth—matters we treat in some detail in the chapters on revising and editing—make for clarity. On the whole, this part of style is inconspicuous when present; when absent, the effect ranges from mildly distracting to ruinous. Clarity is the foundation of style. It can be achieved by anyone willing to make the effort.

Among the things that give texture, or individuality, are effective repetition, variety in sentence structure, wordplay, and so forth. This second group of devices, on the whole more noticeable, makes the reader aware of the writer's particular voice. These devices can be learned too, but seldom by effort alone. In fact, playfulness helps here more than doggedness. Students who work at this part of style usually enjoy hanging around words. At the same time, they're likely to feel that when they put words on paper, even in a casual letter to a friend, they're putting themselves on the line. Serious, as most people are about games they really care about, but not solemn, they'll come to recognize the rules of play in John Holmes's advice to young poets: "You must believe that your feelings and your words for your feelings are important . . . . That they are unique is a fact; that you believe they are unique is necessary."

A Repertory of Styles

We make a second distinction: between style as the reader perceives it from the written word, and style as the writer experiences it. The first is static: It's fixed in writing or print; we can point to it, discuss it, analyze it. The second, the writer's experience of his or her own style, changes as the writer changes. In his essay "Why I Write" George Orwell said, "I find that by the time you have perfected any style of writing, you have always outgrown it." An exaggeration that deposits a truth. The essay concludes, however, "Looking back through my work, I see that it is invariably where I lacked a political purpose that I wrote lifeless books and was betrayed into purple passages, sentences without meaning, decorative adjectives and humbug generally." A suggestion surely, that through trial and error, and with maturity, a writer comes to a sense of self, a true style, not static and not constantly changing, but achieved.

Undergraduates seldom know what purpose, in Orwell's sense, they will have. You may be inclined toward some subjects and against others, you may have decided on a career—many times. But if your education is worth anything like the money and time invested in it, your ideas and feelings will change more rapidly in the next few years than ever before in your memory, and perhaps more than they ever will again. Make use of the confusion you're in. Reach out for new experiences to assimilate; make whatever connections you can from your reading to your inner life, reaching back into your past and forward into your future. And keep writing.

To keep pace with your changing ideas—and here is our main point— you'll need to acquire not one style, but a repertory of styles, a store of writing habits on which you can draw as the need arises.

Originality and Imitation

Finally, a paradox: One starts to acquire an individual style by studying and imitating the style of others. The paradox isn't limited to writing. Stylists in all fields begin as apprentices. The young ball player imitates the movements of Nomar Garciaparra; the chess player hangs around the park or club watching the old pros, then finds a book that probably recommends beginning with Ruy Lopez's opening. When Michelangelo was an apprentice he copied works by his predecessors; when Millet was young he copied works by Michelangelo; when Van Gogh was young he copied works by Millet. The would-be writer may be lucky enough to have a teacher, one he can imitate; more likely he will, in W. H. Auden's words, "serve his apprenticeship in the library."

PART TWO

COLLEGE WRITING

CHAPTER SEVEN

ANALYZING TEXTS

Look at this drawing by Pieter Brueghel the Elder, titled *The Painter and the Connoisseur* (about 1565), and then jot down your responses to the questions that follow.

Graphische Sammlung Albertina, Wien.

Analyzing a Drawing

1. One figure is given considerably more space than the other. What may be implied by this fact?

2. What is the painter doing (besides painting)?

3. What is the connoisseur doing?

4. What does the face of each figure tell you about the character of each figure? The figures are physically close; are they mentally close? How do you know?

Now consider this brief discussion of the picture.

> The painter, standing in front of the connoisseur and given more than two-thirds of the space, dominates this picture. His hand holds the brush with which he creates, while the connoisseur's hand awkwardly fumbles for money in his purse. The connoisseur apparently is pleased with the picture he is looking at, for he is buying it, but his parted lips give him a stupid expression and his eyeglasses imply defective vision. In contrast, the painter looks away from the picture and fixes his eyes on the model (reality) or, more likely, on empty space, his determined expression suggesting that he possesses an imaginative vision beyond his painting and perhaps even beyond earthly reality.

The author of this paragraph uses analysis to interpret the drawing, to discover its meaning. The paragraph doesn't simply tell us that the picture shows two people close together—that would be a *description*, not an analysis. This analytic paragraph separates the parts of the picture, pointing out that the two figures form a contrast. It explains why one figure gets much more space than the other, and it explains what the contrasting gestures and facial expressions imply. The writer of the comment has "read" or interpreted the drawing by examining how the parts function, that is, how they relate to the whole.

Analyzing Texts

Much of academic reading and writing is analytical. You read of the causes of a revolution, of the effects of inflation, or of the relative importance of heredity and environment; you write about the meaning of a short story, the causes and effects of poverty, the strengths and weaknesses of some proposed legislative action. And much of this reading and writing is based on the analysis of *texts*. As we note in Chapter 1, the word "text" derives from the Latin for "woven" (as in textile), and it has come to refer not only to words stitched together into sentences (whether novels or letters or advertisements), but also to all kinds of objects of interpretation: films, paintings, music videos, even food on a plate.

For that reason, much of our discussion in this chapter focuses on textual analysis. Of course writing an analysis of a drawing differs from writing an analysis of a poem (or, for that matter, a legislative proposal or an argument about the causes of inflation). Nevertheless, we believe that there are important similarities between these processes. In all cases, the reader must be able to envision the object under scrutiny, so the writer must summarize it or describe it precisely. In all cases, the writer must be able to explain what the text *means*, so the writer must pay close attention to its details, to its parts—to how they work, to what they imply or suggest, to their relationship to each other and to the whole.

It's worth keeping in mind, though, that when academic writers write analytically, their purpose is to persuade readers to see things *their* way: to understand the poem the way they do; to reach their conclusion about the causes of poverty; to adopt their position on the proposed legislative action. The analysis helps the writer to make a larger point: It provides the evidence for the argument. In Chapter 8, "Persuading Readers," we discuss argument in more detail. But for now, we'll focus on analysis, and we'll begin with a look at a brief essay on a short text.

Analysis at Work: A Student Analyzes a Short Story

Here is a very short story, followed by an essay that a student, Antonia Tenori, wrote for an assignment in a first-year composition class. We reprint the story with the student's annotations, which record her first steps toward analyzing this text.

Kate Chopin
Ripe Figs

Maman-Nainaine said that when the figs were ripe Babette might go to visit her cousins down on the Bayou Lafourche where the sugar cane grows. Not that the ripening of figs had the least thing to do with it, but that is the way Maman-Nainaine was.

strange

It seemed to Babette a very long time to wait; for the leaves upon the trees were tender yet, and the figs were like little hard, green marbles.

But warm rains came along and plenty of strong sunshine, and though Maman-Nainaine was as patient as the statue of la Madone, and Babette as restless as a hummingbird, the first thing they both knew it was hot summer-time. Every day Babette danced out to where the fig-trees were in a long line against the fence. She walked slowly beneath them, carefully peering between the gnarled, spreading branches. But each time she came disconsolate away again. What she saw there finally was something that made her sing and dance the whole long day.

contrast between M-N and B

When Maman-Nainaine sat down in her stately way to breakfast, the following morning, her muslin cap standing like an aureole about her white, placid face, Babette approached. She bore a dainty porcelain platter, which she set down before her god-mother. It contained a dozen purple figs fringed around with their rich, green leaves.

another contrast

check this?

ceremonious

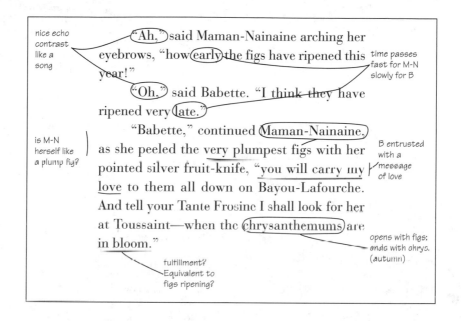

Now for the student's analysis of Chopin's story. As you read the analysis, notice that the first paragraph orients the reader by naming the author and the title of the story and by very briefly summarizing it. Further, in the opening paragraph, Antonia provides her reader with an answer to the reader's implicit question: "Why should I read this essay?" In this case, as you will see, the answer to this question is, in effect, "You may think this story is just a character sketch, but Chopin is doing much more than contrasting two figures." The idea, of course, is to get the readers' attention and to hold it, by promising to teach them something interesting, something that they might not see or understand on their own.

Images of Ripening in Kate Chopin's "Ripe Figs"

1   Very little happens in Kate Chopin's one-page story, "Ripe Figs." Maman-Nainaine tells her goddaughter Babette that she may "visit her cousins down on the Bayou-Lafourche" "when the figs were ripe";

the figs ripen, and Babette is given permission to go. So little happens in "Ripe Figs" that the story at first appears merely to be a character sketch that illustrates, through Babette and her godmother, the contrast between youth and age. But by means of the natural imagery of the tale, Chopin suggests more than this: she asks her readers to see the relationship of human time to nature's seasons, and she suggests that, try as we may to push the process of maturity, growth or "ripening" happens in its own time.

2   The story clearly contrasts the impatience of youth with the patience and dignity that come with age. Babette, whose name suggests she is still a "little baby," is "restless as a humming-bird." Each day when she eagerly goes to see if the figs have ripened, she doesn't simply walk but she dances. By contrast, Maman-Nainaine has a "stately way," she is "patient as the statue of la Madone," and there is an "aureole"--a radiance--"about her white, placid face." The brief dialog near the end of the story also emphasizes the difference between the two characters. When the figs finally ripen, Maman-Nainaine is surprised (she arches her eyebrows), and she exclaims, "how early the figs have ripened this year!" Babette replies, "I think they have ripened very late."

3   Chopin is not simply remarking here that time passes slowly for young people, and quickly for old people. She suggests that nature moves at its own pace regardless of human wishes. Babette, young and "tender" as the fig leaves, can't wait to "ripen." Her visit to Bayou-Lafourche is not a mere pleasure trip, but represents her coming into her own season of maturity. Babette's desire to rush this process is tempered by a condition that her godmother sets: Babette must wait until the figs ripen, since everything comes in its own season. Maman-Nainaine recognizes the patterns of the natural world, the rhythms of life. By asking Babette to await the ripening, the young girl is asked to pay attention to the patterns as well.

4   Chopin further suggests that if we pay attention and wait with patience, the fruits of our own growth will be sweet, plump, and beautiful, like the "dozen purple figs, fringed around with their rich, green leaves," that Babette finally offers her grandmother. Chopin uses natural imagery effectively, interweaving the young girl's growth with the rhythms of the seasons. In this way, the reader is connected with both processes in an intimate and inviting way.

A Brief Analysis of the Student's Analysis

In our introductory paragraph we mentioned that the student's first paragraph oriented readers and gave them a reason to continue reading. Here are some other important features of the essay:

- The **title** is informative; it clearly indicates the focus of the analysis.

- The second sentence offers enough **plot summary** to enable readers to follow the discussion.

- The opening paragraph presents one view (the view Antonia believes is inadequate); then, after a transitional "but," offers a second view and presents a **thesis**.

- Brief **quotations** in this paragraph and the next provide **evidence.**

- The third paragraph **develops thesis** ("Chopin is not simply . . . . She suggests . . . .")

- The final paragraph begins with a helpful **transition** ("Chopin *further* suggests"), offers additional evidence, and ends with a **new idea** (about the reader's response to the story) that takes the discussion a step further. (The conclusion doesn't simply summarize the essay.)

A Note on the Use of Summary in the Analytic Essay

When writers analyze an image, they must first describe it, must make it present to the reader. When writers analyze a written text, they must do something similar, and that is provide enough information about the text at hand to enable a reader to follow the discussion. This information often appears in the form of a brief *summary* at or near the beginning of an essay.

A summary is a condensation or abridgment; it briefly gives the reader the gist of a longer work. Or, to change the figure, it boils down the longer work, resembling the longer work as a bouillon cube resembles a bowl of soup. For example, in the preceding essay, the student summarizes "Ripe Figs" in the second sentence of her essay:

```
Maman-Nainaine tells her goddaughter Babette that
she may "visit her cousins down on the Bayou-
Lafourche" "when the figs were ripe"; the figs
ripen, and Babette is given permission to go.
```

She is *summarizing* because she is briefly reporting what happens in the story, and of course her readers need to know what happens before they can make sense of what she'll say about it. On the other hand, she is *analyzing* when she writes:

```
Chopin is not simply remarking here that time
passes slowly for young people, and quickly for
old people. She suggests that nature moves at its
own pace regardless of human wishes.
```

In this sentence, the writer is not reporting *what happens* but is explaining *what the story means.*

Most of your writing about other writing will be analytical, but for the benefit of the reader, it will probably include an occasional sentence or even a paragraph of summary. (And part of your preparation for writing your essay may involve writing summaries as you take notes on the reading you are going to analyze.) Needless to say, if the assignment calls for an analysis, it will not be enough simply to write a summary.

Classifying and Thinking

Analysis (literally a separating into parts) is not only the source of much writing that seeks to explain, it is also a way of thinking, a way of arriving at conclusions (generalizations), a way of discovering meaning.

Much of what we normally mean by analysis requires classifying things into categories and seeing how the categories relate to each other. Writers who analyze texts, must, of course, classify their observations. When Antonia Tenori annotates Chopin's "Ripe Figs," she notes that many images in the story have to do with the natural world; she narrows this category to words and images that have to do with growth or "ripening" as she continues to ponder the meaning of the story. Other kinds of analysis require classifying things or ideas as well. When you think about choosing courses, for example, you classify the courses by subject matter, or by degree of difficulty ("Since I'm taking two hard courses, I ought to look for an easy one"), or by the hour at which they are offered, or by the degree to which they interest you, or by their merit as determined through the grapevine. When you classify, you establish categories by breaking down the curriculum into parts, and by then putting into each category courses that significantly resemble each other but that are not identical. We need categories: We simply cannot get through life treating every object as unique.

Examples of Classifying

Suppose you were asked to write an essay putting forth your ideas about punishment for killers. You would need to distinguish between those killers whose actions are premeditated and those killers whose actions are not. And in the first category you might make further distinctions:

1. Professional killers who carefully contrive a death

2. Killers who are irrational except in their ability to contrive a death

3. Robbers who contrive a property crime and who kill only when they believe that killing is necessary in order to commit that crime

You can hardly talk usefully about capital punishment or imprisonment without making some such analysis of killers. You have, then, taken killers and *classified* them, for the sake of educating yourself and those persons with whom you discuss the topic. Unless your attitude is the mad Queen of Hearts's "Off with their heads," you will be satisfied with your conclusion only after you have tested it by dividing your topic into parts, each clearly distinguished from the others, and then showed how they are related.

A second example: If you think about examinations you may find that they can serve several purposes. Examinations may test knowledge, intelligence, or skill in taking examinations; or they may stimulate learning. Therefore, if you wish to discuss what constitutes a good examination, you must decide what purpose an examination *should* serve. Possibly you will decide that in a particular course an examination should chiefly stimulate learning, but that it should also test the ability to reason. To arrive at a reasonable conclusion, a conclusion worth sharing and, if need be, defending, you must first recognize and sort out the several possibilities.

Often the keenest analytical thinking considers not only what parts are in the whole, but also what is *not* there—what is missing in relation to a larger context that we can imagine. For example, if we analyze the women in the best-known fairy tales, we will find that most are either sleeping beauties or wicked stepmothers. These categories are general: "Sleeping beauties" includes all passive women valued only for their appearance, and "wicked stepmothers" includes Cinderella's cruel older sisters. (Fairy godmothers form another category, but they are not human beings.) Analysis helps us to discover the almost total absence of resourceful, productive women. You might begin a thoughtful essay with a general statement to this effect and then support the statement with an analysis of "Cinderella," "Little Red Riding Hood," and "Snow White."

Cause and Effect

Analytical reasoning from cause to effect is also often expected in academic discussions, which are much given to questions such as the following:

> What part did the Bay of Pigs attack on Cuba play in the Cuban missile crisis of 1962?
>
> What is the function of Mrs. Linde in Ibsen's *A Doll's House?*
>
> How does the death penalty affect jury verdicts?
>
> Why do people enjoy horror movies?
>
> What are the effects of billboard advertising?

Let's look at the first eight paragraphs of an essay, by the architect and scholar Dolores Hayden, that addresses the last question on the list, arguing from cause to effect.

Dolores Hayden
Advertisements, Pornography, and Public Space

1   Americans need to look more consciously at the ways in which the public domain is misused for spatial displays of gender stereotypes: These appear in outdoor advertising, and to a lesser extent in commercial displays, architectural decoration, and public sculpture. While the commercial tone and violence of the American city is often

criticized, there is little analysis of the routine way that crude stereo-types appear in public, urban spaces as the staple themes of commercial art. Most Americans are accustomed to seeing giant females in various states of undress smiling and caressing products such as whiskey, food, and records. Male models also sell goods, but they are usually active and clothed—recent ad campaigns aimed at gay men seem to be the first major exception. Several geographers have established that men are most often shown doing active things, posed in the great outdoors; women are shown in reflective postures responding to male demands in interior spaces. As the nineteenth-century sexual double standard is preserved by the urban advertising, many twentieth-century urban men behave as if good women are at home while bad ones adorn the billboards and travel on their own in urban space; at the same time, many urban women are encouraged to think of emotionlessness, war-mongering, and sexual inexhaustibility as natural to the Marlboro cowboy, war heroes' statues, and every other male adult.

2   This double standard is the result of advertising practices, graphic design, and urban design. Sanctioned by the zoning laws, billboards are approved by the same urban planning boards who will not permit child care centers or mother-in-law apartments in many residential districts. But the problem with billboards is not only aesthetic degradation. By presenting gender stereotypes in the form of non-verbal body language, fifty feet long and thirty feet high, billboards turn the public space of the city into a stage set for a drama starring enticing women and stern men.

3   Let us observe outdoor advertising and other urban design phenomena with similar effects, as they are experienced by two women on an urban commuting trip along the Sunset Strip in Los Angeles in June 1981. Standing on a street corner, the two women are waiting for a bus to go to work. The bus arrives, bearing a placard on the side advertising a local nightclub. It shows strippers doing their act, their headless bodies naked from neck to crotch except for a few blue sequins. The two women get on the bus and find seats for the ride along Sunset Boulevard. They look out the windows. As the bus pulls away, their heads appear incongruously above the voluptuous cardboard female bodies displayed on the side. They ride through a district of record company headquarters and film offices, one of the most prosperous in L.A.

4   Their first views reveal rows of billboards. Silent Marlboro man rides the range; husky, khaki-clad Camel man stares at green hills; gigantic, uniformed professional athletes catch passes and hit home runs on behalf of booze. These are the male images. Then, on a billboard for whiskey, a horizontal blonde in a backless black velvet dress, slit to the thigh, invites men to "Try on a little Black Velvet." Next, a billboard shows a well-known actress, reclining with legs spread, who notes that avocados are only sixteen calories a slice. "Would this body lie to you?" she asks coyly, emphasizing that the body language which communicates blatant sexual availability is only meant to bring attention to her thin figure. Bo Derek offers a pastoral contrast garbed in nothing but a few bits of fur and leather, as she swings on a vine of green leaves, promoting *Tarzan, the Ape Man.*

5   Next the bus riders pass a club called the Body Shop that advertises "live, nude girls." Two reclining, realistic nudes, one in blue tones in front of a moonlight cityscape, one in orange sunshine tones, stretch their thirty-foot bodies along the sidewalk. This is the same neighborhood where a billboard advertising a Rolling Stones' record album called "Black and Blue" made news ten years ago. A manacled, spread-legged woman with torn clothes proclaimed "I'm Black and Blue from the Rolling Stones—and I love it!" Members of a group called Women Against Violence Against Women (WAVAW) arrived with cans of spray paint and climbed the scaffolding to make small, uneven letters of protest: "This is a crime against women." Demonstrations and boycotts eventually succeeded in achieving the removal of that image, but not in eliminating the graphic design problem. "Black and Blue" has been replaced by James Bond in a tuxedo, pistol in hand, viewed through the spread legs and buttocks of a giant woman in a bathing suit and improbably high heels, captioned "For Your Eyes Only."

6   When the two women get off the bus in Hollywood, they experience more gender stereotypes as pedestrians. First, they walk past a department store. In the windows mannequins suggest the prevailing ideals of sartorial elegance. The male torsos lean forward, as if they are about to clinch a deal. The female torsos, pin-headed, tip backward and sideways, at odd angles, as if they are about to be pushed over onto a bed. The themes of gender advertisements are trumpeted here in the mannequins' body language as well as on

billboards. Next, the women pass an apartment building. Two neo-classical caryatids support the entablature over the front door. Their breasts are bared, their heads carry the load. They recall the architecture of the Erechtheum on the Acropolis in Athens, dating from the 5th century B.C., where the sculptured stone forms of female slaves were used as support for a porch in place of traditional columns and capitals. This is an ancient image of servitude.

7   After the neo-classical apartment house, the commuters approach a construction site. Here they are subject to an activity traditionally called "running the gauntlet," but referred to as "girl watching" by urban sociologist William H. Whyte. Twelve workers stop whatever they are doing, whistle, and yell: "Hey, baby!" The women put their heads down, and walk faster, tense with anger. The construction workers take delight in causing exactly this response: "You're cute when you're mad!" Whyte regards this type of behavior as charming, pedestrian fun in "Street Life," where he even takes pleasure in tracing its historic antecedents, but he has never been whistled at, hooted at, and had the dimensions of his body parts analyzed out loud on a public street.[1]

8   Finally, these women get to the office building where they work. It has two statues out front of women. Their bronze breasts culminate in erect nipples. After they pass this last erotic public display of women's flesh, sanctioned as fine art, they walk in the door to begin the day's work. Their journey has taken them through an urban landscape filled with images of men as sexual aggressors and women as submissive sexual objects.

Now let's analyze these paragraphs. In the first paragraph Hayden introduces the question her essay will address: "How do billboards and other outdoor representations of male and female bodies perpetuate gender stereotypes?" (our paraphrase). She points out that there has been "little analysis" of this problem, thus suggesting that it is worth investigating. In the last sentence of the second paragraph, she states an argument: "billboards turn the public space of the city into a stage set for a

---

[1]William H. Whyte, "Street Life," *Urban Open Spaces* (Summer 1980); for a more detailed critique of hassling: Lindsy Van Gelder, "The International Language of Street Hassling," *Ms.* 9 (May 1981), 15–20, and letters about this article, *Ms.* (September 1981); and Cheryl Benard and Edith Schlaffer, "The Man in the Street: Why He Harasses," *Ms.* 9 (May 1981), 18–19.

drama starring enticing women and stern men." Paragraphs 4 through 8 discuss the "causes." We note Hayden classifies these images fairly methodically: paragraphs 4 and 5 focus on billboards representing women as "available"; paragraph 6 focuses first on mannequins that represent women as vulnerable, and then on architectural elements that represent women as subservient; paragraph 8 focuses on bronze statues of female torsos.

In the last three paragraphs of the essay, Hayden discusses the effects of these representations: "women guard themselves," "men assume that ogling is part of normal public life," and the "sexual double standard" is maintained "in a brutal and vulgar way."

9   The transient quality of male and female interaction in public streets makes the behavior provoked by billboards and their public design images particularly difficult to attack. Psychologist Erving Goffman has analyzed both print ads and billboards as *Gender Advertisements* because art directors use exaggerated body language to suggest that consumers buy not products but images of masculinity or femininity.[2] If passers-by are driving at fifty miles per hour, these gender cues cannot be subtle. In *Ways of Seeing*, art historian John Berger describes the cumulative problem that gender stereotypes in advertising create for woman as "split consciousness."[3] While many women guard themselves, some men assume that ogling is part of normal public life. Women are always wary, watching men watch them, and wondering if and when something is going to happen to them.

10   Urban residents also encounter even more explicit sexual images in urban space. Tawdry strip clubs, X-rated films, "adult" bookstores and sex shops are not uncommon sights. Pornographic video arcades are the next wave to come. Pornography is a bigger, more profitable industry in the United States than all legitimate film and record business combined.[4] It spills over into soft-porn, quasi-porn, and tasteless public imagery everywhere. In the midst of this sex-exploitation, if one sees a real prostitute, there is mild surprise. Yet

[2]Erving Goffman, *Gender Advertisements* (New York: Harper Colphon, 1976), pp. 24–27; Nancy Henley, *Body Politics: Power, Sex, and Nonverbal Communication* (Englewood Cliffs, NJ: Prentice-Hall, 1977), p. 30; Marianne Wex, *Let's Take Back Our Space* (Berlin: Movimento Druck, 1979).
[3]John Berger et al., *Ways of Seeing* (Harmondsworth, Eng.: BBC and Penguin, 1972), pp. 45–64.
[4]Tom Hayden, *The American Future: New Visions Beyond Old Frontiers* (Boston: South End Press, 1980), p. 15.

soliciting is still a crime. Of course, the male customer of an adult prostitute is almost never arrested, but the graphic designer, the urban designer, and the urban planner never come under suspicion for their contributions to a commercial public landscape that preserves the sexual double standard in a brutal and vulgar way.

11   Feminist Laura Shapiro calls our society a "rape culture."[5] Adrienne Rich has written of "a world masculinity made unfit for women or men."[6] But surely most Americans do not consciously, deliberately accept public space given over to commercial exploitation, violence and harassment of women. Indeed, the success of the "Moral Majority" displays how a few activists were able to tap public concern effectively about commercialized sexuality, albeit in a narrow, antihumanist way. In contrast, the example of the Women's Christian Temperance Union under Frances Willard's leadership, and the parks movement under Olmsted's,[7] show religious idealism, love of nature, and concern for female safety can be activated into dynamic urban reform movements that enlarge domestic values into urban values, instead of diminishing them into domestic pieties.

Analysis and Description

Analysis differs from description, as we note on page 142, but passages of description are commonly used in essays to support analysis of visual texts. In the preceding essay, for example, a writer asks and answers the question "What are the effects of representations of women in public space?"; as she answers this question, she presents us with brief but vivid descriptions of billboards, mannequins, and architectural elements. Hayden's essay is primarily analytical; reading it, we share the writer's thoughts, but these thoughts are not the random and fleeting notions of reverie. The thoughts have been organized for us; the effects of billboards and other images on both women and men have been classified and presented to us in an orderly and coherent account made vivid by passages of description. Even if we have never seen the advertisement for the James Bond film or the Rolling Stones album, we can visualize these images because Hayden has made

[5]Laura Shapiro, "Violence: The Most Obscene Fantasy," in Jo Freeman, ed., *Women: A Feminist Perspective*, 2nd ed. (Palo Alto, CA: Mayfield, 1979), pp. 469–73.
[6]Ibid., p. 469.
[7]Frederick Law Olmsted (1822–1903) was an American landscape architect. Among his noble works are Central Park in Manhattan and Prospect Park in Brooklyn.

them present to us. Through these passages, we share at least imaginatively in the experiences that gave rise to her thinking. And through description, if the communication between writer and reader has been successful, we are persuaded to share the writer's opinions.

Description at Work in the Analytic Essay

In the essay "Advertisements, Pornography, and Public Space," Hayden uses description to support her analysis of the effects of certain kinds of representations of women—the kind of analysis that might be written for a course in sociology or popular culture.

But because description is not analysis, if you are asked to analyze a painting for your art history class or an advertisement for your media studies class, it won't be enough simply to describe the thing in detail. It may be useful, then, to make some distinctions between the two processes, *description* and *analysis*. Hayden *describes* a billboard when she says, "a horizontal blonde in a backless black velvet dress, slit to the thigh, invites men to 'Try on a little Black Velvet' "; she *describes* mannequins in a department store window: "The female torsos, pin-headed, tip backward and sideways, at odd angles." She reports what any viewer might see if he or she looked closely enough. These statements do not offer inferences, and they don't offer evaluations, although Hayden's diction and tone—the words "slit" and "pin-headed," for example—do begin to shape our responses to these images. But when Hayden goes on to say that those mannequins look "as if they are about to be pushed over onto a bed" she is making an *inference*, she's telling her readers what the image *implies* or *suggests;* she is *analyzing*. Likewise, she *describes* the caryatids on the front door of an apartment building when she says,

> Their breasts are bared, their heads carry the load.

But she's *analyzing* when she says,

> They recall the architecture of the Erechtheum on the Acropolis in Athens, dating from the 5th century B.C., where the sculptured stone forms of female slaves were used as support for a porch in place of traditional columns and capitals. This is an ancient image of servitude.

She's comparing (a common analytic procedure) the modern caryatids to those on the Acropolis, and she's offering an evaluation, a judgment: The caryatids at the entrance of the modern building present an "image of servitude." In another sense, she's explaining how the caryatids function. She not only answers the question "what do these images mean?" she explains *how* they mean.

Comparing

If you want to really see something, look at something else.

—*Howard Nemerov*

We began this chapter with a brief analysis of a Brueghel drawing. We *compared* Brueghel's handling of the two figures: the amount of space each figure occupied, their activities, their facial expressions, the directions of their gaze; we thereby arrived at an interpretation of the *meaning* of Brueghel's drawing. We might say that the drawing invites the comparison, and in so doing communicates Brueghel's understanding of the artist's vision, or of the value of art.

Writers, too, often use comparisons to explain a concept or idea or to arrive at a judgment or conclusion. As in drawing or painting, the point of a comparison in writing is not simply to list similarities or differences, but to explain something, to illuminate what the similarities and differences add up to. What the comparison—or analysis—adds up to is sometimes referred to as a *synthesis*, literally, a combination of separate elements to form a coherent whole.

Notice in the following paragraph, from an essay titled "England, Your England," written during World War II, how George Orwell clarifies our understanding of one kind of military march, the Nazi goose-step, by calling attention to how it differs from the march used by English soldiers. Notice, too, the point of his comparison, which he makes clear in his second sentence, and which resonates throughout the comparison.

One rapid but fairly sure guide to the social atmosphere of a country is the parade-step of its army. A military parade is really a kind of ritual dance, something like a ballet, expressing a certain philosophy of life. The goose-step, for instance, is one of the most horrible sights in the world, far more terrifying than a dive-bomber. It is simply an affirmation of naked power; contained in it, quite consciously and intentionally, is the vision of a boot crashing down on a face. Its ugliness is part of its essence, for what it is saying is "Yes, I *am* ugly, and you daren't laugh at me," like the bully who makes faces at his victim. Why is the goose-step not used in England? There are, heaven knows, plenty of army officers who would be only too glad to introduce some such thing. It is not used because the people in the street would laugh. Beyond a certain point, military display is only possible in countries where the common people dare not laugh at the army. The Italians adopted the goose-step at about the time when Italy passed definitely under German control, and, as one would expect, they do it less well than the Germans. The Vichy government, if it survives, is bound to introduce a stiffer parade-ground discipline into what is left of the French army. In the British army the drill is rigid and complicated, full of memories of the eighteenth century, but without definite swagger; the march is merely a formalised walk. It belongs to a society which is ruled by the sword, no doubt, but a sword which must never be taken out of the scabbard.

—*George Orwell*

Organizing Short Comparisons

An essay may be devoted entirely to a comparison, say of two kinds of tribal organization. But such essays are relatively rare. More often, an essay includes only a paragraph or two of comparison—for example, explaining something unfamiliar by comparing it to something familiar. Let's spend a moment discussing how to organize a paragraph that makes a comparison—though the same principles can be applied to entire essays.

The first part may announce the topic, the next part may discuss one of the two items being compared, and the last part may discuss the other. We can call this method *lumping*, because it presents one item in a lump, and then the other in another lump. Thus Orwell says all that he wishes to say about the goose-step in one lump, and then says what he wishes to say about the British parade-step in another lump. But in making a comparison a writer may use a different method, which we'll call *splitting*. The discussion of the two items may run throughout the paragraph, the writer perhaps devoting alternate sentences to each.

Because almost all writing is designed to help the reader to see what the writer has in mind, it may be especially useful here to illustrate this second structure, splitting, with a discussion of visible distinctions. The following comparison of a Japanese statue of a Buddha with a Chinese statue of a bodhisattva (a slightly lower spiritual being, dedicated to saving humankind) treats the Buddha first, and then the bodhisattva.

The Buddha, recognizable by a cranial bump that indicates a sort of supermind, sits erect and austere in the lotus position (legs crossed, each foot with the sole upward on the opposing thigh), in full control of his body.

The carved folds of his garments, in keeping with the erect posture, are severe, forming a highly disciplined pattern that is an outward expression of his remote, constrained, austere inner nature. The bodhisattva, on the other hand, sits in a languid, sensuous posture known as "royal ease," the head pensively tilted downward, one knee elevated, one leg hanging down. He is accessible, relaxed, and compassionate.

The structure is, simply this:

The Buddha (posture, folds of garments, inner nature)

The bodhisattva (posture, folds of garments, inner nature)

If, however, the writer had wished to split rather than to lump, she would have compared an aspect of the Buddha with an aspect of the bodhisattva, then another aspect of the Buddha with another aspect of the bodhisattva, and so on, perhaps ending with a synthesis to clarify the point of the comparison. The paragraph might have read like this:

Shaka, the Historical Buddha, Japan, Heian period, late 10th-early 11th century; cherry with polychrome and gold; single woodblock construction; 83 cm (height of figure); 72.5 cm (height of hairline). Denman Waldo Ross Collection, 09.72.

The Buddha, recognizable by a cranial bump that indicates a sort of supermind, sits erect and austere, in the lotus position (legs crossed, each foot with the sole upward on the opposing thigh), in full control of his body. In contrast, the bodhisattva sits in a languid, sensuous posture known as "royal ease," the head pensively tilted downward, one knee elevated, one leg hanging down. The carved folds of the Buddha's garments, in keeping with his erect posture, are severe, forming a highly disciplined pattern, whereas the bodhisattva's garments hang naturalistically. Both figures are spiritual but the Buddha is remote, constrained, and austere; the bodhisattva is accessible, relaxed, and compassionate.

In effect the structure is this:

The Buddha (posture)

The bodhisattva (posture)

The Buddha (garments)

The bodhisattva (garments)

The Buddha and the bodhisattva (synthesis)

Guanyin, China, Jin Dynasty, 12th century; wood with traces of polychrome and gold, 141 x 88 x 88 cm. Gift of Harvey Edward Wetzel, 20.590.

Whether in any given piece of writing you should compare by lump-ing or by splitting will depend largely on your purpose and on the com-plexity of the material. We can't even offer the rule that splitting is good for brief, relatively obvious comparisons, lumping for longer, more complex ones, though such a rule usually works. We can, however, give some advice:

1. If you split, in rereading your draft

- *imagine your reader*, and ask yourself if it is likely that this reader can keep up with the back-and-forth movement. Make sure (perhaps by a summary sentence at the end) that the larger picture is not obscured by the zigzagging;

- *don't leave any loose ends*. Make sure that if you call attention to points 1, 2, and 3 in *X*, you mention all of them (not just 1 and 2) in *Y*.

2. If you lump, do not simply comment first on *X* and then on *Y*.

- *Let your reader know where you are going*, probably by means of an introductory sentence;

- *Don't be afraid in the second half to remind your reader of the first half.* It is legitimate, and even desirable, to relate the second half of the comparison to the first half. A comparison organized by lumping will not break into two separate halves if the second half develops by reminding the reader how it differs from the first half.

Longer Comparisons

Now let's think about a comparison that extends through two or three paragraphs. If you are comparing the indoor play (for instance, board games or play with toys) and the sports of girls with those of boys, you can, for example, devote one paragraph to the indoor play of girls, a second paragraph to the sports of girls, a third to the indoor play of boys, and a fourth to the sports of boys. If you are thinking in terms of com-paring girls and boys, such an organization uses lumps, girls first and then boys (with a transition such as "Boys on the other hand . . ."). But you might split, writing four paragraphs along these lines:

indoor play of girls

indoor play of boys

sports of girls

sports of boys

Or you might organize the material into two paragraphs:

play and sports of girls

play and sports of boys

There is no rule, except that the organization and the point of the comparison be clear.

Consider these paragraphs from an essay by Sheila Tobias on the fear of mathematics. The writer's thesis in the essay is that although this fear is more commonly found in females than in males, biology seems not to be the cause. After discussing some findings (for example, that girls compute better than boys in elementary school, and that many girls tend to lose interest in mathematics in junior high school), the writer turns her attention away from the schoolhouse. Notice that whether a paragraph is chiefly about boys or chiefly about girls, the writer keeps us in mind of the overall point: reasons why more females than males fear math.

Not all the skills that are necessary for learning mathematics are learned in school. Measuring, computing, and manipulating objects that have dimensions and dynamic properties of their own are part of the everyday life of children. Children who miss out on these experiences may not be well primed for math in school.

Feminists have complained for a long time that playing with dolls is one way of convincing impressionable little girls that they may only be mothers or housewives—or, as in the case of the Barbie doll, "pinup girls"—when they grow up. But doll-playing may have even more serious consequences for little girls than that. Do girls find out about gravity and distance and shapes and sizes playing with dolls? Probably not.

A curious boy, if his parents are tolerant, will have taken apart a number of household and play objects by the time he is ten, and, if his parents are lucky, he may even have put them back together again. In all of this he is learning things that will be useful in physics and math. Taking parts out that have to go back in requires some examination of form. Building something that stays up or at least stays put for some time involves working with structure.

Sports is another source of math-related concepts for children which tends to favor boys. Getting to first base on a not very well hit grounder is a lesson in time, speed, and distance. Intercepting a football thrown through the air requires some rapid intuitive eye calculations based on the ball's direction, speed, and trajectory. Since physics is partly concerned with velocities, trajectories, and collisions of objects, much of the math taught to prepare a student for physics deals with relationships and formulas that can be used to express motion and acceleration.

The first paragraph offers a generalization about "children," that is, about boys and girls. The second paragraph discusses the play of girls with dolls, but discusses it in a context of its relevance, really irrelevance, to mathematics. The third paragraph discusses the household play of boys, again in the context of mathematics. The fourth paragraph discusses the outdoor sports of boys, but notice that girls are not forgotten, for its first sentence is "Sports is another source of math-related concepts for children which tends to favor boys." In short, even when there is a sort of seesaw structure, boys on one end and girls on the other, we never lose sight of the thesis that comprises both halves of the comparison.

Ways of Organizing an Essay Devoted to a Comparison

Let's now talk about organizing a comparison or contrast that runs through an entire essay, say a comparison between two political campaigns, or between the characters in two novels. Remember, first of all, one writes such a comparison not as an exercise, but in order to make a point, let's say to demonstrate the superiority of X to Y.

Probably your first thoughts, after making some jottings, will be to lump rather than to split, that is, to discuss one half of the comparison and then to go on to the second half. We'll discuss this useful method of organization in a moment, but here we want to point out that many instructors and textbooks disapprove of such an organization, arguing that the essay too often breaks into two parts and that the second part involves a good deal of repetition of categories set up in the first part. They prefer splitting. Let's say you are comparing the narrator of *Huckleberry Finn* with the narrator of *The Catcher in the Rye*, in order to show that despite superficial similarities, they are very different, and that the difference is partly the difference between the nineteenth century and the twentieth. An organization often recommended is something like this:

1. first similarity (the narrator and his quest)
    a. Huck
    b. Holden

2. second similarity (the corrupt world surrounding the narrator)

    a. society in *Huckleberry Finn*

    b. society in *The Catcher in the Rye*

3. first differences (degree to which the narrator fulfills his quest and escapes from society)

    a. Huck's plan to "light out" to the frontier

    b. Holden's breakdown

And so on, for as many additional differences as seem relevant. Here is another way of splitting and organizing a comparison:

1. first point: the narrator and his quest

    a. similarities between Huck and Holden

    b. differences between Huck and Holden

2. second point: the corrupt world

    a. similarities between the worlds in *Huck* and *The Catcher*

    b. differences between the worlds in *Huck* and *The Catcher*

3. third point: degree of success

    a. similarities between Huck and Holden

    b. differences between Huck and Holden

But a comparison need not employ either of these methods of splitting. There is even the danger that an essay employing either of them may not come into focus until the essayist stands back from the seven-layer cake and announces, in the concluding paragraph, that the odd layers taste better. In your preparatory thinking you may want to make comparisons in pairs, but you must come to some conclusions about what these add up to before writing the final version. The final version should not duplicate the thought processes; rather, it should be organized so as to make the point clearly and effectively. The point of the essay is not to list pairs of similarities or differences, but to illuminate a topic by making thoughtful comparisons. Although in a long essay you cannot postpone until page 30 a discussion of the second half of the comparison, in an essay of, say, fewer than ten pages, nothing is wrong with setting forth half of the comparison and then, in the light of what you've already said, discussing the second half. True, an essay that uses lumping will break into two unrelated parts if the second half makes no use of the first or fails to modify it; but the essay will hang together if the second half looks back to the first half and calls attention to differences that the new material reveals.

The danger of organizing the essay into two unrelated lumps can be avoided if in formulating your thesis you remember that the point of a comparison is to call attention to the unique features of something by holding it up against something similar but significantly different. If the differences are great and apparent, a comparison is a waste of effort. ("Blueberries are different from elephants. Blueberries do not have trunks. And elephants do not grow on bushes.") Indeed, a comparison between essentially and evidently unlike things can only obscure, for by making the comparison the writer implies there are significant similarities, and readers can only wonder why they do not see them. The essays that do break into two halves are essays that make *un*instructive comparisons: The first half tells the reader five things about baseball, the second half tells the reader five unrelated things about football.

CHECKLIST FOR REVISING COMPARISONS

✔ Is the point of the comparison—your reason for making it—clear?
✔ Do you cover all significant similarities and differences?
✔ Is the comparison readable, that is, is it clear and yet not tediously mechanical?
✔ Is lumping or is splitting (see pp. 153–157) the best way to make this comparison?
✔ If you are offering a value judgment, is it fair? Have you overlooked weaknesses in your preferred subject, and strengths in your less preferred subject?

Analyzing a Process

Popular writing offers many examples of the form of writing known as process analysis. Newspaper articles explain how to acquire a home aquarium or how to "detail" your car to improve its resale value; magazine articles explain how to begin a program of weight training or how to make a safe exit in an airplane emergency. The requirements for writing such an article, sometimes called a *directive process analysis*, can be simply stated. The writer must:

Know the material thoroughly

Keep his or her audience in mind

Set forth the steps clearly, usually in chronological order

Define unfamiliar terms

In addition, in the introductory paragraph or in the conclusion writers often express their pleasure in the process or their sense of its utility or value. But such comments must be brief, must not interrupt the explanation of the process, and must not gush. Surely everyone has one such article to write, and you may be asked to write one.

Explaining a process is common in academic writing too, though usually the explanation is of how something happens or has happened, and it is thus sometimes called an *informative process analysis.* The writer's purpose is for the reader to understand the process, not to perform it. You may find yourself reading or writing about a successful election strategy or a botched military campaign. In an exam you may be explaining your plan to solve a mathematical problem, or you may be explaining how the imagery works in a Shakespearean sonnet. You might write an essay on the camera techniques Hitchcock used in a sequence, or a term paper based on your research in marine biology. Once again, you will need to keep your reader in mind, to organize your explanation clearly and logically, and, of course, to write with expert knowledge of your subject.

The essay below, "It's the Portly Penguin That Gets the Girl, French Biologist Claims," reports on a lecture that was, from the evidence, an entertaining example of an *informative process analysis.*

Anne Hebald Mandelbaum
It's the Portly Penguin That Gets the Girl, French Biologist Claims

1   The penguin is a feathered and flippered bird who looks as if he's on his way to a formal banquet. With his stiff, kneeless strut and nat-

ural dinner jacket, he moves like Charlie Chaplin in his heyday dressed like Cary Grant in his.

2   But beneath the surface of his tuxedo is a gallant bird indeed. Not only does he fast for 65 days at a time, sleep standing up, and forsake all others in a lifetime of monogamy, but the male penguin also guards, watches over, and even hatches the egg.

3   We owe much of our current knowledge of the life and loves of the king and emperor penguins to—*bien sûr*—a Frenchman. Twenty-eight-year-old Yvon Le Maho is a biophysiologist from Lyons who visited the University last week to discuss his discoveries and to praise the penguin. He had just returned from 14 months in Antarctica, where he went to measure, to photograph, to weigh, to take blood and urine samples of, to perform autopsies on—in short, to study the penguin.

4   Although his original intent had been to investigate the penguin's long fasts, Monsieur Le Maho was soon fascinated by the amatory aspect of the penguin. Copulating in April, the female produces the egg in May and then heads out to sea, leaving her mate behind to incubate the egg. The males huddle together, standing upright and protecting the 500-gram (or 1.1-pound) egg with their feet for 65 days. During this time, they neither eat nor stray: each steadfastly stands guard over his egg, protecting it from the temperatures which dip as low as −40 degrees and from the winds which whip the Antarctic wilds with gusts of 200 miles an hour.

5   For 65 days and 65 nights, the males patiently huddle over the eggs, never lying down, never letting up. Then, every year on July 14th—Bastille Day, the national holiday of France—the eggs hatch and thousands of penguin chicks are born, M. Le Maho told his amused and enthusiastic audience at the Biological Laboratories.

6   The very day the chicks are born—or, at the latest, the following day—the female penguins return to land from their two-and-a-half month fishing expedition. They clamber out of the water and toboggan along the snow-covered beaches toward the rookery and their mates. At this moment, the males begin to emit the penguin equivalent of wild, welcoming cheers—*"comme le cri de trompette,"* M. Le Maho later told the *Gazette* in an interview—"like the clarion call of the trumpet."

7   And, amid the clamorous thundering of 12,000 penguins, the female recognizes the individual cry of her mate. When she does, she begins to cry to him. The male then recognizes *her* song, lifts the newborn chick into his feathered arms, and makes a beeline for the female. Each singing, each crying, the males and females rush toward each other, slipping and sliding on the ice as they go, guided all the while by the single voice each instinctively knows.

8   The excitement soon wears thin for the male, however, who hasn't had a bite to eat in more than two months. He has done his duty and done it unflaggingly, but even penguins cannot live by duty alone. He must have food, and quickly.

9   Having presented his mate with their newborn, the male abruptly departs, heading out to sea in search of fish. The female, who has just returned from her sea-going sabbatical, has swallowed vast quantities of fish for herself and her chick. Much of what she has eaten she has not digested. Instead, this undigested food becomes penguin baby food. She regurgitates it, all soft and pap-like, from her storage throat right into her chick's mouth. The chicks feed in this manner until December, when they first learn to find food on their own.

10   The penguins' reproductive life begins at age five, and the birds live about 25 years. Their fasting interests M. Le Maho because of its close similarities with fasting in human beings. And although many migratory birds also fast, their small size and indeed their flight make it almost impossible to study them closely. With the less-mobile and non-flying penguin, however, the scientist has a relatively accessible population to study. With no damage to the health of the penguin, M. Le Maho told the *Gazette*, a physiobiologist can extract blood from the flipper and sample the urine.

11   "All fasting problems are the same between man and the penguin," M. Le Maho said. "The penguin uses glucose in the brain, experiences ketosis as does man, and accomplishes gluconeogenesis, too." Ketosis is the build-up of partially burned fatty acids in the blood, usually as a result of starvation; gluconeogenesis is the making of sugar from non-sugar chemicals, such as amino acids. "The penguin can tell us a great deal about how our own bodies react to fasting conditions," M. Le Maho said.

12   He will return to Antarctica, M. Le Maho said, with the French government-sponsored *Expéditions Polaires Françaises* next December. There he will study the growth of the penguin chick, both inside the egg and after birth; will continue to study their mating, and to examine the penguin's blood sugar during fasting.

13   During the question-and-answer period following his talk, M. Le Maho was asked what the female penguin looks for in a mate. Responding, M. Le Maho drew himself up to his full five-foot-nine and said, *"La grandeur."*

Explaining An Analysis

As we have suggested, the writer of an analytical essay arrives at a thesis by asking questions and answering them, by separating the topic into parts and by seeing—often through the use of lists and scratch outlines—how those parts relate. Or, we might say, analytic writing presupposes detective work: The writer looks over the evidence, finds some clues, pursues the trail from one place to the next, and makes the arrest. Elementary? Perhaps.

You may recall that Sherlock Holmes customarily searches for evidence, finds it, and then—and this is important—explains it to his listener, usually Dr. Watson. When you write an analytic essay, you are Holmes, and your reader is Watson. That is, even when as a writer, after preliminary thinking you have solved a problem—that is, focused on a topic and formulated a thesis—you are, as we have said before, not yet done. It is, alas, not enough simply to present the results of your analytical thinking to a reader who, like Dr. Watson, will surely want to know "How in the world did you deduce that?" And like Holmes, writers are often impatient; we long to say with him "I have no time for trifles." But the real reason for our impatience is, as Holmes is quick to acknowledge, that "It was easier to know it than to explain why I know it." But explaining to readers why or how, presenting both the reasoning that led to a thesis and the evidence that supports the reasoning, is the writer's job.

In your preliminary detective work (that is, in reading, taking notes, musing, jotting down some thoughts, and writing rough drafts) some insights (perhaps including your thesis) may come swiftly, apparently spontaneously, and in random order. You may be unaware that you have been thinking analytically at all. In preparing your essay for your reader, however, you become aware, in part because *you must become aware.* You must persuade *your* Dr. Watson that what you say is not "brag and bounce." To replace your reader's natural suspicion with respect for your analysis, you must explain your reasoning in an orderly and interesting fashion and you must present your evidence.

CHAPTER EIGHT

PERSUADING READERS

To persuade readers is to convince them of the merit of your point of view, whether you're arguing against censorship, or for capital punishment, or in favor of a particular interpretation of a short story. To be persuasive, you must present *reasonable arguments*, supported with *evidence*. In academic essays, the distinction between argument and analysis is often blurry. In the preceding chapter, for example, the analytic essay on "Ripe Figs" puts forth an **argument** (that the story is more than a mere character sketch, that it says something about time and human nature); the writer supports that argument with **evidence** from the text—brief passages that have been carefully analyzed. In the next chapter, we'll examine a research essay in which the writer uses analysis and argument in roughly equal proportion. In this chapter, after a brief comment on persuasion by emotional appeal, we'll focus on the elements of argument: on the distinction between claims and evidence, on the importance of defining terms and of avoiding fallacies, and on the use of wit in persuasive writing.

Emotional Appeals

It is often said that good argumentative writing appeals only to reason, never to emotion, and that any sort of emotional appeal is illegitimate, irrelevant, fallacious. Logic textbooks may even stigmatize with Latin labels the various sorts of emotional appeal, for instance *argumentum ad populam* (appeal to the prejudices of the mob, as in "Come on, we all know that schools don't teach anything anymore") and *argumentum ad misericoridam* (appeal to pity, as in "No one can blame this poor kid for stabbing a classmate because his mother was often institutionalized and his father beat him").

True, appeals to emotion may get in the way of the facts of the case; they may blind the audience by stimulating tears. When an emotional argument confuses the issue or shifts attention away from the facts of the issue, we can reasonably speak of the fallacy of emotional appeal. But no fallacy is involved when an emotional appeal heightens the facts, bringing them home to the audience rather than masking them. If we are talking about legislation that would govern police actions, it is legitimate to show a photograph of the battered, bloodied face of a victim of alleged police brutality. Of course such a photograph cannot tell if the subject threatened the officer with a gun or repeatedly resisted an order to surrender. But it can tell us that the victim was severely beaten and (like a comparable description in words) evoke in us emotions that may properly enter into our decision about what sorts of limitations on police actions are appropriate. Similarly, an animal rights activist who is arguing that calves are cruelly confined might reasonably tell us the size of the pen in which the beast—unable to turn around or even to lie down—is kept. Others may argue that calves don't much care about turning around or have no right to turn around, but the verbal description, which unquestionably makes an emotional appeal, can hardly be called fallacious or irrelevant.

In appealing to emotions, then, the important things are

• not to falsify (especially by oversimplifying) the issue, and

• not to distract attention from the facts of the case

For the most part, you should focus on the facts and concentrate on offering reasons (essentially, statements linked with "because"), but you may also legitimately bring the facts home to your readers by seeking to induce in them the appropriate emotions. Your words will be fallacious only if you stimulate emotions that are not rightly connected with the facts of the case.

Making Reasonable Arguments

Persuasive writing that offers evidence and relies chiefly on reasoning rather than on appeals to the emotions is usually called *argument*. What distinguishes argument from exposition is this: Whereas both consist of statements, in argument some statements are offered as *reasons* for other statements. Another way of characterizing argument is that argument assumes there is or may be substantial disagreement between informed readers. To overcome this disagreement, the writer of an argument offers reasons that seek to convince by their validity. Here, for example, is C. S. Lewis arguing against vivisection, the experimentation on live animals for scientific research:

> A rational discussion of this subject begins by inquiring whether pain is, or is not, an evil. If it is not, then the case against vivisection falls. But then so does the case for vivisection. If it is not defended on the ground that it reduces human suffering, on what ground can it be defended? And if pain is not an evil, why should human suffering be reduced? We must therefore assume as a basis for the whole discussion that pain is an evil, otherwise there is nothing to be discussed.
>
> Now if pain is an evil then the infliction of pain, considered in itself, must clearly be an evil act. But there are such things as necessary evils. Some acts which would be bad, simply in themselves, may be excusable and even laudable when they are necessary means to a greater good. In saying that the infliction of pain, simply in itself, is bad, we are not saying that pain ought never to be inflicted. Most of us think that it can rightly be inflicted for a good purpose—as in dentistry or just and reformatory punishment. The point is that it always requires justification. On the man whom we find inflicting pain rests the burden of showing why an act which in itself would be simply bad is, in those particular circumstances, good. If we find a man giving pleasure it is for us to prove (if we criticize him) that his action is wrong. But if we find a man inflicting pain it is for him to prove that his action is right. If he cannot, he is a wicked man.

And here is Supreme Court Justice Louis Brandeis, concluding his justly famous argument that government may not use evidence illegally obtained by wiretapping:

> Decency, security and liberty alike demand that government officials shall be subjected to the same rules of conduct that are commands to the citizen. In a government of laws, existence of the government will be imperiled if it fails to observe the law scrupulously. Our Government is the potent, the omnipresent teacher. For good or for ill, it teaches the whole people by its example. Crime is contagious. If the Government becomes

a lawbreaker, it breeds contempt for law; it invites every man to become a law unto himself; it invites anarchy. To declare that in the administration of the criminal law the end justifies the means—to declare that the Government may commit crimes in order to secure the conviction of a private criminal—would bring terrible retribution. Against that pernicious doctrine this Court should resolutely set its face.

Notice here that Brandeis's reasoning is highlighted by his forceful style. Note the resonant use of parallel constructions ("Decency, security and liberty," "For good or for ill," "it breeds . . . it invites," "To declare . . . to declare") and the variation between long and short sentences. Note too the wit in his comparisons: Government is a teacher, crime is like a disease.

Claims and Evidence

A **claim** is an assertion—usually that something is true, or right, or good. *Evidence* is what the writer offers in support of that claim, and it usually comes in the form of examples, testimony, and statistics.

Three Kinds of Claims: Claims of Fact, Value, and Policy

We can usually distinguish between two kinds of claims, claims of fact and claims of value, and we can sometimes distinguish these from a third kind of claim, claims of policy.

Claims of Fact

Claims of fact assert that something is or was or will be. They include, for instance, arguments about cause and effect, correlation, probability, and states of affairs. The following examples can be considered claims of fact:

Vanilla is the most popular flavor of ice cream in the United States.

Pornography stimulates violence against women.

Pornography has the potential of leading to violence.

Pornography serves a useful social purpose for it offers a harmless release of impulses that might otherwise be released in such activities as molestation or rape.

Capital punishment reduces crime.

Capital punishment does not reduce crime.

Racial integration of the armed forces was achieved with very little conflict during the Korean War.

To support a claim of this sort, you must provide (probably after defining any terms that may be in doubt) evidence. Such evidence might, for instance, be testimony (for instance, your own experience, or statements by men who have said that pornography stimulated them to violence), or it might be statistics (gathered from a report in a scholarly journal). Even if the claim has to do with the future—let's say the claim that gun control will not reduce crime—you try to offer evidence. For example, you might gather information about the experiences of other countries, or even of certain states, that have adopted strict regulations concerning the sale of guns.

Claims of Value

Claims of value concern what is right or wrong, good or bad, better or worse than something else:

Country music deserves to be taken seriously.

Rock is better than country music.

Capital punishment is barbaric.

Euthanasia is immoral.

Some claims of value may be mere expressions of taste: "Vanilla is better than chocolate." It is hard to imagine how one could go about supporting such a claim—or refuting it. One probably can do no better than reply with the Latin proverb, *"De gustibus non est disputandum."* (There is no disputing about tastes.) Notice, however, that the claim that vanilla is better than chocolate is quite different from the claim that most Americans prefer vanilla to chocolate. The last statement is a claim of fact, not of value, and it can be proved or disproved with evidence—for example, with information provided by the makers of ice cream.

Claims of value that go beyond the mere expression of taste—for instance, claims of morality or claims of artistic value—are usually supported by appeals to standards ("Such-and-such a proposal is bad *because* governments should not restrict the rights of individuals," or

"Such-and-such music is good *because* it is complex."). In supporting claims of value, writers usually appeal to standards that they believe are acceptable to their readers. Examples:

Sex-education programs in schools are inappropriate *because* aspects of moral education should properly be given only by parents.

Sex-education programs in schools are appropriate *because* society has a duty to provide what most parents obviously are reluctant to provide.

Doctors should be permitted to end a patient's life if the patient makes such a request, *because* each of us should be free to make the decisions that most concern us.

Euthanasia is unacceptable *because* only God can give or take life.

In arguing a claim of value, be sure you have clearly in your mind the standards that you believe support the claim. You may find it appropriate to explain *why* you hold these standards, and *how* adherence to these standards will be of benefit.

Claims of Policy

Claims of policy assert that a policy, law, or custom should be initiated or altered or dropped. Such claims usually are characterized by words like "should," "must," and "ought."

Children should be allowed to vote, if they wish to.

A course in minority cultures ought to be required.

The federal tax on gasoline must be raised.

In defending an unfamiliar claim of policy, you may want to begin by pointing out that there is a problem that is usually overlooked. For instance, if you urgently believe that children should have the right to vote—a view almost never expressed—you'll probably first have to convince your audience that there really is an arguable issue here, an issue concerning children's rights, an issue that deserves serious thought.

In defending a claim of policy you will probably find yourself providing information, just as you would do in support of a claim of fact. For instance, if your topic is children and the vote, you might point out that until 1920 women could not vote in the United States, the usual arguments being that they were mentally unfit and that they would vote the way their men told them to vote. Experience has proven that these low estimates of the capabilities of the disenfranchised were absurd.

But in defending a claim of policy you will probably have to consider values as well as facts. Thus, in arguing for an increase in the gasoline tax, you might want not only to provide factual information about how much money a five-cents-per-gallon tax would raise, but also to argue that such an increase is *fairer* than an alternative such as reducing social security benefits.

Three Kinds of Evidence: Examples, Testimony, Statistics

Writers of arguments seek to persuade by offering evidence. The three chief forms of evidence used in argument are:

- Examples
- Testimony, the citation of authorities
- Statistics

We'll briefly consider each of these.

Examples

"Example" is from the Latin *exemplum*, which means "something taken out." An example is the sort of thing, taken from among many similar things, that one selects and holds up for view, perhaps after saying "For example," or "For instance."

Three categories of examples are especially common in written arguments:

- Real examples
- Invented instances
- Analogies

Real examples are just what they sound like, instances that have occurred. If, say, we are arguing that gun control won't work, we point to those states that have adopted gun control laws and that nevertheless have had no reduction in crimes using guns. Or, if we want to support the assertion that a woman can be a capable head of state, we may find ourselves pointing to women who actually served as heads of state, such as Golda Meir and Indira Ghandi (prime ministers of Israel and India) and to Margaret Thatcher (prime minister of England).

The advantage of using real example is, clearly, that they are real. Of course an opponent might stubbornly respond that Golda Meir, Indira Gandhi, and Margaret Thatcher for some reason or other could not function as the head of state in *our* country. Someone might argue, for instance, that the case of Golda Meir proves nothing, since the role of women in Israeli society is different from the role of women in the United States (a country in which a majority of the citizens are Christians). And another person might argue that much of Mrs. Gandhi's power came from the fact that she was the daughter of Nehru, an immensely popular Indian statesman. Even the most compelling real example inevitably will in some ways be special or particular, and in the eyes of some readers may not seem to be a fair example.

Consider, for instance, a student who is arguing that peer review should be part of the writing course. The student points out that he or she found it of great help in high school. An opponent argues that things in college are different—college students should be able to help themselves, even highly gifted college students are not competent to offer college-level instruction, and so on. Still, as the feebleness of these objections (and the objections against Meir and Gandhi) indicates, real examples can be very compelling.

Invented instances are exempt from the charge that, because of some detail or other, they are not relevant as evidence. Suppose, for example, you are arguing against capital punishment, on the grounds that if an innocent person is executed, there is no way of even attempting to rectify the injustice. If you point to the case of X, you may be met with the reply that X was not in fact innocent. Rather than get tangled up in the guilt or innocence of a particular person, it may be better to argue that we can suppose—we can imagine—an innocent person convicted and executed, and we can imagine that evidence later proves the person's innocence.

Invented instances have the advantage of presenting an issue clearly, free from all of the distracting particularities and irrelevancies that are bound up with any real instance. But invented instances have the disadvantage of being invented, and they may seem remote from the real issues being argued.

Analogies are comparisons pointing out several resemblances between two rather different things. For instance, one might assert that a government is like a ship, and in times of stress—if the ship is to weather the storm—the authority of the captain must not be questioned.

But don't confuse an analogy with proof. An analogy is an extended comparison between two things; it can be useful in exposition, for it explains the unfamiliar by means of the familiar: "A government is like a ship, and just as a ship has a captain and a crew, so a government has . . ."; "Writing an essay is like building a house; just as an architect must begin with a plan, so the writer must . . ." Such comparisons can be useful, helping to clarify what otherwise might be obscure, but their usefulness goes only so far. Everything is what it is, and not another thing. A government is not a ship, and what is true of a captain's power need not be true of a president's power; and a writer is not an architect. Some of what is true about ships may be roughly true of governments, and some of what is true about architects may be true of writers, but there are differences too. Consider the following analogy between a lighthouse and the death penalty:

> The death penalty is a warning, just like a lighthouse throwing its beams out to sea. We hear about shipwrecks, but we do not hear about the ships the lighthouse guides safely on their way. We do not have proof of the number of ships it saves, but we do not tear the lighthouse down.
>
> —*J. Edgar Hoover*

How convincing is Hoover's analogy as an argument, that is, as a reason for retaining the death penalty?

Testimony

Testimony, or the citation of authorities, is rooted in our awareness that some people are recognized as experts. In our daily lives we constantly turn to experts for guidance: We look up the spelling of a word in the dictionary, we watch weather forecasts on television, we take an ailing cat to the vet for a checkup. Similarly, when we wish to become informed about controversial matters, we often turn to experts, first to help educate ourselves, and then to help convince others.

Don't forget that *you* are an authority on many things. For example, today's newspaper includes an article about the cutback in funding
for the teaching of the arts in elementary and secondary schools. Art educators are responding that the arts are not a frill, and that in fact the
arts provide the analytical thinking, teamwork, motivation, and self-dis-
cipline that most people agree are needed to reinvigorate American
schools. If you have been involved in the arts in school—for instance, if
you studied painting or learned to play a musical instrument—you are in
a position to evaluate these claims. Similarly, if you have studied in a
bilingual educational program, your own testimony will be invaluable
in any discussion of the merits of bilingual programs.

There are at least two reasons for offering testimony in an argument.
The obvious one is that expert opinion carries some weight with any audience; the less obvious one is that a change of voice (if the testimony is not
your own) in an essay may afford the reader a bit of pleasure. No matter how engaging your own voice may be, a fresh voice—whether that
of Thomas Jefferson, Ruth Bader Ginsburg, or Alice Walker—may provide a refreshing change of tone.

But, of course, there are dangers: The chief danger is that the words of
authorities may be taken out of context or otherwise distorted, and the
second is that the authorities may not be authorities on the present topic.
Quite rightly we are concerned with what Jefferson said, but it is not clear
that his words can be fairly applied, on one side or the other, to such an issue
as abortion. Quite rightly we are concerned with what Einstein said, but it
is not clear that his eminence as a physicist constitutes him an authority
on, say, world peace. In a moment, when we discuss errors in reasoning, we'll
have more to say about the proper and improper use of authorities.

Statistics

Statistics, another important form of evidence, are especially useful in
arguments concerning social issues. If we want to argue for raising the
driving age, we will probably do some research in the library, and will
offer statistics about the number of accidents caused by people in certain age groups.

But a word of caution: The significance of statistics may be difficult
to assess. For instance, opponents of gun control legislation have pointed
out, in support of the argument that such laws are ineffectual, that

homicides in Florida *increased* after Florida adopted gun control laws. Supporters of gun control laws cried "Foul," arguing that in the years after adopting these laws Miami became (for reasons having nothing to do with the laws) the cocaine capital of the United States, and the rise in homicide was chiefly a reflection of murders involved in the drug trade. That is, a significant change in the population has made a comparison of the figures meaningless. This objection seems plausible, and probably the statistics therefore should carry little weight.

A Note on Definition in the Persuasive Essay

To argue a point or to explain an idea, writers frequently need to define words. Defining the terms of an argument is one of the persuasive writer's most useful strategies: A writer making an argument for or against abortion would be likely at some point in the essay to define the term "life."

The words may be *specialized* or unfamiliar to the writer's intended audience—for example, the words "venture capitalist" or "enterprise zones." Or, we might define a word that the audience may think it knows but that (in the writer's opinion) the audience may misunderstand. For instance, a writer might argue that the words "guerrilla" and "terrorist" are not synonyms, and then go on to define each word, showing the differences between them.

In addition to defining a word because it is specialized ("venture capitalist"), or because we want to distinguish it from another word ("guerrilla" and "terrorist"), we may define a word because the word has many meanings, and we want to make sure that readers take the word in a particular way. A word like "ability," for example, may require defining in a discussion of the Scholastic Aptitude Test. To argue that the SAT does or does not measure "academic ability," the writer and reader need, in a sense, to agree on a specific meaning for "ability." This kind of definition, where the writer specifies or stipulates a meaning ("By 'ability' I mean . . .), is called a *stipulative definition*.

The word "stipulate," by the way, comes from a Latin word meaning "to bargain." Explaining a word's *etymology*, its *history* or its *origin*, as we have just done, is often an aid in definition.

In short, in defining a word or term, writers have many options and they need to take into account both their own purposes in writing and their readers' needs.

Definition at Work

In the following brief essay, a student, Lena Flora, defines the term *political correctness.*

The Plight of the Politically Correct

Political correctness is a style of language, an attitude, and a standard of ethics that people have now been struggling with for years. Part of the reason for this struggle lies in the fact that no one is exactly sure what is and what is not politically correct. The phrase <u>political correctness</u> might be defined as "conformity to a body of liberal or radical opinion, especially on social matters." Political correctness also involves the avoidance of anything, even established vocabulary, that might be construed as discriminatory or pejorative. In effect, political correctness seems to mean taking every word in the English language, scrutinizing it for any way that it could possibly offend any one person, and using this criterion to ban its use in day-to-day speech. For example, I can no longer grow up and be a fireman, a policeman, a mailman, or a woman. I may not even be allowed to call myself female. Does this mean that I am fated to call myself testosteronally-challenged, or maybe x-chromosomally gifted? Am I a chauvinist pig if I like to be known as a woman, or if I refer to my daughter as my little girl? By some strict politically correct standards, yes. Also, political correctness forces me to refrain from using many adjectives I might use to describe myself. I am not Oriental, short, or near-sighted. Instead, I am an Asian-American, vertically-challenged, and distant-visually-challenged person of feminine gender. I certainly don't feel challenged in any of these areas, only in the area of speaking with political correctness.

How Much Evidence Is Enough?

If you allow yourself ample time to write your essay, you probably will turn up plenty of evidence to illustrate your arguments, such as examples drawn from your own experience and imagination, from your reading, and from your talks with others. Evidence will not only help to clarify and to support your assertions, but it will also provide a concreteness that will be welcome in a paper that might be on the whole fairly abstract. Your sense of your audience will have to guide you as you select your evidence. Generally speaking, a single example may not fully illuminate a difficult point, and so a second example, a clincher, may be desirable. If you offer a third or fourth example you probably are succumbing to a temptation to include something that tickles your fancy. If it is as good as you think it is, the reader probably will accept the unnecessary example and may even be grateful. But before you heap up examples, try to imagine yourself in your reader's place, and ask if the example is needed. If it is not needed, ask yourself if the reader will be glad to receive the overload.

One other point. On most questions, say on the value of bilingual education or on the need for rehabilitation programs in prisons, it's not possible to make a strictly logical case, in the sense of an absolutely airtight proof. Don't assume that it is your job to make an absolute proof. What you are expected to do is to offer a reasonable argument.

Two Kinds of Reasoning: Induction and Deduction

We have just said that you are expected to offer a reasonable argument, which means that your essay will probably demonstrate two kinds of thinking, inductive and deductive. **Induction** is the process of reasoning from particular to general, or drawing a conclusion about all members of a class from a study of some members of the class. Every elephant I have seen is grayish, so by induction (from Latin for "lead into," "lead up to") I conclude that all elephants are grayish. Another example: I have met ten graduates of Vassar College and all are females, so I conclude that all Vassar graduates are females. This conclusion, however, happens to be incorrect; Vassar originally admitted only women, but it now admits men, and so although male graduates of Vassar are relatively few, they do exist. Induction is valid only if the sample is representative.

Because we can rarely be certain that a sample is representative, induced conclusions are usually open to doubt. Still, we live our lives largely by induction; we have dinner with a friend, we walk the dog, we write home for money—all because these actions have produced certain results in the past and we assume that actions of the same sort will produce results consistent with our earlier experience. Nelson Algren's excellent advice must have been arrived at inductively: "Never eat at a place called Mom's, and never play cards with a man called Doc." In developing our argument, we draw on experience—"Policy X has been successful in all ten instances where it was tried, so we can assume it will probably succeed here too"—but we must understand that we are not dealing with certainties.

Deduction is the process of reasoning from premises to a logical conclusion. Here is the classic example: "All men are mortal" (the major premise); "Socrates is a man" (the minor premise); "Therefore Socrates is mortal" (the conclusion). Such an argument, which takes two truths and joins them to produce a third truth, is called a syllogism (from Greek for "a reckoning together"). Deduction (from Latin for "lead down from") moves from a general statement to a specific application; it is, therefore, the opposite of induction, which moves from specific instances to a general conclusion.

Notice that if a premise of a syllogism is not true, one can reason logically and still come to false conclusion. Example: "All teachers are members of a union"; "Jones is a teacher"; "Therefore Jones is a member of a union." Although the formal process of reasoning is correct here, the major premise is false—not all teachers are members of a union—and so the conclusion is worthless. (Jones may or may not be a member of a union.) In other words, "Garbage in, garbage out."

Let's now look at some common errors in thinking, whether inductive or deductive.

Avoiding Fallacies

Let's further examine writing reasonable arguments by considering some obvious errors in reasoning. In logic these errors are called *fallacies* (from a Latin verb meaning "to deceive"). As Tweedledee says in *Through the Looking-Glass*, "If it were so, it would be; but as it isn't, it ain't. That's logic."

To persuade readers to accept your opinions you must persuade them that you are reliable; if your argument includes fallacies, thoughtful readers will not take you seriously. More important, if your argument includes fallacies, you are misleading yourself. When you search your draft for fallacies, you are searching for ways to improve the quality of your thinking.

1. False authority. Don't try to borrow the prestige of authorities who are not authorities on the topic in question—for example, a heart surgeon speaking on politics. Similarly, some former authorities are no longer authorities, because the problems have changed or because later knowledge has superseded their views. Adam Smith, Jefferson, Eleanor Roosevelt, and Einstein remain persons of genius, but an attempt to use their opinions when you are examining modern issues—even in their fields—may be questioned. Remember the last words of John B. Sedgwick, a Union Army general at the Battle of Spotsylvania in 1864: "They couldn't hit an elephant at this dist—." In short, before you rely on an authority, ask yourself if the person in question *is* an authority on the topic. And don't let stereotypes influence your idea of who is an authority. Remember the Yiddish proverb: "A goat has a beard, but that doesn't make him a rabbi."

2. False quotation. If you do quote from an authority, don't misquote. For example, you may find someone who grants that "there are strong arguments in favor of abolishing the death penalty"; but if she goes on to argue that, on balance, the arguments in favor of retaining it seem stronger to her, it is dishonest to quote her words so as to imply that she favors abolishing it.

3. Suppression of evidence. Don't neglect evidence that is contrary to your own argument. You owe it to yourself and your reader to present all the relevant evidence. Be especially careful not to assume that every question is simply a matter of *either/or.* There may be some truth on both sides. Take the following thesis: "Grades encourage unwholesome competition, and should therefore be abolished." Even if the statement about the evil effect of grading is true, it may not be the whole truth, and therefore it may not follow that grades should be abolished. One might point out that grades do other things too: They may stimulate learning, and they may assist students by telling them how far they have progressed. One might nevertheless conclude, on balance, that the fault outweighs the benefits. But the argument will be more persuasive now that the benefits of grades have been considered.

Concede to the opposition what is due it, and then outscore the opposition. If you don't discuss the opposing evidence, your readers will keep wondering why you do not consider this point or that, and may consequently dismiss your argument. Confronting the opposition will almost surely strengthen your own argument. As Edmund Burke said 200 years ago, "He that wrestles with us strengthens our nerves, and sharpens our skill. Our antagonist is our helper."

4. Generalization from insufficient evidence. In rereading a draft of an argument that you have written, try to spot your own generalizations. Ask yourself if a reasonable reader is likely to agree that the generalization is based on an adequate sample.

A visitor to a college may sit in on three classes, each taught by a different instructor, and may find all three stimulating. That's a good sign, but can we generalize and say that the teaching at this college is excellent? Are three classes a sufficient sample? If all three are offered by the Biology Department, and if the Biology Department includes only five instructors, perhaps we can tentatively say that the teaching of biology at this institution is good. If the Biology Department contains twenty instructors, perhaps we can still say, though more tentatively, that this sample indicates that the teaching of biology is good. But what does the sample say about the teaching of other subjects at the college? It probably does say something—the institution may be much concerned with teaching across the board—but then again it may not say a great deal, since the Biology Department may be exceptionally concerned with good teaching.

5. The genetic fallacy. Don't assume that something can necessarily be explained in terms of its birth or origin. "He wrote the novel to make money, so it can't be any good" is not a valid inference. The value of a novel does not depend on the author's motivations in writing it. Indeed, the value or worth of a novel needs to be established by reference to other criteria. Neither the highest nor the lowest motivations guarantee the quality of the product. Another example: "Capital punishment arose in days when people sought revenge, so now it ought to be abolished." Again an unconvincing argument: Capital punishment may have some current value; for example, it may serve as a deterrent to crime. But that's another argument, and it needs evidence if it is to be believed.

6. Begging the question and circular reasoning. Don't assume the truth of the point that you should prove. The term "begging the question" is a trifle odd. It means, in effect, "You, like a beggar, are asking me to grant you something at the outset."

Examples: "The barbaric death penalty should be abolished"; "This senseless language requirement should be dropped." Both of these statements assume what they should prove—that the death penalty is bar-

"Look, maybe you're right, but for the sake of argument let's assume you're wrong and drop it." © The New Yorker Collection 1983 Robert Mankoff from Cartoonbank.com. All Rights Reserved.

baric, and that the language requirement is senseless. You can of course make assertions such as these, but you must go on to prove them.

Circular reasoning is usually an extended form of begging the question. What ought to be proved is covertly assumed. Example: "X is the best-qualified candidate for the office, because the most informed people say so." Who are the most informed people? Those who recognize X's superiority. Circular reasoning, then, normally includes intermediate steps absent from begging the question, but the two fallacies are so closely related that they can be considered one. Another example: "I feel sympathy for her because I identify with her." Despite the "because," no reason is really offered. What follows "because" is merely a restatement, in slightly different words, of what precedes; the shift of words, from "feel sympathy" to "identify with," has misled the writer into thinking she is giving a reason. Other examples: "Students are interested in courses when the subject matter and the method of presentation are interesting"; "There cannot be peace in the Middle East because the Jews and the Arabs will always fight." In each case, an assertion that ought to be proved is reasserted as a reason in support of the assertion.

7. *Post hoc ergo propter hoc* (Latin for "after this, therefore because of this"). Don't assume that because X precedes Y, X must cause Y. For example: "He went to college and came back a boozer; college corrupted him." He might have taken up liquor even if he had not gone to college. Another example: "When a fifty-five-mile-per-hour limit was imposed in 1974, after the Arab embargo on oil, the number of auto fatalities decreased sharply, from 55,000 deaths in 1973 to 46,000 in 1974, so it is evident that a fifty-five-mile-per-hour limit—still adhered to in some states—saves lives." Not quite. Because gasoline was expensive after the embargo, the number of miles traveled decreased. The number of fatalities *per mile* remained constant. The price of gas, not the speed limit, seems responsible for the decreased number of fatalities. Moreover, the national death rate has continued to fall. Why? Several factors are at work: seat-belt and child-restraint laws, campaigns against drunk driving, improved auto design, and improved roads. Medicine, too, may have improved so that today doctors can save accident victims who in 1974 would have died. In short, it probably is impossible to isolate the correlation between speed and safety.

8. *Argumentum ad hominem* (Latin for "argument toward the man"). Here the argument is directed toward the person rather than toward the issue. Don't shift from your topic to your opponent. A speaker argues against legalizing abortions and her opponent, instead of facing the merits of the argument, attacks the character or the associations of the opponent: "You're a Catholic, aren't you?"

9. False assumption. Consider the Scot who argued that Shakespeare must have been a Scot. Asked for his evidence, he replied, "The ability of the man warrants the assumption." Or take a statement such as "She goes to Yale, so she must be rich." Possibly the statement is based on faulty induction (the writer knows four Yale students, and all four are rich) but more likely he is just passing on a cliché. The Yale student in question may be on a scholarship, may be struggling to earn the money, or may be backed by parents of modest means who for eighteen years have saved money for her college education. Other examples: "I haven't heard him complain about French 10, so he must be satisfied"; "She's a writer, so she must be well read." A little thought will show how weak such assertions are; they *may* be true, but they may not.

The errors we have discussed are common. In revising, try to spot them and eliminate or correct them. You have a point to make, and you should make it fairly. If it can be made only unfairly, you do an injustice not only to your reader but also to yourself; you should try to change your view of the topic. You don't want to be like the politician whose speech had a marginal note: "Argument weak; shout here."

Wit

In addition to using sound argument and other evidence, writers often use wit, especially irony, to persuade. In irony, the words convey a meaning somewhat different from what they explicitly say. Wry understatement is typical. Here, for instance, is Thoreau explaining why in *Walden*, his book about his two years in relative isolation at Walden Pond, he will talk chiefly about himself:

> In most books, the *I*, or first person, is omitted; in this it will be retained; that, in respect to egotism, is the main difference. We commonly do not remember that it is, after all, always the first person that is speaking. I should not talk so much about myself if there were anybody else whom I knew as well. Unfortunately, I am confined to this theme by the narrowness of my experience.

Notice the wry apology in his justification for talking about himself: He does not know anyone else as well as he knows himself. Similarly, in "unfortunately" ("Unfortunately, I am confined to this theme by the narrowness of my experience") we again hear a wry voice. After all, Thoreau knows, as we know, that *no one* has experience so deep or broad that he or she knows others better than himself or herself. Thoreau's presentation of himself as someone who happens not to have had the luck of knowing others better than himself is engagingly clever.

Avoiding Sarcasm

Because writers must, among other things, persuade readers that they are humane, sarcasm has little place in persuasive writing. Although desk dictionaries usually define sarcasm as "bitter, caustic irony" or "a kind of satiric wit," if you think of a sarcastic comment that you have heard you will probably agree that "a crude, sneering remark" is a better definition. Lacking the wit of good satire and the carefully controlled mockery of irony, sarcasm usually relies on gross overstatement and intends simply to humiliate. *Sarcasm* is derived from a Greek word meaning "to tear flesh" or "to bite the lips in rage," altogether an unattractive

"Please forgive Edgar. He has no verbal skills." (c) The New Yorker Collection 1980
Lee Lorenz from Cartoonbank.com. All Rights Reserved.

business. Sarcasm is unfair, for it dismisses an opponent's arguments with ridicule rather than with reason; it is also unwise, for it turns the reader against the speaker or writer. Readers hesitate to ally themselves with a writer who apparently enjoys humiliating the opposition. A sarcastic remark can turn the hearers against the speaker and arouse sympathy for the victim. In short, sarcasm usually doesn't work.

Tone and Ethical Appeal

Although this chapter is chiefly about persuasion in the sense of rational discourse—the presentation of reasons in support of a thesis or conclusion—there are other forms of persuasion. We've already mentioned one of them: the *appeal to emotion*. The *appeal to force* is another: As Al Capone put it, "You can get a lot more done with a kind word and a gun, than with a kind word alone." But, in a sense, kind words themselves can do quite a lot. A moment ago we cautioned against the use of sarcasm, on the grounds that the satirist is perceived as an unattractive character, and this caution can now be put into a larger context, something that Aristotle called the **ethical appeal,** from the Greek work for "character," *ethos*. The ethical appeal is based on the idea that effective speakers and writers convey the suggestion that they are good people, specifically that they are

- informed
- intelligent
- benevolent
- honest

Because they are perceived as trustworthy, their words inspire confidence in their listeners and their readers. When we read an argument, we hear or sense a *voice* or *persona* behind the words, and our assent to the argument depends partly on the extent to which we trust this speaker, this voice, this character.

How can you inspire this trust? To begin with, you should indeed be informed, intelligent, benevolent, and honest. Still, possession of these qualities does not guarantee that you will convey them in your writing. You will have to revise your drafts so that these qualities become apparent to your audience—so that nothing in your essay causes your reader to doubt your knowledge, intelligence, good intentions, and integrity. A blunder in logic, a misleading quotation, a sarcastic remark—all such slips can cause readers to withdraw their trust from the writer.

Our general advice: When you argue, be courteous, respectful of your topic, of your audience, and of the people who hold views you are arguing against. It's generally not persuasive to present as villains or fools all persons who hold views different from your own, especially if some of them are your readers. Recognize opposing views, assume they are held in good faith, state them fairly, and be temperate in arguing your own position: "If I understand their view correctly . . ."; "It seems reasonable to conclude that . . ."; "Perhaps, then, we can agree that . . . ."

Later, in our comments on Diane Ravitch's "In Defense of Testing," we will call attention to her use of ethical appeal.

Organizing an Argument

As we have said earlier, writers find out what they think partly by means of the act of putting words on paper. But in presenting arguments for their readers, writers rarely duplicate their own acts of discovery. To put it another way, the process of setting forth ideas, and supporting them, does not follow the productive but untidy, repetitive, often haphazard process of preliminary thinking. For instance, a point that did not strike us until the middle of the third draft may, in the final version, appear in the opening paragraph. Or an example that seemed useful early in our thinking may, in the process of revision, be omitted in favor of a stronger example. Through a series of revisions, large and small, we try to work out the best strategy for persuading our readers to accept our reasoning as sound, our conclusion as valid. Unfortunately, we find, an argument cannot be presented either as it occurs to us or all at once.

No simple formula governs the organization of all effective argumentative essays. An essay may begin by announcing its thesis and then set forth the supporting reasons. Or it may begin more casually, calling attention to specific cases, and then generalize from these cases. Probably it will then go on to reveal an underlying unity that brings the thesis into view, and from here it will offer detailed reasoning that supports the thesis.

As the writer of a persuasive essay, you almost always have to handle, in some sequence or other, the following matters:

- The context of the argument (for instance, an explanation of why the
  issue should be considered, or reconsidered)
- The thesis
- The evidence that supports the thesis
- The counterevidence
- The response to counterclaims and counterevidence (either a refu-
  tation or a concession that there *is* merit to the counterclaims but
  not as much as to the writer's thesis)
- Some sort of reaffirmation, perhaps that the topic needs attention or
  that the thesis advanced is the most plausible or the most workable
  or the most moral, or that the ball is now in the reader's court

Three methods of organizing arguments are fairly common, and
one or another may suit an essay you're working on.

**1. Begin with the context of the argument, then set forth the
thesis statement and work from the simplest argument up to the
most complex, taking account of opposing arguments as you set
forth your own arguments.** Such an arrangement will keep your reader
with you, step by step.

**2. After setting forth the context and your thesis, arrange the
arguments in order of increasing strength.** The danger in following
this plan is that you may lose the reader from the start, because you begin
with a weak argument. Avoid this problem by telling your reader that
indeed the first argument is relatively weak (if it is terribly weak, it isn't
an argument at all, so scrap it), but that you offer it for the sake of com-
pleteness or because it is often given, and that you will soon give the
reader far stronger arguments. Face the opposition to this initial argument, grant that opposition as much as it deserves, and salvage what is
left of the argument. Then proceed to the increasingly strong arguments,
devoting at least one paragraph to each. Introduce each argument with
an appropriate transition ("another reason," "even more important,"
"most convincing of all"). State it briefly, summarize the opposing view,
and then demolish this opposition. With this organization, your discussion of each of your own arguments ends affirmatively.

3. After sketching the background and stating your thesis in an introductory paragraph, mass all of the opposing arguments, and then respond to them one by one.

In short, when you (1) think you have done your initial thinking and your rethinking, (2) have, if appropriate, consulted some published sources, (3) have talked with friends and perhaps with experts, and (4) have moved from random notes and lists to fairly full drafts, you are not quite done.

You still must check what you hope is your last draft to see if you have found the best possible order for the arguments, have given effective examples, and have furnished transitions. In short, you must check to see that you have produced an argument that will strike a reasonable reader as courteous, clear, and concrete.

CHECKLIST FOR REVISING DRAFTS
OF PERSUASIVE ESSAYS

✔ Are the terms clearly defined? (See pp. 176–78.)

✔ Is the thesis stated promptly and clearly? (See pp. 187–89.)

✔ Are the assumptions likely to be shared by your readers? If not, are they reasonably argued rather than merely stated? (See pp. 179–80; 184.)

✔ Are the facts verifiable? Is the evidence reliable? (No out-of-date statistics, no generalizations from insufficient evidence?) (See pp. 169–70; 181–82.)

✔ Is the reasoning sound? (See pp. 180–84.)

✔ Are the authorities really authorities on this matter? (See p. 180.)

✔ Are all of the substantial counterarguments recognized and effectively responded to? (See p. 181.)

✔ Does the essay make use, where appropriate, of concrete examples? (See pp. 172–73.)

✔ Is the organization effective? Does the essay begin interestingly, keep the thesis in view, and end interestingly? (See pp. 187–89.)

✔ Is the tone appropriate? (Avoid sarcasm. Present yourself as fair-minded, and assume that those who hold a view opposed to yours are also fair-minded.) (See pp. 184–87.)

Persuasion at Work: Two Writers Consider the Death Penalty

We reprint below two essays, the first arguing in favor of the death penalty, the second arguing against it. Following each essay, we offer a brief analysis of the writers, persuasive devices and strategies.

Edward Koch

Death and Justice: How Capital Punishment Affirms Life

Edward Koch, born in New York City, was mayor of New York from 1978 to 1989. This essay first appeared in the New Republic.

1   Last December a man named Robert Lee Willie, who had been convicted of raping and murdering an 18-year-old woman, was executed in the Louisiana state prison. In a statement issued several minutes before his death, Mr. Willie said: "Killing people is wrong.... . It makes no difference whether it's citizens, countries, or governments. Killing is wrong." Two weeks later in South Carolina, an admitted killer named Joseph Carl Shaw was put to death for murdering two teenagers. In an appeal to the governor for clemency, Mr. Shaw wrote: "Killing is wrong when I did it. Killing is wrong when you do it. I hope you have the courage and moral strength to stop the killing."

2   It is a curiosity of modern life that we find ourselves being lectured on morality by cold-blooded killers. Mr. Willie previously had been convicted of aggravated rape, aggravated kidnapping, and the murders of a Louisiana deputy and a man from Missouri. Mr. Shaw committed another murder a week before the two for which he was executed, and admitted mutilating the body of the 14-year-old girl he killed. I can't help wondering what prompted these murderers to speak out against killing as they entered the death-house door. Did their newfound reverence for life stem from the realization that they were about to lose their own?

3   Life is indeed precious, and I believe the death penalty helps to affirm this fact. Had the death penalty been a real possibility in the minds of these murderers, they might well have stayed their hand. They might have shown moral awareness before their victims died, and not after. Consider the tragic death of Rosa Velez, who happened to be home when a man named Luis Vera burglarized her apartment in Brooklyn. "Yeah, I shot her," Vera admitted. "She knew me, and I knew I wouldn't go to the chair."

4   During my twenty-two years in public service, I have heard the pros and cons of capital punishment expressed with special intensity. As a district leader, councilman, congressman, and mayor, I have represented constituencies generally thought of as liberal. Because I support the death penalty for heinous crimes of murder, I have sometimes been the subject of emotional and outraged attacks by voters who find my position reprehensible or worse. I have listened to their ideas. I have weighed their objections carefully. I still support the death penalty. The reasons I maintain my position can be best understood by examining the arguments most frequently heard in opposition.

5   1. *The death penalty is "barbaric."* Sometimes opponents of capital punishment horrify with tales of lingering death on the gallows, of faulty electric chairs, or of agony in the gas chamber. Partly in response to such protests, several states such as North Carolina and Texas switched to execution by lethal injection. The condemned person is put to death painlessly, without ropes, voltage, bullets, or gas. Did this answer the objections of death penalty opponents? Of course not. On June 22, 1984, the *New York Times* published an editorial that sarcastically attacked the new "hygienic" method of death by injection, and stated that "execution can never be made humane through science." So it's not the method that really troubles opponents. It's the death itself they consider barbaric.

6   Admittedly, capital punishment is not a pleasant topic. However, one does not have to like the death penalty in order to support it any more than one must like radical surgery, radiation, or chemotherapy in order to find necessary these attempts at curing cancer. Ultimately we may learn how to cure cancer with a simple pill. Unfortunately, that day has not yet arrived. Today we are faced with the choice of letting the cancer spread or trying to cure it with the methods available, methods that one day will almost certainly

be considered barbaric. But to give up and do nothing would be far more barbaric and would certainly delay the discovery of an eventual cure. The analogy between cancer and murder is imperfect, because murder is not the "disease" we are trying to cure. The disease is injustice. We may not like the death penalty, but it must be available to punish crimes of cold-blooded murder, cases in which any other form of punishment would be inadequate and, therefore, unjust. If we create a society in which injustice is not tolerated, incidents of murder—the most flagrant form of injustice—will diminish.

7   2. *No other major democracy uses the death penalty.* No other major democracy—in fact, few other countries of any description—are plagued by a murder rate such as that in the United States. Fewer and fewer Americans can remember the days when unlocked doors were the norm and murder was a rare and terrible offense. In America the murder rate climbed 122 percent between 1963 and 1980. During that same period, the murder rate in New York City increased by almost 400 percent, and the statistics are even worse in many other cities. A study at M.I.T. showed that based on 1970 homicide rates a person who lived in a large American city ran a greater risk of being murdered than an American soldier in World War II ran of being killed in combat. It is not surprising that the laws of each country differ according to differing conditions and traditions. If other countries had our murder problem, the cry for capital punishment would be just as loud as it is here. And I daresay that any other major democracy where 75 percent of the people supported the death penalty would soon enact it into law.

8   3. *An innocent person might be executed by mistake.* Consider the work of Hugo Adam Bedau, one of the most implacable foes of capital punishment in this country. According to Mr. Bedau, it is "false sentimentality to argue that the death penalty should be abolished because of the abstract possibility that an innocent person might be executed." He cites a study of the 7,000 executions in this country from 1893 to 1971, and concludes that the record fails to show that such cases occur. The main point, however, is this. If government functioned only when the possibility of error didn't exist, government wouldn't function at all. Human life deserves special protection, and one of the best ways to guarantee that protection is to assure that convicted murderers do not kill again. Only the death penalty can accomplish this end. In a recent case in New Jersey, a man named Richard

Biegenwald was freed from prison after serving 18 years for murder; since his release he has been convicted of committing four murders. A prisoner named Lemuel Smith, who, while serving four life sentences for murder (plus two life sentences for kidnapping and robbery) in New York's Green Haven Prison, lured a woman corrections officer into the chaplain's office and strangled her. He then mutilated and dismembered her body. An additional life sentence for Smith is meaningless. Because New York has no death penalty statute, Smith has effectively been given a license to kill.

9   But the problem of multiple murder is not confined to the nation's penitentiaries. In 1981, 91 police officers were killed in the line of duty in this country. Seven percent of those arrested in the cases that have been solved had a previous arrest for murder. In New York City in 1976 and 1977, 85 persons arrested for homicide had a previous arrest for murder. Six of these individuals had two previous arrests for murder, and one had four previous murder arrests. During those two years the New York police were arresting for murder persons with a previous arrest for murder on the average of one every 8.5 days. This is not surprising when we learn that in 1975, for example, the median time served in Massachusetts for homicide was less than two and a half years. In 1976 a study sponsored by the Twentieth Century Fund found that the average time served in the United States for first-degree murder is ten years. The median time served may be considerably lower.

10   *4. Capital punishment cheapens the value of human life.* On the contrary, it can be easily demonstrated that the death penalty strengthens the value of human life. If the penalty for rape were lowered, clearly it would signal a lessened regard for the victims' suffering, humiliation, and personal integrity. It would cheapen their horrible experience, and expose them to an increased danger of recurrence. When we lower the penalty for murder, it signals a lessened regard for the value of the victim's life. Some critics of capital punishment, such as columnist Jimmy Breslin, have suggested that a life sentence is actually a harsher penalty for murder than death. This is sophistic nonsense. A few killers may decide not to appeal a death sentence, but the overwhelming majority make every effort to stay alive. It is by exacting the highest penalty for the taking of human life that we affirm the highest value of human life.

11   5. *The death penalty is applied in a discriminatory manner.* This
factor no longer seems to be the problem it once was. The appeals
process for a condemned prisoner is lengthy and painstaking. Every
effort is made to see that the verdict and sentence were fairly arrived
at. However, assertions of discrimination are not an argument for ending the death penalty but for extending it. It is not justice to exclude
everyone from the penalty of the law if a few are found to be so
favored. Justice requires that the law be applied equally to all.

12   6. *Thou shalt not kill.* The Bible is our greatest source of moral
inspiration. Opponents of the death penalty frequently cite the sixth
of the Ten Commandments in an attempt to prove that capital punishment is divinely proscribed. In the original Hebrew, however, the
Sixth Commandment reads "Thou shalt not commit murder," and the
Torah specifies capital punishment for a variety of offenses. The bib-
lical viewpoint has been upheld by philosophers throughout history.
The greatest thinkers of the nineteenth century—Kant, Locke,
Hobbes, Rousseau, Montesquieu, and Mill—agreed that natural law
properly authorizes the sovereign to take life in order to vindicate justice. Only Jeremy Bentham was ambivalent. Washington, Jefferson,
and Franklin endorsed it. Abraham Lincoln authorized executions for
deserters in wartime. Alexis de Tocqueville, who expressed profound
respect for American institutions, believed that the death penalty was
indispensable to the support of social order. The United States Constitution, widely admired as one of the seminal achievements in the
history of humanity, condemns cruel and inhuman punishment, but
does not condemn capital punishment.

13   7. *The death penalty is state-sanctioned murder.* This is the defense
with which Messrs. Willie and Shaw hoped to soften the resolve of those
who sentenced them to death. By saying in effect, "You're no better
than I am," the murderer seeks to bring his accusers down to his own
level. It is also a popular argument among opponents of capital punishment, but a transparently false one. Simply put, the state has rights
that the private individual does not. In a democracy, those rights are
given to the state by the electorate. The execution of a lawfully condemned killer is no more an act of murder than is legal imprisonment
an act of kidnapping. If an individual forces a neighbor to pay him
money under threat of punishment, it's called extortion. If the state does
it, it's called taxation. Rights and responsibilities surrendered by the

individual are what give the state its power to govern. This contract is the foundation of civilization itself.

14   Everyone wants his or her rights, and will defend them jealously. Not everyone, however, wants responsibilities, especially the painful responsibilities that come with law enforcement. Twenty-one years ago a woman named Kitty Genovese was assaulted and murdered on a street in New York. Dozens of neighbors heard her cries for help but did nothing to assist her. They didn't even call the police. In such a climate the criminal understandably grows bolder. In the presence of moral cowardice, he lectures us on our supposed failings and tries to equate his crimes with our quest for justice.

15   The death of anyone—even a convicted killer—diminishes us all. But we are diminished even more by a justice system that fails to function. It is an illusion to let ourselves believe that doing away with capital punishment removes the murderer's deed from our conscience. The rights of society are paramount. When we protect guilty lives, we give up innocent lives in exchange. When opponents of capital punishment say to the state: "I will not let you kill in my name," they are also saying to murderers: "You can kill in your *own* name as long as I have an excuse for not getting involved."

16   It is hard to imagine anything worse than being murdered while neighbors do nothing. But something worse exists. When those same neighbors shrink back from justly punishing the murderer, the victim dies twice.

An Analysis of Koch's Argument

Koch uses a range of devices to persuade readers to his point of view. In the first paragraph he uses two quotations by murderers, and thereby begins to establish his authority on the topic. He uses mild **irony** in the second paragraph when he writes, "It is a curiosity of modern life that we find ourselves being lectured on morality by cold-blooded killers." (Although retaining his composure, Koch conveys indignation that we can all share, for "we" are all subject to these lectures.) Koch cites another killer in the third paragraph, one who provides **evidence** for Koch's thesis by saying, in effect, that if the death penalty had been in place he might not have committed murder. In the fourth paragraph the writer presents himself as a man of honor ("During my twenty-two years in public service"—not "During my twenty-two years as a politician"), a man who has often been subject to "emotional and outraged attacks." So the speaker is himself a sort of victim, not a man who lashes out at others. (Writers of persuasive essays seek to present themselves as persons of good will, and, if possible, as persons who have been wronged by their opponents.)

Note, too, Koch's style. After giving us a sentence in which he tells of the trials he has undergone, he gives us three short sentences, each of six words, and each beginning with "I":

> "I have listened to their ideas."
> "I have weighed their objections carefully."
> "I still support the death penalty."

Not quite *veni, vidi, vici,* but firm, concise, deliberate. What more can a reader want than a man who listens to his opponents and weighs their objections carefully?

Later paragraphs use, among other persuasive devices, an **analogy** (between cancer and murder in paragraph 6); **statistics** (in paragraphs 7 and 9); **authority** (in paragraph 8 he cites Hugo Bedau, "one of the most implacable foes of capital punishment in this country"); and a **hypothetical situation** (in paragraph 7 he speculates, "If other countries had our murder problem . . ."). There is even, in paragraph 13, one touch of **wit:** "If an individual forces a neighbor to pay him money under threat of punishment, it's called extortion. If the state does it, it's called taxation."

Koch's statistics are impressive, though on further thought, we find them a bit puzzling. He tells us that in 1981, ninety-one police officers were killed in the line of duty, and that seven percent of those arrested in the cases that have been solved had already been arrested for a murder. Possibly only eighteen cases were solved; if so, a single person previously arrested for murder would give us Koch's seven percent. Another odd thing about this evidence: Koch says that seven percent had a "previous arrest for murder"—which is not at all the same as a previous conviction for murder. A person arrested for murder but acquitted is, in our system, not to be thought of as a murderer, only as a person wrongly accused of murder. The statistics do indeed lend weight to Koch's argument, but we think he could have been clearer and used them more effectively.

David Bruck

The Death Penalty

David Bruck, born in 1949, holds a law degree from the University of South Carolina. After serving four years as a public defender in South Carolina he entered private practice in order to devote all of his efforts to defending inmates on death row. This essay was written as a direct response to the essay by Edward Koch, beginning on page 190.

1   Mayor Ed Koch contends that the death penalty "affirms life." By failing to execute murderers, he says, we "signal a lessened regard for the value of the victim's life." Koch suggests that people who oppose the death penalty are like Kitty Genovese's neighbors, who heard her cries for help but did nothing while an attacker stabbed her to death.

2   This is the standard "moral" defense of death as punishment: even if executions don't deter violent crime any more effectively than imprisonment, they are still required as the only means we have of doing justice in response to the worst of crimes.

3   Until recently, this "moral" argument had to be considered in the abstract, since no one was being executed in the United States. But the death penalty is back now, at least in the southern states, where every one of the more than 30 executions carried out over the last two years has taken place. Those of us who live in those states are getting to see the difference between the death penalty in theory, and what happens when you actually try to use it.

4   South Carolina resumed executing prisoners in January with the electrocution of Joseph Carl Shaw. Shaw was condemned to death for helping to murder two teenagers while he was serving as a military policeman at Fort Jackson, South Carolina. His crime, propelled by mental illness and PCP, was one of terrible brutality. It is Shaw's last words ("Killing was wrong when I did it. It is wrong you do it . . . .") that so outraged Mayor Koch: he finds it "a curiosity of modern life that we are being lectured on morality by cold-blooded killers." And so it is.

5   But it was not "modern life" that brought this curiosity into being. It was capital punishment. The electric chair was J. C. Shaw's

platform. (The mayor mistakenly writes that Shaw's statement came in the form of a plea to the governor for clemency: actually Shaw made it only seconds before his death, as he waited, shaved and strapped into the chair, for the switch to be thrown.) It was the chair that provided Shaw with celebrity and an opportunity to lecture us on right and wrong. What made this weird moral reversal even worse is that J. C. Shaw faced his own death with undeniable dignity and courage. And while Shaw died, the TV crews recorded another "curiosity" of the death penalty—the crowd gathered outside the death-house to cheer on the executioner. Whoops of elation greeted the announcement of Shaw's death. Waiting at the penitentiary gates for the appearance of the hearse bearing Shaw's remains, one demonstrator started yelling, "Where's the beef?"

6   For those who had to see the execution of J. C. Shaw, it wasn't easy to keep in mind that the purpose of the whole spectacle was to affirm life. It will be harder still when Florida executes a cop-killer named Alvin Ford. Ford has lost his mind during his years of death-row confinement, and now spends his days trembling, rocking back and forth, and muttering unintelligible prayers. This has led to litigation over whether Ford meets a centuries-old legal standard for mental competency. Since the Middle Ages, the Anglo-American legal system has generally prohibited the execution of anyone who is too mentally ill to understand what is about to be done to him and why. If Florida wins its case, it will have earned the right to electrocute Ford in his present condition. If it loses, he will not be executed until the state has nursed him back to some semblance of mental health.

7   We can at least be thankful that this demoralizing spectacle involves a prisoner who is actually guilty of murder. But this may not always be so. The ordeal of Lenell Jeter—the young black engineer who recently served more than a year of a life sentence for a Texas armed robbery that he didn't commit—should remind us that the system is quite capable of making the very worst sort of mistake. That Jeter was eventually cleared is a fluke. If the robbery had occurred at 7 P.M. rather than 3 P.M., he'd have had no alibi, and would still be in prison today. And if someone had been killed in that robbery, Jeter probably would have been sentenced to death. We'd have seen the usual execution-day interviews with state officials and the victim's relatives, all complaining that Jeter's appeals took too

long. And Jeter's last words from the gurney would have taken their place among the growing literature of death-house oration that so irritates the mayor.

8   Koch quoted Hugo Adam Bedau, a prominent abolitionist, to the effect that the record fails to establish that innocent defendants have been executed in the past. But this doesn't mean, as Koch implies, that it hasn't happened. All Bedau was saying was that doubts concerning executed prisoners' guilt are almost never resolved. Bedau is at work now on an effort to determine how many wrongful death sentences may have been imposed: his list of murder convictions since 1900 in which the state eventually *admitted* error is some 400 cases long. Of course, very few of these cases involved actual executions: the mistakes that Bedau documents were uncovered precisely because the prisoner was alive and able to fight for his vindication. The cases where someone is executed are the very cases in which we're least likely to learn that we got the wrong man.

9   I don't claim that executions of entirely innocent people will occur very often. But they will occur. And other sorts of mistakes already have. Roosevelt Green was executed in Georgia two days before J. C. Shaw. Green and an accomplice kidnapped a young woman. Green swore that his companion shot her to death after Green had left, and that he knew nothing about the murder. Green's claim was supported by a statement that his accomplice made to a witness after the crime. The jury never resolved whether Green was telling the truth, and when he tried to take a polygraph examination a few days before his scheduled execution, the state of Georgia refused to allow the examiner into the prison. As the pressure for symbolic retribution mounts, the courts, like the public, are losing patience with such details. Green was electrocuted on January 9, while members of the Ku Klux Klan rallied outside the prison.

10   Then there is another sort of arbitrariness that happens all the time. Last October, Louisiana executed a man named Ernest Knighton. Knighton had killed a gas station owner during a robbery. Like any murder, this was a terrible crime. But it was not premeditated, and is the sort of crime that very rarely results in a death sentence. Why was Knighton electrocuted when almost everyone else who committed the same offense was not? Was it because he was black? Was it because his victim and all 12 members of the jury that

sentenced him were white? Was it because Knighton's court-appointed lawyer presented no evidence on his behalf at his sentence hearing? Or maybe there's no reason except bad luck. One thing is clear: Ernest Knighton was picked out to die the way a fisherman takes a cricket out of a bait jar. No one cares which cricket gets impaled on the hook.

11   Not every prisoner executed recently was chosen that randomly. But many were. And having selected these men so casually, so blindly, the death penalty system asks us to accept that the purpose of killing each of them is to affirm the sanctity of human life.

12   The death penalty states are also learning that the death penalty is easier to advocate than it is to administer. In Florida, where executions have become almost routine, the governor reports that nearly a third of his time is spent reviewing the clemency requests of condemned prisoners. The Florida Supreme Court is hopelessly backlogged with death cases. Some have taken five years to decide, and the rest of the Court's work waits in line behind the death appeals. Florida's death row currently holds more than 230 prisoners. State officials are reportedly considering building a special "death prison" devoted entirely to the isolation and electrocution of the condemned. The state is also considering the creation of a special public defender unit that will do nothing else but handle death penalty appeals. The death penalty, in short, is spawning death agencies.

13   And what is Florida getting for all of this? The state went through almost all of 1983 without executing anyone: its rate of intentional homicide declined by 17 percent. Last year [1984] Florida executed eight people—the most of any state, and the sixth highest total for any year since Florida started electrocuting people back in 1924. Elsewhere in the U.S. last year, the homicide rate continued to decline. But in Florida, it actually rose by 5.1 percent.

14   But these are just the tiresome facts. The electric chair has been a centerpiece of each of Koch's recent political campaigns, and he knows better than anyone how little the facts have to do with the public's support for capital punishment. What really fuels the death penalty is the justifiable frustration and rage of people who see that the government is not coping with violent crime. So what if the death penalty doesn't work? At least it gives us the satisfaction of knowing that we got one or two of the sons of bitches.

15   Perhaps we want retribution on the flesh and bone of a handful of convicted murderers so badly that we're willing to close our eyes to all of the demoralization and danger that come with it. A lot of politicians think so, and they may be right. But if they are, then let's at least look honestly at what we're doing. This lottery of death both comes from and encourages an attitude toward human life that is not reverent, but reckless.

16   And that is why the mayor is dead wrong when he confuses such fury with justice. He suggests that we trivialize murder unless we kill murderers. By that logic, we also trivialize rape unless we sodomize rapists. The sin of Kitty Genovese's neighbors wasn't that they failed to stab her attacker to death. Justice does demand that murderers be punished. And common sense demands that society be protected from them. But neither justice nor self-preservation demands that we kill men whom we have already imprisoned.

17   The electric chair in which J. C. Shaw died earlier this year was built in 1912 at the suggestion of South Carolina's governor at the time, Cole Blease. Governor Blease's other criminal justice initiative was an impassioned crusade in favor of lynch law. Any lesser response, the governor insisted, trivialized the loathsome crimes of interracial rape and murder. In 1912 a lot of people agreed with Governor Blease that a proper regard for justice required both lynching and the electric chair. Eventually we are going to learn that justice requires neither.

An Analysis of Bruck's Response to Koch

Although Bruck wrote this essay as a response to Koch's essay, he does not respond point-by-point to all of Koch's arguments. For instance, he does not take up Koch's **assumption** (paragraphs 3, 6) that the death penalty is a deterrent to would-be murderers. Or consider his response to Koch's argument that even if the death penalty is now administered in an almost random way, the proper thing to do is to administer it more justly, that is, more widely. Bruck does not discuss Koch's proposal; rather, he simply argues that because the penalty is administered in what seems to be a random way, it ought not to be administered at all. On the other hand, Bruck does vigorously challenge Koch's **claim** that the death penalty "affirms life." Bruck's fifth paragraph, which ends with a description of the crowd waiting at the penitentiary gates for the hearse bearing Shaw's remains, strikes us as especially effective.

Some additional comments may be useful. We find it odd that Bruck cites the case of Lenell Jeter in order to show that "the system is quite capable of making the very worst sort of mistake" (paragraph 7). Jeter was not executed, and in fact he was not even sentenced to execution. Jeter was sentenced to life imprisonment for an armed robbery that he didn't commit. But what does this case have to do with murderers and with capital punishment? It shows only that someone can be wrongly convicted of a crime—a point that no one would deny. What Bruck needs, if his case is to be strong, is an **example** of an innocent person who was not only convicted of murder but was also sentenced to death and who was in fact executed, but he offers no such example.

In paragraph 8 Bruck speaks of murder cases in which the state admitted error. He says that "very few . . . involved actual executions." Why doesn't he specify the number? We don't know why, but probably it is indeed so small a number that it would be unimpressive and thus would not strongly buttress his case. In paragraph 9 he grants that executions of "entirely innocent people" will not occur very often, but he insists "they will occur." This assertion may be true, but it would be more convincing if he could point to **examples** from the past, if he could offer **statistics.**

Bruck is careful to indicate that he is fully aware of the brutality of the murders he discusses; he thus **concedes to the opposition its due.** Thus, in paragraph 4 he says that a certain murder "was one of terrible brutality," and in paragraph 10, speaking of another murder, he says that "Like any murder, this was a terrible crime." Nothing in the essay suggests that he sentimentalizes murderers, is unsympathetic to their victims, or is soft on crime—unless one assumes, in a circular fashion, that anyone who opposes the death penalty is therefore soft on crime.

Paragraph 10 suggests that those who are executed are unfairly chosen from a pool of comparable candidates. Bruck says that Knighton may have been chosen because he was black and his victim was white, or because his lawyer was particularly unpersuasive, or perhaps simply because of bad luck. Bruck's point, then, is not that Knighton was necessarily the victim of racial prejudice, but that local conditions and chance seem to determine who gets executed. That's probably true, but it doesn't address Koch's objection. Koch, you'll recall, said that if capital punishment now is administered at random, the thing that needs reform is the way it is administered. Or put it this way: If capital punishment is indeed just, the fact that X is executed and Y (a comparable offender) is not executed does not mean that X is unjustly treated; it means that justice has not been done to Y (or to Y's victims).

The final paragraph seems to us to be effective rhetoric, though one can quarrel with some of the **logic**. By talking about "the electric chair in which J. C. Shaw died earlier this year," Bruck returns us to the early part of his essay (that is, to paragraph 4, in which Shaw was introduced), and thus he tends to wrap up his essay. That's nice. On the other hand, by telling us that the chair was built in 1912 at the suggestion of Governor Cole Blease, who led "an impassioned crusade in favor of lynch law," he is engaging in the **fallacy** that logicians call "poisoning the well" (an attempt to discredit a proposition by associating it with something unattractive). Whether Blease was a saint or a monster is of no relevance to the issue of whether capital punishment is just.

Now let's look at a brief essay on a different topic, and then we will comment briefly on some of the writer's ways of presenting her argument.

Diane Ravitch
In Defense of Testing

Diane Ravitch, a Distinguished Visiting Fellow at the Hoover Institution and a research professor at New York University, served as assistant secretary of education in the administration of George Herbert Walker Bush. She is the author of many books — the most recent is Left Back: A Century of Failed School Reforms *(2000) — and of many articles. The following essay was originally published in* Time, *September 11, 2000.*

1   No one wants to be tested. We would all like to get a driver's license without answering questions about right of way or showing that we can parallel park a car. Many future lawyers and doctors probably wish they could join their profession without taking an exam.

2   But tests and standards are a necessary fact of life. They protect us—most of the time—from inept drivers, hazardous products, and shoddy professionals. In schools too, exams play a constructive role. They tell public officials whether new school programs are making a difference and where new investments are likely to pay off. They tell teachers what their students have learned—and have not. They tell parents how their children are doing compared with others their age. They encourage students to exert more effort.

3   It is important to recall that for most of this century, educators used intelligence tests to decide which children should get a high-quality education. The point of IQ testing was to find out how much children were capable of learning rather than to test what they had actually learned. Based on IQ scores, millions of children were assigned to dumbed-down programs instead of solid courses in science, math, history, literature, and foreign languages.

4   This history reminds us that tests should be used to improve education, not ration it. Every child should have access to a high-quality education. Students should have full opportunity to learn what will be tested; otherwise their test scores will merely reflect whether they come from an educated family.

5   In the past few years, we have seen the enormous benefits that flow to disadvantaged students because of the information provided by state tests. Those who fall behind are now getting extra instruction in after-school classes and summer programs. In their efforts to student performance, states are increasing teachers' salaries, testing new teachers, and insisting on better teacher education.

6   Good tests should include a mix of essay, problem-solving, short-answer, and even some multiple-choice questions. On math quizzes, students should be able to show how they arrived at their answer. The tests widely used today often rely too much on multiple-choice questions, which encourage guessing rather than thinking. Also, they frequently ignore the importance of knowledge. Today's history tests, for example, seldom expect the student to know any history—sometimes derided as "mere facts"—but only to be able to read charts, graphs, and cartoons.

7   Performance in education means the mastery of both knowledge and skills. This is why it is reasonable to test teachers to make sure they know their subject matter, as well as how to teach it to young

children. And this is why it is reasonable to assess whether students are ready to advance to the next grade or graduate from high school. To promote students who cannot read or do math is no favor to them. It is like pushing them into a deep pool before they have learned to swim. If students need extra time and help, they should get it, but they won't unless we first carefully assess what they have learned.

A Brief Examination of Ravitch's Ways of Presenting an Argument

Paragraph 1. Ravitch gets our goodwill by identifying herself with us, or, to put it the other way around, by getting us to identify with her: "No one wants to be tested." Readers are almost surely drawn to agree with her thus far. (She seems reasonable, she understands human nature, she is someone we can trust—which is to say, she has set forth an ethical appeal.) She then goes on to give examples, the first of which is something almost all of us have experienced: "We would all like to get a driver's license without answering questions about right of way or showing that we can parallel park a car."

Paragraph 2. Having won our agreement, Ravitch now asserts her thesis: "But tests and standards are a necessary fact of life." She picks up an example (driving) asserted in her first paragraph, and says of tests, "They protect us . . . from inept drivers . . . ." Surely we must agree with her thus far. Then, picking up the construction used in "They protect us," she speaks of school tests; using a parallel construction (thereby suggesting that driving test and academic tests are indeed parallel), she says: "They tell public officials . . . . They tell teachers . . . . They tell parents . . . ."

Paragraphs 3 and 4. Again, ethical appeal: Ravitch tells us that in the past tests have been used to harm students, whereas of course they should be used to help students. That is, she reveals that she knows that tests were used this way—she thus disarms us from offering this objection—and she also assures us that she disapproves of those tests.

Paragraph 5. Tests, Ravitch claims, offer "enormous benefits . . . to disadvantaged students." Why does she make this claim? Because she knows that the chief criticism of tests comes from advocates for disadvantaged students, who say that the tests discriminate against these students. The tests, they sometimes argue, are biased in favor of whites, or even if the tests are not biased, the tests favor students in affluent families because the parents of such families can afford to give their kids tutoring that raises test scores. Ravitch does not go into these objections, but she knows that her readers are aware of them, hence she pointedly claims that tests help *dis*advantaged students.

Paragraph 6. Here Ravitch briefly offers her ideas of what a good test is, and of what a bad test is, thus reassuring her readers that she knows that not all tests are fair or useful.

Paragraph 7. Having asserted that we should test students, Ravitch now extends the idea of testing and asserts that we should test teachers— an idea that most students and their parents can easily subscribe to. But notice that she again uses a parallel construction to suggest, in effect, that if you accept *A* you will also accept *B* and *C:* "This is why it is reasonable to test teachers . . . . And this is why it is reasonable to assess whether students are ready . . . ."

As we suggest above, offering an airtight proof on a controversial matter may be an impossible proposition. Virginia Woolf put it this way: "When a subject is highly controversial . . . one cannot hope to tell the truth. One can only show how one came to hold whatever opinion one does hold."

CHAPTER NINE

USING SOURCES

> Research is formalized curiosity. It is poking
> and prying with a purpose.
> —*Zora Neale Hurston*, Dust Tracks on a Road *(1942)*

Why Use Sources?

In preparing to write, academic writers use sources to enlarge and refine their ideas. These sources can include facts, opinions, and the ideas of others, recorded in print or in bytes, and in the form of books, articles, lectures, reports, reviews, and interviews. Research essays—which are also sometimes called "researched essays" or "documented essays"—are based in part on such sources, and you'll write them in many of your college courses.

Even an essay that is primarily persuasive or analytical may be in part based on research. For example, if you have been asked to write an essay in which you state your position on the death penalty, you will probably need to take into consideration the arguments of others who have written on the topic. If you've been asked to analyze a novel by Kate Chopin, it may be useful to read what current literary critics have said about it. If you don't consider any source, you risk taking a very uninformed position. Considering what others have said and developing your own position in relation to their ideas is central to academic writing.

Not everyone likes research, of course. There are hours spent reading books and articles that prove to be contradictory or irrelevant. When the project is large, you may feel that there isn't enough time to read all the material that's available—or even to get your hands on it. Regardless of the scope of the project, some of the books may be dull. The poet William Butler Yeats, though an indefatigable worker on projects that interested him, engagingly expressed an indifference to the obligation that confronts every researcher: to look carefully at all the relevant evidence. Running over the possible reasons why Jonathan Swift did not marry (that he had syphilis, for instance, or that he feared he would transmit a hereditary madness), Yeats says: "Mr. Shane Leslie thinks that Swift's relation to Vanessa was not platonic, and that whenever his letters speak of a cup of coffee they mean the sexual act; whether the letters seem to bear him out I do not know, for those letters bore me."

Though research sometimes requires one to read boring things, those who engage in it feel, at other times, an exhilaration, a sense of triumph at becoming expert on something. When you know what others have said about your topic, you are in a position to say: "Here is how other people have thought about this question; their ideas are all very interesting, but I see the matter differently: Let me tell you what *I* think."

In the following paragraph, the second paragraph of a research essay we reprint in full at the end of this chapter, a student does just that, more or less. In the essay, Beatrice Cody argues against interpretations of the Chopin's *The Awakening* as a feminist political statement—the prevailing view. Instead, she contends that the suicide of Chopin's protagonist, Edna Pontellier, "resulted from the torments of her individual psyche, her inability to cope with the patriarchal expectations, which most women in fact were able to tolerate."

> It is difficult to say how Chopin wished <u>The Awakening</u> to be interpreted. Heroines who explore their own individuality (with varying degrees of success and failure) abound in her work (Shinn 358); Chopin herself, though married, was a rather nontraditional wife who smoked cigarettes, and, like Edna Pontellier, took walks by herself (Nissenbaum 333–34). One might think therefore

that Chopin was making a political statement in
The Awakening about the position of women in
society based on her own rejection of that
position. But aside from slim biographical
evidence and the assertions of some critics such
as Larzer Ziff and Daniel S. Rankin that Chopin
sympathized with Edna, we have no way of knowing
whether she regarded this protagonist as a victim
of sexist oppression or simply, to quote her
family doctor in the novel itself, as "a
sensitive and highly organized woman [. . . who] is
especially peculiar" (66). It is therefore
necessary to explore the two possibilities, using
evidence from the novel to determine whether Edna
Pontellier's awakening is political or peculiarly
personal in nature.

Note the authority with which the student writes as she (respectfully)
calls into question the conclusions of others who have written about the
novel she's studied and researched. She has read enough to know that the
biographical evidence supporting a feminist reading of *The Awakening*
is "slim"; she has found enough evidence to say (persuasively, we think)
that "It is . . . necessary to explore" the matter further. She knows a lot
about her topic. She has become, over the course of several weeks, a kind
of expert on it.

There can be great satisfaction in knowing enough about a topic to
contribute to the store of knowledge and ideas about it. There can also
be great satisfaction in simply learning to use the seemingly infinite
resources now available to researchers—in print or electronic formats—
as well as in learning to document and to acknowledge your research
accurately and responsibly.

In this chapter we discuss

- how to find and evaluate sources, both print and electronic,
- how to take useful notes,
- how to use others' ideas to help you develop your own, and
- how to paraphrase, summarize, and quote the work of others, so that
  their words and ideas are distinct from yours.

What Is a Source? Primary and Secondary Materials

Sources are usually divided into two categories, primary and secondary. The primary sources are the real subject of study; the secondary sources are critical and historical accounts written about these primary materials. For example, if you want to know whether Shakespeare's attitude toward Julius Caesar was highly traditional or highly original, or a little of each, you would read *Julius Caesar*, other Elizabethan writings about Caesar, and translations of Latin writings known to the Elizabethans. These are primary materials. In addition to these primary materials you would read secondary material such as modern books on Shakespeare and on Elizabethan attitudes toward Rome and toward monarchs.

Similarly, the primary material for an essay on Kate Chopin's *The Awakening* novel, is of course the novel itself; the secondary material consists of such things as biographies of Chopin and critical essays on the novel. But the line between these two kinds of sources is not always sharp. For example, if you are concerned with the degree to which *The Awakening* is autobiographical, primary materials include not only the novel and also Chopin's comments on her writing but perhaps also the comments of people who knew her. Thus the essays—based on interviews with Chopin—that two of her friends published in newspapers probably can be regarded as primary material because they were contemporary with the novel and because they give direct access to Chopin's views, while the writings of later commentators constitute secondary material.

Developing a Research Topic

Your instructor may assign a topic, in which case, you'll be saved some work. (On the other hand, you may find yourself spending a lot of time with material you don't find exciting. On yet another hand, you may become interested in something you'd otherwise never have known about.) More likely, you'll need to develop your own topic, a topic related to the subject of the course for which the research essay has been assigned. Some possibilities:

- Perhaps you've read Maxine Hong Kingston's *The Woman Warrior* (1976) for a Women's Studies course, and you have become interested in Confucian or Buddhist ideas that inform the narrative.

- Perhaps your Government course has touched on the internment of Japanese-Americans during World War II, and you'd like to know more about what happened.

- Perhaps you have read Chopin's *The Awakening* for a literature course, and you're wondering what readers thought about the novel when it was first published.

Any of these interests could well become a topic for a research essay. But how do you find the relevant material?

Finding Sources

We can't give you a roadmap or a recipe for finding the sources you need. The number of possible topics is infinite, as is the number of sources. Research approaches vary widely. And the Internet—the vast network of interconnected computers that has made an extraordinary amount of information available to researchers and everyone else—complicates things further. The Internet, by its very nature, is constantly changing; guides to research on the Internet are generally out of date even before they appear in print.

Nevertheless, we do have some general suggestions. One good rule of thumb is to begin with what you already know, with what you already have at hand. For instance, the textbook for your Government course may cite official documents on the relocation and internment of Japanese Americans. Or your edition of Chopin's *The Awakening* may contain an introduction that references some critical essays on the novel; it's also likely to contain a selected bibliography, a list of books and articles about Chopin and her work. If you have already identified a few titles, you can go directly to your library's on-line catalog, and begin your search there. (We'll have a bit more to say about on-line searches in a moment.)

If, however, you know very little about the topic, and haven't yet identified any possible sources (let's say you know nothing or almost nothing about Confucianism, but Maxine Hong Kingston's *The Woman Warrior* has made you want to learn about it), it's not a bad idea to begin with an encyclopedia—the *Encyclopaedia Britannica*, perhaps—which you'll find in the reference area of your college or university library. In addition to providing you with basic information about your topic, encyclopedia articles usually include cross-references to other articles within the encyclopedia, as well as suggestions for further reading. These suggestions can help you begin to compose a list of secondary sources for your essay. And of course you need not limit yourself to this one encyclopedia: There are hundreds of invaluable specialized encyclopedias, such as *Encyclopedia of Anthropology, Encyclopedia of Crime and Justice, Encyclopedia of Psychology, Encyclopedia of Religion* (a good place to go for an introduction to Confucianism), and *Kodansha Encyclopedia of Japan,* and several of them are certain to be available in your library's reference area. Encyclopedias are also available on-line, in full-text versions you can access through your library's central information system.

The Library's Central Information System

All libraries used to work in more or less the same way. Each one had a card catalog, a set of hundreds of little drawers containing thousands (even millions) of alphabetically arranged three-by-five cards. When you wanted a book, you went to the card catalog and looked it up by title, author, or subject. Because books would of course differ from library to library, the cards would also of course differ. But the system in every library was pretty much the same.

In recent years, on-line catalogs have replaced card catalogs in college and university libraries, and in most public libraries as well. And the on-line catalog constitutes only a tiny fraction of the information available to you through your institution's library. From a computer terminal in your library (or from home via an Internet connection), you can access bibliographies and indexes, full-text versions of encyclopedias and dictionaries and academic journals, the catalogs of *other* libraries—and much more.

Unlike card catalogs, each library's central information system is a bit different. Resources differ from one library to the next. And like the Internet itself, your library's central information system is changing every day. For these reasons, the best advice we can give you about learning to find books and articles in your library is to go to your college or university's research librarian and ask for help.

Using the Internet

As we've noted, the Internet can be a tremendous resource for researchers. But because anyone, anywhere, can post pretty much anything, the information available on the Internet can be difficult to evaluate. When you're working with secondary sources that have been published in journals or in book form, for the most part you're working with material that experts in that field have judged to be worth reading. Before it's published, an article in such a journal as *Society* or *College English*, for example, will have been read by a number of reviewers (most or all of them college professors in the field), as well as by members of an advisory board and several editors. If *Society* or *College English* is in your institution's library—and we bet it is—it's there in part because librarians have decided it's worth including in the serials collection. An article in one of these journals may have weaknesses, but several experts have thought it was pretty good.

Much of the information available on the Internet has not been similarly vetted. Advertisements coexist with course syllabi. One could (if one wanted to) access a chat group on Russell Crowe as easily as one could find photographs of people's pets. Or an interview with Jamaica Kincaid. Or the full text of *Romeo and Juliet*. Or an essay on your research topic, written by your professor—or by the person who sits next to you in your biology class.

How do you judge what may be worth considering? In part by using the analytic skills we discuss elsewhere in this book. The following checklist will help you focus your analysis.

CHECKLIST FOR EVALUATING WEBSITES

✔ Who produced the site (a teacher, a commercial entity, a student)?

✔ Who sponsored the site?

✔ For whom is the author writing? What is the intended audience?

✔ Can you tell if the author of the document is an authority in the field? (Perhaps the document is linked to the author's homepage.)

✔ Does he or she reference other critics or writers? Good ones?

✔ Is the text well written?

✔ Do arguments seem well supported, or is the document full of vague generalizations?

✔ When was the site created or last updated?

For more on this matter, we recommend (appropriately enough) that you consult documents available on the Web, such as "Evaluating

Information Found on the Internet" (http://milton.mse.jhu.edu:8001/ research/education/net.html). It *should* still be available—but that's the other problem with Internet sources: What's here today may be gone tomorrow.

Reading and Taking Notes on Secondary Sources

Almost all researchers—professionals as well as beginners—find that they end up with some notes that are irrelevant, and, on the other hand, find, when drafting the paper, that they vaguely remember certain material they now wish they had taken notes on. Especially in the early stages of one's project, when the topic and thesis may still be relatively unfocused, it's hard to know what is noteworthy and what is not. You simply have to flounder a bit.

It may be helpful to skim an article or book all the way through the first time around without taking notes. By the time you reach the end, you may find it isn't noteworthy. Or you may find a useful summary near the end that will contain most of what you can get from the piece. Or you may find that, having a sense of the whole, you can now quickly reread the piece and take notes on the chief points that concern you.

Even if you follow this procedure, a certain amount of inefficiency is inevitable; therefore plenty of time should be allowed. And it's worth keeping in mind that different people really do work differently. We list here three strategies; we suspect that, over time, you'll develop your own.

- Take notes using four-by-six-inch cards, writing on one side only, because material on the back of a card is usually neglected when you come to write the paper. (Taking notes by hand offers several advantages—not least of which is that you don't need access to a computer to do it.)

- Take notes on your computer, keeping a separate file for each book or article. Material can be easily moved from one file to another as the organization of the essay begins to take shape.

- Don't take notes—or take very few notes. Photocopy secondary material you think you might use, if it is brief, and underline and annotate that material as you read and think about it. (Material from electronic sources can be downloaded and later printed out and annotated as well.) The disadvantage here is obvious: This method uses a

Verrett, pp. 152-154 ✓   botulism argument
                               search for substitute
p.152 Industry and gov't approved nitrite as color
fixer. Now shifting ground, saying it prevents
botulism. Verrett points out "legal snag." New
approval needed for new use.
(Thus public hearing and unwanted attention)

p.154 "... the industry--USDA-FDA coalition seems
firm in its position that there is no substitute for
nitrate, now or ever. Their posture is misdirected
at defending nitrites, devising ways to keep it
in food rather than ways to get it out. ✓

     Verrett and Carper, Eating May Be Hazardous

lot of paper. But there are two big advantages. Passages from the
sources are transcribed (or, in the cases of downloaded material,
moved) only once, into the draft itself, so there's less risk of mistakes
and distortions. And the research—the collecting of information—can
go very quickly. **A word of caution** though: It's crucial that you think
carefully about the material you're collecting and that you annotate
it thoroughly. If you don't—that is, if you merely photocopy and
mindlessly highlight vast areas—you'll find yourself with a pile of
paper, and no idea of what to do with it.

A Guide to Note-Taking

1. Scan the work before you start taking notes. Before assiduously
taking notes from the first paragraph onward, or highlighting long
passages, try to get a sense of the author's thesis. You may find an early
paragraph that states the thesis outright; you may also find a concluding
paragraph that offers a summary of the evidence that supports the thesis.
Having gained a general idea of the work, you can now take notes
sparingly while you read the material carefully and critically.

2. Read critically. Read thoughtfully, continually asking yourself
if the author supports assertions with adequate evidence. Be especially
sure to ask what can be said *against* assertions that coincide with your
own beliefs. The heart of critical thinking is a willingness to face objections to one's own beliefs.

3. Be sure to record the title and author of the source. If you're using notecards, specify the source in an abbreviated form in the upper left corner. If you're taking notes on your computer, make a separate file for each book or article, and use the author's name and the first significant word of the title to identify the file. If you're using photocopies or downloaded material, make sure that you also photocopy the bibliographic information—which usually appears in full on the title page of a book and often (but not always) appears on the first page of a journal article. (And be sure to make a record of the full span of the article, not just the pages that you have copied.)

4. Write summaries, not paraphrases (that is, write abridgments rather than restatements, which in fact may be as long as or longer than the original). There is rarely any point to paraphrasing. Generally speaking, either quote exactly (and put the passage in quotation marks, with a notation of the source, including the page number or numbers) or summarize, reducing a page or even an entire article or chapter of a book to a few sentences that can be written on a notecard, typed into your computer, or squeezed into the margin of a photocopied page. Even when you summarize, record your source (including the page numbers), so that you can give appropriate credit in your essay.

5. Quote sparingly. Of course in your summary you will sometimes quote a phrase or a sentence—putting it in quotation marks—but quote sparingly. You are not simply transcribing what you read; rather you are assimilating knowledge and you are thinking, and so for the most part your source should be chewed and digested rather than swallowed whole. Thinking now, while taking notes, will also help you later to avoid plagiarism. If, on the other hand, when you take notes you mindlessly copy material at length, later when you are writing the essay you may be tempted to copy it yet again, perhaps without giving credit. Likewise, if you simply photocopy pages from articles or books, and then merely underline some passages without annotating your reading, you probably will not be thinking; you will just be underlining. But if you make a terse summary you will be forced to think and to find your own words for the idea. Quote directly only those passages that are particularly effective, or crucial, or memorable. In your finished essay these quotations will provide authority and emphasis.

6. Quote accurately. After copying a quotation, check your transcription against the original, and correct any misquotation. Verify the page number also. If a quotation runs from the bottom of, say, page 306 to the top of 307, make a distinguishing mark (for instance two backslashes after the last word of the first page), so that if you later use only part of the quotation, you will know the page on which it appeared.

7. Use ellipses to indicate the omission of any words within a sentence. If the omitted words are at the end of the quoted sentence, put a period immediately at the point where you end the sentence, and then add three spaced periods.

```
If the . . . words are at the end of the quoted sen-
tence, put a period immediately at the point where you
end. . . .
```

Note: the MLA requires that you enclose your ellipsis within square brackets to distinguish your ellipsis from an ellipsis that appeared in the original text. And if the ellipsis appears at the end of the quoted sentence, the sentence period appears *after* the three spaced periods:

```
If the ellipsis appears at the end [. . .], the sen-
tence period appears after [. . .].
```

Use square brackets to indicate your additions to the quotations. Here is an example:

```
Here is an [uninteresting] example.
```

8. *Never* copy a passage by changing an occasional word, under the impression that you are thereby putting it into your own words. Notes of this sort may find their way into your essay, your reader will sense a style other than your own, and suspicions (and perhaps even charges) of plagiarism will follow. (For a detailed discussion of plagiarism, see below).

9. Comment on your notes. Consider it your obligation to *think* about the material as you take notes, evaluating it and using it as a stimulus to further thought. For example, you may want to say "Tyler seems to be generalizing from insufficient evidence," or "Corsa made the same point five years earlier"; but make certain that later you will be able to distinguish between these comments and the notes summarizing or quoting your source. A suggestion: Surround all comments recording your responses with double parentheses, thus: ((. . .)).

10. Write a keyword on each card or at the beginning of each section of notes in your computer file. A brief key—for example "effect on infants' blood"—can help you to tell at a glance what is on the card or in the file.

Acknowledging Sources

Using Sources without Plagiarizing

Your purpose as an academic writer is to develop *your own ideas* about
the topic you're writing about. Secondary sources will help you shape and
develop your thoughts about your topic, but your purpose is to develop
an argument and an analysis that's your own. It's crucial, then, to be clear
about the distinction between your words and ideas and those of your
sources. Not to do so is to risk charges of plagiarism. (The institutional
consequences of plagiarism vary from school to school, and from case
to case. In the university where one of us teaches, students who are found
guilty of plagiarism are, among other things, banned from the campus
for a year; at other schools, students can be expelled for good; at still others, they simply receive a failing grade for the course and are put on
academic probation.)

Respect for your readers and for your sources requires that you
acknowledge your indebtedness for material when

1. you quote directly from a work, or

2. you paraphrase or summarize someone's words (the words of your
   paraphrase or summary are your own, but the points are not), or

3. you appropriate an idea that is not common knowledge.

Most commonly, the words, ideas, and information you'll cite in a
research essay will come from printed and electronic sources. But you
must also acknowledge the advice of peer editors and ideas that come
from lectures and class discussions unless your instructor tells you not
to do so. (We explain how to format the citations for all these sources
in Chapter 12, "Documentation.")

Let's suppose you are going to make use of William Bascom's comment on the earliest responses of Europeans to African art:

> The first examples of African art to gain public attention were the bronzes
> and ivories which were brought back to Europe after the sack of Benin
> by a British military expedition in 1897. The superb technology of the
> Benin bronzes won the praise of experts like Felix von Luschan who wrote
> in 1899, "Cellini himself could not have made better casts, nor anyone
> else before or since to the present day." Moreover, their relatively realis-
> tic treatment of human features conformed to the prevailing European

aesthetic standards. Because of their naturalism and technical excellence, it was at first maintained that they had been produced by Europeans— a view that was still current when the even more realistic bronze heads were discovered at Ife in 1912. The subsequent discovery of new evidence has caused the complete abandonment of this theory of European origins of the bronzes of Benin and Ife, both of which are cities in Nigeria.

> —*William Bascom*, African Art in Cultural Perspective
> *(New York: Norton, 1973), p. 4*

Acknowledging a Direct Quotation   You may want to use some or all of Bascom's words, in which case you will write something like this:

```
As William Bascom says, when Europeans first
encountered Benin and Ife works of art in the late
nineteenth century, they thought that Europeans
had produced them, but the discovery of new
evidence "caused the complete abandonment of this
theory of European origins of the bronzes of Benin
and Ife, both of which are cities in Nigeria" (4)
```

In this example, the writer introduces Bascom with a signal phrase ("As William Bascom says"); then he summarizes several sentences from Bascom; then he uses quotation marks to indicate the passage that comes directly from Bascom's book. Note that the summary does not borrow Bascom's language; the words are all the writer's own. Note also that what appears inside the quotation marks is an exact transcription of Bascom's words: The writer has not changed any word endings, or omitted any words, or inserted any punctuation of his own. (The "4" inside parentheses at the end of the passage is the page reference. Again, we explain how to use the MLA system of parenthetic citation in Chapter 12, "Documentation.")

Acknowledging a Paraphrase or Summary   Summaries (abridgments) are usually superior to paraphrases (rewordings, of approximately the same length as the original) because summaries are briefer. But occasionally you may find that you cannot abridge a passage in your source and yet you don't want to quote it word for word—perhaps because it is too technical or because it is poorly written. Even though you are putting the idea into your own words, you must give credit to the source because the idea is not yours.

Here is an example of an **acceptable summary:**

```
William Bascom, in African Art, points out that
the first examples of African art--Benin bronzes
and ivories--brought to Europe were thought by
Europeans to be of European origin, because they
were realistic and well made, but evidence was
later discovered that caused this theory to be
abandoned (4).
```

The summary is adequate, and the page reference indicates where the source is to be found. But if the writer had omitted the signal phrase "William Bascom, in *African Art*, points out that," the result would have been plagiarism. Not to give Bascom credit would be to plagiarize, even if the words were the writer's own. The offense is just as serious as not acknowledging a direct quotation.

The following is an example of an **unacceptable summary.** The writer uses too much of Bascom's language and gives Bascom no credit for his ideas:

```
The earliest examples of African art to become
widely known in Europe were bronzes and ivories
that were brought to Europe in 1897. These works
were thought to be of European origin, and one
expert said that Cellini could not have done
better work. Their technical excellence, as
well as their realism, fulfilled the European
standards of the day. The later discovery of new
evidence at Benin and Ife, both in Nigeria,
refuted this belief.
```

Again, one problem here is that all the *ideas* are Bascom's—and his name appears neither in a signal phrase, nor in a citation. Another problem is that the writer doesn't, strictly speaking, paraphrase Bascom; she doesn't put the passage entirely into her own words. Rather, she simply substitutes one phrase for another, maintaining much of the structure and organization of Bascom's sentences.

She substitutes

> "The earliest examples of African art"

for Bascom's

> "The first examples of African art";

she substitutes

> "to become widely known"

for

> "to gain public attention";

she substitutes

> "Their technical excellence, as well as their realism"

for

> "their naturalism and technical excellence."

The writer here is plagiarizing—perhaps without even knowing it. But it should be clear that neither the words nor the ideas in this passage are the writer's own. (This form of plagiarism, where a writer simply substitutes his or her own phrases here and there, but retains the form and content of the original passage, is one of the most common forms of plagiarism that writing instructors see. Much of it occurs, we believe, because students don't know it's wrong—and because they don't see their job as developing their *own* ideas in relation to their sources.)

Acknowledging an Idea   Let us say that you have read an essay in which Irving Kristol argues that journalists who pride themselves on being tireless critics of national policy are in fact irresponsible critics because they have no policy they prefer. If this strikes you as a new idea and you adopt it in an essay—even though you set it forth entirely in your own words and with examples not offered by Kristol—you must acknowledge your debt to Kristol. *Not to acknowledge such borrowing is plagiarism.* Your readers will not think the less of you for naming your source; rather, they will be grateful to you for telling them about an interesting writer.

Fair Use of Common Knowledge

If in doubt as to whether or not to give credit (either with formal documentation or merely in a phrase such as "Carol Gilligan says . . ."), give credit. But as you begin to read widely in your field or subject, you will develop a sense of what is considered common knowledge.

Unsurprising definitions in a dictionary can be considered common knowledge, and so there is no need to say "According to Webster, a novel is a long narrative in prose." (That's weak in three ways: It's unnecessary, it's uninteresting, and it's inexact since "Webster" appears in the titles of several dictionaries, some good and some bad.)

Similarly, the date of Freud's death can be considered common knowledge. Few can give it when asked, but it can be found out from innumerable sources, and no one need get the credit for providing you with the date. Again, if you simply *know*, from your reading of Freud, that Freud was interested in literature, you need not cite a specific source for an assertion to that effect, but if you know only because some commentator on Freud said so, and you have no idea whether the fact is well known or not, you should give credit to the source that gave you the information. Not to give credit—for ideas as well as for quoted words—is to plagiarize.

"But How Else Can I Put It?"

If you have just learned—say from an encyclopedia—something that you sense is common knowledge, you may wonder, How can I change into my own words the simple, clear words that this source uses in setting forth this simple fact? For example, if before writing an analysis of a photograph of Buffalo Bill and Sitting Bull, you look up these names in the *Encyclopaedia Britannica*, you will find this statement about Buffalo Bill (William F. Cody): "In 1883 Cody organized his first Wild West exhibition." You could not use this statement as your own, word for word, without feeling uneasy. But to put in quotation marks such a routine statement of what can be considered common knowledge, and to cite a source for it, seems pretentious. After all, the *Encyclopedia Americana* says much the same thing in the same routine way: "In 1883, . . . Cody organized Buffalo Bill's Wild West." It may be that the word "organized" is simply the most obvious and the best word, and perhaps you will end up using it. Certainly to change "Cody organized" into "Cody presided over the organization of" or "Cody assembled" or some such thing, in an effort to avoid plagiarizing, would be to make a change for the worse and still to be guilty of plagiarism. But you won't get yourself into this mess of wondering whether to change clear, simple wording into awkward wording if in the first place, when you take notes, you *summarize* your sources, thus: "1883: organized Wild West," or "first Wild West: 1883." Later (even if only thirty minutes later), when drafting your paper, if you turn this nugget—probably combined with others—into the best sentence you can, you will not be in danger of plagiarizing, even if the word "organized" turns up in your sentence.

Of course, even when dealing with material that can be considered common knowledge—and even when you have put it into your own words—you probably *will* cite your source if you are drawing more than just an occasional fact from a source. If, for instance, your paragraph on Buffalo Bill uses half a dozen facts from a source, cite the source. You do this both to avoid charges of plagiarism and to protect yourself in case your source contains errors of fact.

Writing the Essay

When you use sources, you are not merely dumping on the table the contents of a shopping cart filled at the scholar's supermarket, the library. You are cooking a meal. You must have a point, an opinion, a thesis. You are working toward a conclusion, and your readers should always feel they are moving toward that conclusion rather than reading an anthology of commentary on the topic. You've become an expert on your topic; you now know what others have to say about it, but if you've been *thinking* about what the secondary sources have said about your primary material, it's likely that you've noticed contradictions and gaps, that you agree with some opinions and arguments (and disagree with others), that you've begun to develop your *own* ideas about your topic.

There remains the difficult job of writing the essay. Beyond referring you to the rest of this book, we can offer only seven pieces of advice.

1. With a tentative thesis in mind, begin by rereading your notes and sorting them by topic. Put together what belongs together. Don't hesitate to reject interesting material that now seems irrelevant or redundant. After sorting, resorting, and rejecting, you will have a kind of first draft without writing a draft.

2. From your notes you can make a first outline. Although you can't yet make a paragraph outline, you may find it useful to make a fairly full outline, indicating not only the sequence of points but also the quotations that you will use. In sketching the outline, of course you will be guided by your *thesis.* As you worked, you probably modified your tentative ideas in the light of what your further research produced, but by now you ought to have a relatively firm idea of what you want to say. Without a thesis you will have only the basis for a *report*, not a potential essay.

3. Transcribe or download quotations, even in the first draft, exactly as you want them to appear in the final version. Of course this takes some time, and the time will be wasted if, as may well turn out, you later see that the quotation is not really useful. (On the other hand, the time has not really been wasted, since it helped you ultimately to delete the unnecessary material.)

If at this early stage you just write a note reminding yourself to include the quotation—something like "here quote Jackson on undecided voters"—when you reread the draft you won't really know how the page sounds. You won't, for instance, know how much help your reader needs by way of a lead-in to the quotation, or how much discussion should follow. Only if you actually see the quotation are you in the position of your audience, and it's a good idea to try to imagine your audience, even at this early stage.

4. Include, right in the body of the draft, all of the relevant citations so that when you come to revise you don't have to start hunting through your notes to find who said what, and where. You can, for the moment, enclose these citations within diagonal lines, or within double parentheses—anything to remind you that they will be your documentation.

5. Resist the urge to include every note in your essay. As we suggest in Chapter 1, writing is a way of discovering ideas. Consequently, as you write your first draft, your thesis will inevitably shift, and notes that initially seemed important will now seem irrelevant. Don't stuff them into the draft, even if you're concerned about meeting a page requirement: Readers know padding when they see it.

6. Resist the urge to do more research. As you draft, you may also see places where another piece of evidence, another reference to a source, or another example would be useful. And you may feel compelled to head back to the library. We think that for now you should resist that urge too: It may simply be procrastination in disguise. Continue writing this first draft if possible, and plan to incorporate new material in a later draft.

7. As you revise your draft, make sure that you do not merely tell the reader "A says . . . B says . . . C says . . ." Rather, by using a lead-in or signal phrase such as "A claims," "B provides evidence that," "C gives the usual view," "D concedes that," you help the reader to see the role of the quotation in your paper. Further, after quoting or summarizing a source, you should normally comment on it, thereby making clear the relation between your own ideas, and those of the source.

CHECKLIST FOR READING DRAFTS
OF RESEARCH ESSAYS

✔ Is the tentative title informative and focused?

✔ Does the paper make a point, or does it just accumulate other people's ideas? (See pp. 207–09.)

✔ Does it reveal the thesis early? (See Chapter 8, "Persuading Readers.")

✔ Are claims supported by evidence? (See Chapter 8, "Persuading Readers.")

✔ Are all the *words* and *ideas* of the sources accurately attributed? (See pp. 218–23.)

✔ Are quotations introduced adequately with signal phrases (such as "according to Ziff," or "Smith contends," or "Johnson points out") to indicate who is speaking? (See p. 225.)

✔ Are all of the long quotations necessary, or can some of them be effectively summarized? (See pp. 216–17.)

✔ Are quotations discussed adequately? (See p. 217; see also Chapter 7, "Analyzing Texts.")

✔ Does the paper advance in orderly stages? Can your imagined reader easily follow your thinking? (See Chapter 2, "Drafting and Revising.")

✔ Is the documentation in the correct form? (See Chapter 12, "Documentation.")

A Sample Research Essay (MLA Format)

We began this chapter with a paragraph from the following research essay, "Politics and Psychology in *The Awakening.*" We noted that Beatrice Cody used her research to help her develop her *own* position on the novel. As you read the following essay, be alert to the range of sources Cody uses, and to the range of ways in which she uses them: to establish the critical position she'll be arguing against, to give helpful background on Chopin's life, to provide information on Chopin's contemporaries' responses to the novel, and so on.

A note on the format of the essay: Cody uses the Modern Language Association (MLA) form of in-text citations, which are clarified by a list headed "Works Cited." We explain the MLA system in detail in Chapter 12, "Documentation." In Chapter 12, we also explain and illustrate the American Psychological Association (APA) form of in-text citations, and we offer information on several other systems of documentation.

1/2'

Cody 1

Beatrice Cody
Ms. Bellanca
Writing 125
12 April 2001

Politics and Psychology in

The Awakening

Title announces focus and scope of essay.

At first glance, Kate Chopin's novel The Awakening (1899) poses no problem to the feminist reader. It is the story of Edna Pontellier, a woman living at the turn of the century who, partly through a half-realized summer romance, discovers that sensual love, art, and individuality mean more to her than marriage or motherhood. When she concludes that there can be no compromise between her awakened inner self and the stifling shell of her outer life as a wife and mother, she drowns herself. In such a summary, Edna appears to be yet another victim of the "Feminine Mystique" described by Betty Friedan in the 1950's, a mind-numbing malaise afflicting the typical American housewife whose husband and society expected her to care for family at the expense of personal freedom and fulfillment. However, it is possible that the events leading to Edna's tragic death were not caused solely by the expectations of a sexist society pre-dating Friedan's model, in which a wife was not only dutiful to but also the "property" of her husband (Culley 119),

Plot summary helps orient readers unfamiliar with novel.

← 1" →

← 1" →

1"

Cody 2

Citation includes title because there are two works by Chopin on Works Cited list.

and a mother not only stayed home but also sacrificed even the "essential" for her children (Chopin <u>Awakening</u> 48). Perhaps Edna's suicide resulted from the torments of her individual psyche, her inability to cope with the patriarchal expectations, which most women in fact were able to tolerate.

Clear statement of thesis.

Citation includes name because author isn't cited in the sentence itself.

It is difficult to say how Chopin wished <u>The Awakening</u> to be interpreted. Heroines who explore their own individuality (with varying degrees of success and failure) abound in her work (Shinn 358); Chopin herself, though married, was a rather nontraditional wife who smoked cigarettes, and, like Edna Pontellier, took walks by herself (Nissenbaum 333-34). One might think therefore that Chopin was making a political statement in <u>The Awakening</u> about the position of women in society based on her own rejection of that position. But aside from slim biographical evidence and the assertions of some critics such as Larzer Ziff and Daniel S. Rankin that Chopin sympathized with Edna, we have no way of knowing whether she regarded this protagonist as a victim of sexist oppression or simply, to quote her family doctor in the novel itself, as "a sensitive and highly organized woman [. . . who] is especially peculiar" (66). It is therefore necessary to explore the two possibilities, using

Sources are paraphrased here. Although the words of the sources aren't used, ideas must be acknowledged.

Brackets around "who" indicate that word has been added.

Citation includes page number because title and author are clear from context.

Cody 3

evidence from the novel to determine
whether Edna Pontellier's awakening is
political or peculiarly personal in
nature.

It does not take a deeply feminist
awareness to detect the dominant,
controlling stance Edna's husband,
Leonce, assumes in their marriage.
Throughout the novel Chopin documents
the resulting injustices, both great and
small, which Edna endures. In one
instance Leonce comes home late at night
after Edna has fallen asleep, and, upon
visiting their sleeping children,
concludes that both of them are
feverish. He wakes Edna so that she may
check on them, despite her assertion
that the children are perfectly well.
He chides her for her "inattention" and
"habitual neglect of the children"
(7)--rather than respecting her ability
as their mother to judge the state of
their health or attending to them
himself--and reduces her to tears. She
defers to his judgment, looking at the
boys as he had asked, and, finding them
entirely healthy, goes out to the porch
where "an indescribable oppression
[. . .] filled her whole being with a
vague anguish" (8). Though in some ways
inconsequential, actions such as these
epitomize Leonce Pontellier's attitude
toward women and particularly toward
his wife. It is his belief that she has
a certain role and specific duties

Three spaced periods indicate that words have been omitted from sentence.

Cody 4

(those of a woman) which must be done well--according to his (a man's) standards. Although he would probably claim to love Edna, he does not seem to regard her as an autonomous individual; she is the mother of his children, the hostess of such "callers" as he deems appropriate (i.e., the ones who will bring him influence and esteem) (51) and essentially another decoration in his impeccably furnished house (50). When Edna's awakening leads her to abandon household chores in favor of painting, Chopin exposes Leonce's sexism:

> *Prose quotations longer than four typed lines are indented one inch from the left margin and double-spaced.*

> Mr. Pontellier had been a rather courteous husband so long as he met a certain tacit submissiveness in his wife. But her new and unexpected line of conduct completely bewildered him [. . .] her absolute disregard for her duties as a wife angered him. (57)

> *Block quotations do not need quotation marks. Note that the period precedes the parenthetic citation in a block quotation.*

It would seem from such evidence that Chopin intended The Awakening to depict the wrongs that women suffered at the hands of men in her society. Taking this cue from Chopin, many twentieth-century critics choose to view it in a political light. Larzer Ziff, for example, claims that the novel "rejected the family as the automatic equivalent of feminine self-

Cody 5

Cody quotes opposing views. Note smooth integration of quoted passages. The verbs "claims," "noting," and "states" clearly signal quotations.

fulfillment, and on the very eve of the twentieth century it raised the question of what woman was to do with the freedom she struggled toward" (175). Winfried Fluck, noting Edna's "preference for semi-conscious states of being [. . .] sleeping, dreaming, dozing, or the moment of awakening" (435), argues that she is enacting a "a radical retreat from the imprisonment of all social roles" (435). Marie Fletcher states that "[Edna's] suicide is the last in a series of rebellions which structure her life, give it pathos, and make of the novel [. . .] an interpretation of the 'new woman'" (172)--"the emerging suffragist/woman professional of the late nineteenth century" (Culley 118). Even in 1899 an anonymous reviewer in the <u>New Orleans Times Democrat</u> noticed the political implications of the novel, declaring in his own conservative way that

> a woman of twenty-eight, a
> wife and twice a mother who is
> pondering upon her relations
> to the world about her, fails
> to perceive that the relation
> of a mother to her children is
> far more important than the
> gratification of a passion
> which experience has taught
> her is [. . .] evanescent, can
> hardly be said to be fully
> awake. (150)

Cody 6

These critics lead us to focus on the socio-political implications of the novel, and on the questions it raises about woman's role and responsibility: when if ever does a woman's personal life become more important than her children? or, how does Edna embody the emancipated woman? But I believe that more than just the social pressure and politics of the late nineteenth century were acting on Edna. It was the inherent instability of her own psyche, exacerbated by the oppression she suffered as a woman, that drove her to swim out to her death at the end of The Awakening.

Clear
transition
("despite").

Despite the feminist undertones discernible in Chopin's work, a strong sense prevails that Edna's tragedy is unique, a result of her own psychology, not only of societal oppression. Throughout the novel Chopin describes Edna's agitated state of mind and drops hints about her upbringing and family life before marriage. Upon piecing all the clues to her personality together one gets a troubling, stereotypical picture. Edna's widowed father is a stern colonel from Kentucky who "was perhaps unaware that he had coerced his own wife into her grave" (71). From the scenes in which he appears one deduces that he is harsh and authoritative with his family; the narrator's comment about his wife implies that perhaps

In this paragraph and the next, Cody develops her argument by analyzing the text of the novel.

he was abusive (no doubt psychologically, possibly physically) as well. He gambles compulsively on horseracing (69), which denotes an addictive personality. He also makes his own very strong cocktails-- "toddies"--which he drinks almost all day long (71). He retains the appearance of sobriety, however, which indicates a high tolerance built up over much time. From this evidence one may assume that he suffers from alcoholism.

The rest of Edna's family--two sisters--fit the mold of the dysfunctional family that a violent, alcoholic parent tends to create. Her oldest sister seems to be the hyper-responsible, over-functioning "perfect" daughter. She served as a surrogate mother to Edna and her younger sister, and is described by Edna's husband as the only daughter who "has all the Presbyterianism undiluted" (66). Edna's younger sister is, predictably, exactly the opposite: Leonce Pontellier describes her as a "vixen" (66). She has rebelled against all of the rules and expectations that the eldest daughter obeys and fulfills. Edna, the middle child, is hence a curious case. Chopin tells us that "even as a child she had lived her own small life all within herself" (15). In such family situations the

Cody 8

middle child is usually rather
introverted. Where the two other
siblings strive compulsively either to
correct or create problems, the sibling
in the middle passively escapes from
her painful family situation by
withdrawing into herself (Seixas and
Youcha 48-49).

Evidence from experts offered in support of thesis.

So far this simplistic but
relatively reliable delineation of
personalities works for Edna's
character. Later in life she perpetuates
the patterns of her dysfunctional family
by marrying a man who almost mirrors her
father in personality; he is simply a
workaholic rather than an alcoholic.
Edna gives birth to two children, "a
responsibility which she had blindly
assumed" (20) in her typically passive
way. The first time she truly examines
her role in this marriage and indeed in
the world at large occurs on Grand Isle,
a resort island where she and her family
are vacationing for the summer. There
she begins to spend a great deal of time
with a young man named Robert Lebrun,
and a mutual desire gradually arises
between them. This desire, and the
general sensuality and openness of the
Creole community to which she is
exposed, bring about Edna's sexual,
artistic, and individual awakening.
Although the reader is excited and
inspired by this awakening in Edna--a
woman learning to shed the fetters

Cody 9

of both her oppressive marriage and
society in general--the way it takes
control of her life is disturbingly
reminiscent of mental illness. She
becomes infatuated with Robert, devotes
an inordinate amount of time to
painting, and seeks out classical
music, which wracks her soul in a
torturous ecstasy.

Throughout her awakening, she
experiences myriad moods and feelings
that she had never felt before in her
docile, passive state. Many of these
moods manifest themselves in the form
of mysterious, troubling voices: "the
voices were not soothing that came to
her from the darkness and the sky
above and the stars" (53); "she felt
like one who has entered and lingered
within the portals of some forbidden
temple in which a thousand muffled
voices bade her begone" (84). Behind
the veil of metaphor here one can
detect hints of an almost schizoid
character. Chopin even describes Edna
as two selves, which naturally befits
a woman undergoing an emotional
transformation, but which also
denotes a distinctly schizophrenic
state of mind: "she was becoming
herself and daily casting aside that
fictitious self which we assume like
a garment with which to appear before
the world" (57); "she could only
realize that she herself--her present

self--was in some way different from the other self" (41). Chopin phrases her descriptions of Edna in such a way that they could in fact describe either a woman gaining her emotional autonomy or a woman losing her mind.

As compelling as I find the suggestion of Edna's insanity, I must admit that her struggle between self-hood and motherhood is one too common to all women to be passed off as the ravings of a madwoman. As to which interpretation she preferred, Chopin offered few clues. For example, in February 1898 Chopin responded to a question, posed by the society page of the St. Louis Post-Dispatch, about the possible motives for a recent rash of suicides among young high-society women. Rather than the pressure of society as a likely motive, she suggests a "highly nervous" disposition (qtd. in Toth 120). Indeed, she asserts that "leadership in society is a business...there is nothing about it that I can see that would tend to produce an unhealthy condition of mind. On the contrary, it prevents women from becoming morbid, as they might, had they nothing to occupy their attention when at leisure" (qtd. in Toth 120). Perhaps, then, we are to suppose that a combination of psychic instability and extensive leisure, rather than the oppression of her society, caused Edna

Parenthetic reference to an indirect source. (The quotation from Chopin appears on page 120 of Toth's book.)

Cody 11

to take her own life. And yet this
same response in the Post-Dispatch
includes a counter-question to the
editor: "Business men commit suicide
every day, yet we do not say that
suicide is epidemic in the business
world. Why should we say the feeling
is rife among society women, because
half a dozen unfortunates, widely
separated, take their own lives?"
(qtd. in Toth 120). Her implicit
criticism of the double standard
suggests that Chopin was aware of the
politics of gender relations in her
own society in addition to the
existence of an "hysterical tendency"
in some women (qtd. in Toth 120). One
cannot therefore discount the
possibility that Chopin meant Edna's
suicide to be in part a reaction to
her society's rigid and limiting
expectations of women.

Chopin received such harsh
criticism of Edna Pontellier's sexual
freedom and attitude toward family
that, when The Awakening was published,
if not before, she must have had some
idea of how controversial the issue of
her protagonist's personal freedom
really was: her hometown library banned
the book, and Chopin herself was banned
from a St. Louis arts club (Reuben).
Her critics tend to believe that she
sympathized unreservedly with her
headstrong heroine; but even the

*Citation of
on-line
source.
(Source is
unpagi-
nated, so
citation gives
only the
author's
name.)*

Cody 12

retraction she published soon after her
novel does not reveal whether she
viewed Edna as oppressed or mentally
ill. Apparently written for the benefit
of her scandalized reviewers, the
retraction ironically relieves Chopin
of all responsibility for Edna's
"making such a mess of things and
working out her own damnation" (159).
Again, as in her ambiguous response to
the Post-Dispatch, Chopin leaves
curious readers unsatisfied, and the
motive of Edna's suicide unclear.

It is left to the reader therefore
to decide whether Edna is a martyr to a
feminist cause--the liberation of the
American housewife--or the victim of a
psychological disturbance that drives
her to suicide. I believe that it is
best not to dismiss either possibility.
To begin with, one cannot deny that in
the nineteenth century few options other
than marriage and child-rearing were
open to women. These narrow options were
the result of a societal structure in
which men socially, economically, and
sexually dominated women. In the twenty-
first century we can look back at
Chopin's time and feel confident in
condemning this state of affairs, but
from contemporary criticism of The
Awakening alone, it is clear that this
political view was not so widely
accepted at the turn of the century.
Perhaps Chopin had an unusually clear

and untimely insight into what we now
consider the sexism of her society,
but she chose to condemn it only
implicitly by portraying it as a fact
of life against which her unbalanced
heroine must struggle and perish. As
Larzer Ziff puts it, "Edna Pontellier
is trapped between her illusions and
the condition which society
arbitrarily establishes to maintain
itself, and she is made to pay" (175).
Chopin fused the political and the
personal in Edna Pontellier, who, like
most women in the world, suffers not
only from the pressures of a society
run by and for men, but also from her
own individual afflictions.

Sources are listed in alphabetical order by author.

"Works Cited" is centered.

Three hyphens indicate another work by the author named immediately above.

Second and subsequent lines of entry are indented 5 spaces.

Signed entry in a reference work with alphabetically arranged entries.

Begin Works Cited list on new page. Continue pagination.

Short form of citation. Articles by Cully and Fletcher are reprinted in the Norton edition of The Awakening. The full citation for the volume appears under Chopin.

On-line source (paginated).

On-line source (unpaginated).

Works Cited

Chopin, Kate. <u>The Awakening</u>. 1899. Ed. Margaret Culley. New York: Norton, 1976.

---. "Retraction." 1899. Rpt. in <u>The Awakening</u>. By Kate Chopin. 159.

Culley, Margaret. "The Context of <u>The Awakening</u>." In <u>The Awakening</u>. By Kate Chopin. 119-22.

Fletcher, Marie. "The Southern Woman in the Fiction of Kate Chopin." Rpt. in <u>The Awakening</u>. By Kate Chopin. 170-73.

Fluck, Winfried. "'The American Romance' and the Changing Functions of the Imaginary." <u>New Literary History</u> 27.3 (1996): 415-57. <u>Project Muse</u>. JHU. 1 May 1998. http://muse:jhu.edu:80/journals/ new literary history /v27/ 27.3fluck.html.

"New Publications." <u>New Orleans Times-Democrat</u>. Rpt. in <u>The Awakening</u>. By Kate Chopin. 150.

Nissenbaum, Stephen. "Chopin, Kate O'Flaherty." <u>Notable American Women</u>. 1971 ed.

Rankin, Daniel S. "Influences Upon the Novel." Rpt. in <u>The Awakening</u>. By Kate Chopin. 163-65.

Reuben, Paul P. "Chapter 6: 1890-1910: Kate Chopin (1851-1904)." <u>PAL: Perspectives in American</u>

Cody 15

Literature--A Research and
Reference Guide. 20 Mar. 1998.
http://www.csustan.edu/english/reu
ben/pal/chap6/chopin.html.
Seixas, Judith S., and Geraldine
Youcha. Children of Alcoholism: A
Survivor's Manual. New York:
Harper, 1985.
Shinn, Thelma J. "Kate O'Flaherty
Chopin." American Women Writers.
1979 ed.
Toth, Emily. "Kate Chopin on Divine
Love and Suicide: Two Rediscovered
Articles." American Literature 63
(1991): 115-21.
Ziff, Larzer. Excerpt from The American
1890s: Life and Times of a Lost
Generation, 279-305. Rpt. in The
Awakening. By Kate Chopin. 173-75.

*Journal
article.*

A Brief Analysis of Beatrice Cody's Use of Sources

In our introductory comments, we noted that Cody uses sources in a
range of ways in this essay. Here, we will point to some of the specific
ways in which she uses others' ideas to develop her argument about the
novel and to enrich her analysis of it:

- In paragraph 1, Cody alludes to Betty Friedan's concept of the
"feminine mystique" to help explain the prevailing interpretation of
the novel. Note that the reference to Freidan is general; the idea of the
"feminine mystique" is treated as **common knowledge.**

- In paragraph 2, Cody draws on Chopin's biography to help develop
the interpretation she'll be arguing against. She's **granting the**

opposition what's due to it; she's establishing the merit of the point of view against which she's arguing. (One wouldn't, after all, want to waste time arguing against a foolish position.) She also **quotes the authorities,** the critics Ziff and Rankin, she'll go on to dispute.

- At the end of paragraph 2, Cody **quotes a passage from the novel, evidence** that helps **support** her thesis (stated at the end of paragraph 1) that Edna's suicide in part "resulted from the torments of her individual psyche."

- In paragraphs 3 and 4, Cody **analyzes evidence** from the novel, from contemporary reviews, and from current criticism, that **does not support** her argument, but rather supports the "socio-political" interpretation of *The Awakening*. (Again, she's establishing the merit of the **counterargument.**)

- In paragraph 6, Cody **analyzes** the text of the novel, focusing now on **evidence** that **supports** her position—for example, Chopin's representation of Edna's family members.

- In paragraph 7, Cody refers to what might be called **expert testimony:** a discussion in a psychology textbook that supports her interpretation of Edna's dysfunctional family as a cause of Edna's own disturbed psyche.

- In paragraph 10, Cody **quotes from Chopin** herself to give a somewhat different perspective on Edna's character; she thereby **enriches her analysis** of Chopin's protagonist.

- In paragraph 12, Cody uses a **quotation from Larzer Ziff,** a critic she's been disagreeing with until now, in part to support her larger point. We note that at the end of the essay, she develops a position that strikes a balance between the argument she's been putting forth, and the prevailing view of the novel. Our last impression of Cody, therefore, is that she is a thoughtful and **reasonable** critic.

PART THREE

A
WRITER'S
HANDBOOK

CHAPTER TEN

PUNCTUATION

Speakers can raise or lower the volume or pitch of their voices; they can speak a phrase slowly and distinctly and then (making a parenthetical remark, perhaps) quicken the pace. They can wave their arms, pound a table, or pause, meaningfully. But writers, physically isolated from their audience, can do none of these things. Nevertheless, they can embody some of the tones and gestures of speech—in the patterns of their written sentences, and in the dots, hooks, and dashes of punctuation that clarify those patterns.

Punctuation clarifies, first of all, by removing or reducing ambiguity. Consider this headline from a story in a newspaper:

SQUAD HELPS DOG BITE VICTIM

Of course, there is no real ambiguity here—only a laugh—because the stated meaning is so clearly absurd, and on second reading we supply the necessary hyphen in *dog-bite*. But other ill-punctuated sentences may be troublesome rather than entertaining. Take the following sentence:

He arrived late for the rehearsal didn't end until midnight.

Almost surely you stumbled in the middle of the sentence, thinking that it was about someone arriving tardily at a rehearsal, and then, since what followed made no sense, you probably went back and mentally added the comma (by pausing) at the necessary place:

He arrived late, for the rehearsal didn't end until midnight.

Punctuation helps to keep the reader on the right path. And the path is your train of thought. If your punctuation is faulty, you unintentionally point the reader off your path and toward dead-end streets and quagmires.

Even when punctuation is not the key to meaning, it usually helps you get your meaning across neatly. Consider the following sentence:

> There are two kinds of feminism—one is the growing struggle of women to understand and change the shape of their lives and the other is a narrow ideology whose adherents are anxious to clear away whatever does not conform to their view.

The sentence is clear enough, but by changing the punctuation it can be sharpened. Because a dash usually indicates an abrupt interruption—it usually precedes a sort of afterthought—a colon would be better. The colon, usually the signal of an amplification of what precedes it, here would suggest that the two classifications are not impromptu thoughts but carefully considered ones. Second, and more important, in the original version the two classifications are run together without any intervening punctuation, but since the point is that the two are utterly different, it is advisable to separate them by inserting a comma or semicolon, indicating a pause. A comma before "and the other" would do, but probably a semicolon (without the "and") is preferable because it is a heavier pause, thereby making the separation clearer. Here is the sentence, revised:

> There are two kinds of feminism: one is the growing struggle of women to understand and change the shape of their lives; the other is a narrow ideology whose adherents are anxious to clear away whatever does not conform to their view.

The right punctuation enables the reader to move easily through the sentence.

Now, although punctuation helps a reader to move through a sentence, it must be admitted that some of the rules of punctuation do not contribute to meaning or greatly facilitate reading. For example, in American usage a period never comes immediately after quotation marks; it precedes quotation marks, thus:

> "If you put the period inside the closing quotation mark," the writing instructor said, "I will give you an A."

If you put the period after the closing quotation mark, the meaning remains the same, but you are also informing your reader that you don't know the conventions of American usage—conventions all writers in the United States are expected to adhere to. A pattern of such errors will diminish your authority as a writer: Your reader, noticing that you don't know where to put the period in relation to the quotation mark, may well begin to wonder what else you don't know. Conversely, demonstrating that you know the rules will help to gain your reader's confidence and establish your authority as a writer.

A Word on Computer Grammar and Punctuation Checks

Word-processing programs now include a tool that can check grammar and punctuation. At your request, the program will flag sentences that look faulty and offer suggestions for correcting mistakes. These programs can be very helpful: They can draw your attention to sentence fragments, to problems with plurals and possessives, even to passive verbs. But they don't catch everything, and they don't always know how to fix the problems they identify.

Our advice: Use the tool if you have it, but don't let it do your editing for you. Check the program's suggestions against your own knowledge and the advice offered in this book.

Three Common Errors: Fragments, Comma Splices, and Run-On Sentences

Fragments and How to Correct Them

A fragment is a part of a sentence set off as if it were a complete sentence: *Because I didn't care. Being an accident. Later in the week. For several reasons. My oldest sister.* Fragments are common in speech, but they are used sparingly in writing, usually for emphasis. A fragment used carelessly in writing often looks like an afterthought—usually because it *was* an afterthought, that is, an explanation or other addition that belongs to the previous sentence.

With appropriate punctuation (and sometimes with no punctuation at all) a fragment can usually be connected to the previous sentence:

Incorrect

Many nineteenth-century horror stories have been made into films. Such as *Dracula* and *Frankenstein.*

Correct

Many nineteenth-century horror stories have been made into films, such as *Dracula* and *Frankenstein*.

Incorrect

Many schools are putting renewed emphasis on writing. Because SAT scores have declined for ten years.

Correct

Many schools are putting renewed emphasis on writing because SAT scores have declined for ten years.

Incorrect

She wore only rope sandals. Being a strict vegetarian.

Correct

Being a strict vegetarian, she wore only rope sandals.
She wore only rope sandals because she was a strict vegetarian.

Incorrect

A fragment often looks like an afterthought. Perhaps because it *was* an afterthought.

Correct

A fragment often looks like an afterthought—perhaps because it *was* an afterthought.

Incorrect

He hoped to get credit for two summer courses. Batik and Hang-Gliding.

Correct

He hoped to get credit for two summer courses: Batik and Hang-Gliding.

Notice in the examples above that, depending upon the relationship between the two parts, the fragment and the preceding statement can be joined by a comma, a dash, a colon, or by no punctuation at all.

Notice also that unintentional fragments often follow subordinating conjunctions, such as *because* and *although*. Subordinating conjunctions introduce a subordinate (dependent) clause; such a clause cannot stand as a sentence. Here is a list of the most common subordinating conjunctions:

after	though
although	unless
because	until
before	when
if	where
provided	whereas
since	while

Fragments also commonly occur when the writer, as in the third example, mistakenly uses *being* as a main verb.

Comma Splices and Run-On Sentences, and How to Correct Them

An error known as a *comma splice* or *comma fault* results when a comma is mistakenly placed between two independent clauses that are not joined by a coordinating conjunction: *and, or, nor, but, for, yet, so.* If the comma is omitted, the error is called a *run-on sentence.*

Examples of the two errors:

- *Comma splice* (or *comma fault*): In the second picture the man leans on the woman's body, he is obviously in pain.

- *Run-on sentence:* In the second picture the man leans on the woman's body he is obviously in pain.

Run-on sentences and comma splices may be corrected in five principal ways:

1. Use a **period** to create two sentences:

In the second picture the man leans on the woman's body. He is obviously in pain.

2. Use a **semicolon:**

In the second picture the man leans on the woman's body; he is obviously in pain.

3. Use a **comma and a coordinating conjunction** (*and, or, nor, but, for, yet, so*):

In the second picture the man leans on the woman's body, and he is obviously in pain.

4. Make one of the clauses dependent (subordinate). **Use a subordinating conjunction** such as *after, although, because, before, if, provided, since, though, unless, until, when, where, whereas, while:*

In the second picture the man leans on the woman's body because he is in pain.

5. Reduce one of the independent clauses to a phrase, or even to a single word:

In the second picture the man, obviously in pain, leans on the woman's body.

Run-on sentences and comma splices are especially common in sentences containing transitional words or phrases such as the following:

also	however
besides	indeed
consequently	in fact
for example	nevertheless
furthermore	therefore
hence	whereas

When these words join independent clauses, the clauses cannot be linked by a comma:

Incorrect

She argued from faulty premises, however the conclusions happened to be correct.

Here are five correct revisions, following the five rules we have just given. (In the first two revisions we place "however" after, rather than before, "the conclusions" because we prefer the increase in emphasis, but the grammatical point is the same.)

1. She argued from faulty premises. The conclusions, however, happened to be correct. (Two sentences)

2. She argued from faulty premises; the conclusions, however, happened to be correct. (Semicolon)

3. She argued from faulty premises, but the conclusions happened to be correct. (Coordinating conjunction)

4. Although she argued from faulty premises, the conclusions happened to be correct. (Subordinating conjunction)

5. She argued from faulty premises to correct conclusions. (Reduction of an independent clause to a phrase)

The following sentence contains a comma splice:

The husband is not pleased, in fact, he is embarrassed.

How might it be repaired?

The Period

1. Periods are used to mark the ends of sentences (or intentional sentence fragments) other than questions and exclamations:

A sentence normally ends with a period.

She said, "I'll pass."

Yes.

Once more, with feeling.

But a sentence within a sentence is punctuated according to the needs of the longer sentence. Notice, in the following example, that a period is *not* used after "pass":

She said, "I'll pass," but she said it without conviction.

2. Periods are used with abbreviations of titles and terms of reference:

Dr., Mr., Mrs., Ms.

p., pp. (for "page" and "pages"), i.e., e.g., etc.

But when the capitalized initial letters of the words naming an organization are used in place of the full name, the periods are commonly omitted:

CBS, CORE, IBM, NBA, UCLA, UNICEF, USAF

3. Periods are also used to separate chapter from verse in the Bible:

Genesis 3.2, Mark 6.10

For further details on references to the Bible, see page 364.

The Question Mark

Use a question mark after a direct question:

Did Bacon write Shakespeare's plays?

Do not use a question mark after an indirect question, or after a polite request:

He asked if Bacon wrote Shakespeare's plays.
Would you please explain what the support for Bacon is really all about.

The Colon

The colon has four uses:

- To introduce a list or series of examples
- To introduce an amplification or explanation of what precedes the colon
- To introduce a quotation (though a quotation can be introduced by other means)
- To indicate time

Now let's look at each of those four uses.

1. The colon may introduce a list or series:

Students are required to take one of the following sciences: biology, chemistry, geology, physics.

2. The colon may introduce an explanation. It is almost equivalent to *namely*, or *that is*. What is on one side of the colon more or less

equals what is on the other side. The material on either side of the colon
can stand as a separate sentence:

> She explained her fondness for wrestling: she did it to shock her parents.

> The forces which in China created a central government were absent in
> Japan: farming had to be on a small scale, there was no need for exten-
> sive canal works, and a standing army was not required to protect the
> country from foreign invaders.

> Many of the best of the Civil War photographs must be read as the fos-
> sils of earlier events: The caissons with their mud-encrusted wheels, the
> dead on the field, the empty landscapes, all speak of deeds already past.

> *—John Szarkowski*

Notice in this last example that the writer uses a capital letter after the
colon; the usage is acceptable when a complete sentence follows the colon,
as long as that style is followed consistently throughout a paper.

**3. The colon, like the comma, may be used to introduce a quo-
tation;** it is more formal than the comma, setting off the quotation to a
greater degree:

> The black sculptor Ed Wilson tells his students: "Malcolm X is my
> brother, Martin Luther King is my brother, Eldridge Cleaver is my
> brother! But Michelangelo is my grandfather!"

> *—Albert E. Elsen*

4. A colon is used to separate the hour from the minutes when
the time is given in figures:

> 9:15, 12:00

**Colons (like semicolons) go outside of closing quotation marks if
they are not part of the quotation:**

> "There is no such thing as a free lunch": the truth of these words is con-
> firmed every day.

The Semicolon

There are four main uses of the semicolon. Sheridan Baker (in *The
Practical Stylist*) summed them up in this admirable formula: "Use a

semicolon where you could also use a period, unless desperate." Correctly used, the semicolon can add precision to your writing; it can also help you out of some tight corners.

1. You may use a semicolon instead of a period between closely related independent clauses not joined by a coordinating conjunction:

All happy families resemble one another; every unhappy family is unhappy in its own fashion.

—*Leo Tolstoy*

The demands that men and women make on marriage will never be fully met; they cannot be.

—*Jessie Bernard*

In our fractured culture, we cannot agree on morals; we cannot even agree that moral matters should come before literary ones when there is a conflict between them.

—*Flannery O'Connor*

When a cat washes its face it does not move its paw; it moves its face.

In each of the examples the independent clauses might have been written as sentences separated by periods; the semicolon pulls the statements together, emphasizing their relationship. Alternatively, the statements might have been linked by coordinating conjunctions (*and, or, nor, but, for, yet, so*). For example:

The demands made upon marriage will never be fully met for they cannot be.

When a cat washes its face it does not move its paw but it moves its face.

The sentences as originally written, using semicolons, have more bite.

2. You *must* use a semicolon (rather than a comma) if you use a *conjunctive adverb* to connect independent clauses. (A conjunctive adverb is a transitional word such as *also, consequently, furthermore, however, moreover, nevertheless, therefore.*)

His hair was black and wavy; however, it was false.

We don't like to see our depressed relative cry; nevertheless, tears can provide a healthy emotional outlet.

She said "I do"; moreover, she repeated the words.

Take note of the following three points:

- A comma goes after the conjunctive adverb.

- Semicolons (like colons) go outside of closing quotation marks if they are not part of the quotation.

- A conjunctive adverb requires a semicolon to join independent clauses. A comma produces a comma splice:

Incorrect

His hair was black and wavy, however, it was false.

3. You may use a semicolon to separate a series of phrases with internal punctuation:

He had a car, which he hadn't paid for; a wife, whom he didn't love; and a father, who was unemployed.

4. Use a semicolon between independent clauses linked by coordinating conjunctions if the sentence would otherwise be difficult to read, because it is long and complex or because it contains internal punctuation:

In the greatest age of painting, the nude inspired the greatest works; and even when it ceased to be a compulsive subject it held its position as an academic exercise and a demonstration of mastery.

(Often it is preferable to break such sentences up, or to recast them.)

The Comma

The comma (from a Greek word meaning "to cut") indicates a relatively slight pause within a sentence. If after checking the rules you are still uncertain of whether or not to use a comma in a given sentence, read the sentence aloud and see if it sounds better with or without a pause; you can then add or omit the comma. A women's shoe store in New York has a sign on the door:

NO MEN PLEASE.

If the proprietors would read the sign aloud, they might want to change
it to

NO MEN, PLEASE

When you are typing, always follow a comma with a space.

For your reference, here is an outline for the following pages, which
summarize the correct uses of the comma:

1. with independent clauses, page 256
2. with introductory subordinate clauses or long phrases, page 256
3. with tacked-on subordinate phrases or long clauses, page 257
4. as parentheses, page 257
5. with nonrestrictive modifiers, page 258
6. with a series, page 260
7. with direct discourse, page 260
8. with "yes" and "no," page 261
9. with words of address, page 261
10. with geographical locations, page 261
11. with dates, page 261
12. with other punctuation, page 261

**1. Independent clauses (unless short) joined by a coordinating
conjunction (*and, or, nor, but, for, yet, so*) take a comma before the
conjunction:**

> Most students see at least a few football games, and many go to every
> game of the season.

> Most students seem to have an intuitive sense of when to use a comma,
> but in fact the "intuition" is the result of long training.

If the introductory independent clause is short, the comma is usually
omitted:

> She dieted but she continued to gain weight.

2. An introductory subordinate clause or long phrase is usually
followed by a comma:

Having revised his manuscript for the third time, he went to bed.

In order to demonstrate her point, the instructor stood on her head.

If the introductory subordinate clause or phrase is short, say four words or fewer, the comma may be omitted, provided no ambiguity results from the omission:

Having left he soon forgot.

But compare this last example with the following:

Having left, the instructor soon forgot.

If the comma is omitted, the sentence is misread. Where are commas needed in the following sentences?

Instead of discussing the book she wrote a summary.

When Shakespeare wrote comedies were already popular.

While he ate his poodle would sit by the table.

As we age small things become killers.

3. A subordinate clause or long modifying phrase tacked on as an afterthought is usually preceded by a comma:

I have decided not to be nostalgic about the 1950s, despite the hoopla over Elvis.

Buster Keaton fell down a flight of stairs without busting, thereby gaining his nickname from Harry Houdini.

By the time he retired, Hank Aaron had 755 home runs, breaking Babe Ruth's record by 41.

With afterthoughts, the comma may be omitted if there is a clear sequence of cause and effect, signaled by such words as *because, for,* and *so.* Compare the following examples:

In 1601 Shakespeare wrote *Hamlet*, probably his best-known play.

In 1601 Shakespeare wrote *Hamlet* because revenge tragedy was in demand.

4. A pair of commas can serve as a pair of unobtrusive parentheses. Be sure not to omit the second comma:

Doctors, I think, have an insufficient knowledge of acupuncture.

The earliest known paintings of Christ, dating from the third century, are found in the catacombs outside of Rome.

Medicare and Medicaid, the chief sources of federal support for patients in nursing homes, are frequently confused.

Under this heading we can include a conjunctive adverb (a transitional adverb such as *also, besides, consequently, however, likewise, nevertheless, therefore*) inserted within a sentence. These transitional words are set off between a pair of commas:

Her hair, however, was stringy.

If one of these words begins a sentence, the comma after it is optional. Notice, however, that the presence of such a word as "however" is not always a safeguard against a run-on sentence or comma splice; if the word occurs between two independent clauses and it goes with the second clause, you need a semicolon before it and a comma after it:

His hair was black and wavy; however, it was false.

(See the discussion of comma splices on pages 249–51.)

5. Use a comma to set off a nonrestrictive modifier. A nonrestrictive modifier, as the following examples will make clear, is a sort of parenthetical addition; it gives supplementary information about the subject, but it can be omitted without changing the subject. A restrictive modifier, however, is not supplementary but essential; if a restrictive modifier is omitted, the subject becomes more general. In Dorothy Parker's celebrated poem,

Men seldom make passes

At girls who wear glasses,

"who wear glasses" is a restrictive modifier, narrowing or restricting the subject down from "girls" to a particular group of girls, "girls who wear glasses."

Here is a *non*restrictive modifier:

For the majority of immigrants, who have no knowledge of English, language is the chief problem.

Now a restrictive modifier:

For the majority of immigrants who have no knowledge of English, language is the chief problem.

The first version says—in addition to its obvious message that language is the chief problem—that the majority of immigrants have no knowledge of English. The second version makes no such assertion; it talks not about the majority of immigrants but only about a more restricted group—those immigrants who have no knowledge of English.

Other examples:

Shakespeare's shortest tragedy, *Macbeth*, is one of his greatest plays.

In this sentence, "*Macbeth*" is nonrestrictive because the subject is already as restricted as possible; Shakespeare can have written only one "shortest tragedy." That is, "*Macbeth*" is merely an explanatory equivalent of "Shakespeare's shortest tragedy" and it is therefore enclosed in commas. (A noun or noun phrase serving as an explanatory equivalent to another, and in the same syntactical relation to other elements in the sentence, is said to be in apposition.) But compare

Shakespeare's tragedy *Macbeth* is one of his greatest plays.

with the misleadingly punctuated sentence,

Shakespeare's tragedy, *Macbeth*, is one of his greatest plays.

The first of these is restrictive, narrowing or restricting the subject "tragedy" down to one particular tragedy, and so it rightly does not separate the modifier from the subject by a comma. The second, punctuated so that it is nonrestrictive, falsely implies that *Macbeth* is Shakespeare's only tragedy. Here is an example of a nonrestrictive modifier correctly punctuated:

Women, who constitute 51.3 percent of the population and 53 percent of the electorate, constitute only 2.5 percent of the House of Representatives and 1 percent of the Senate.

In the next two examples, the first illustrates the correct use of commas after a nonrestrictive appositive, and the second illustrates the correct omission of commas after a restrictive appositive:

Hong Yee Chiu, a Chinese-American physicist, abbreviated the compound adjective *quasi-stellar* to *quasar*.

The Chinese-American physicist Hong Yee Chiu abbreviated the compound adjective *quasi-stellar* to *quasar.*

6. Words, phrases, and clauses in series take a comma after each item except the last. The comma between the last two items may be omitted if there is no ambiguity:

Photography is a matter of eyes, intuition, and intellect.

She wrote plays, poems, and stories.

He wrote plays, sang songs, and danced jigs.

She wrote a wise, witty, humane book.

But adjectives in a series may cause difficulty. The next two examples correctly omit the commas:

a funny silent film

a famous French professor

In each of these last two examples, the adjective immediately before the noun forms with the noun a compound that is modified by the earlier adjective. That is, the adjectives are not a coordinate series (what is funny is not simply a film but a silent film, what is famous is not simply a professor but a French professor) and so commas are not used. Compare:

a famous French professor

a famous, arrogant French professor

In the second example, only "famous" and "arrogant" form a coordinate series. If in doubt, see if you can replace the commas with "and"; if you can, the commas are correct. In the example given, you could insert "and" between "famous" and "arrogant," but not between "arrogant" and "French."

Commas are not needed if all the members of the series are connected by conjunctions:

He ate steak for breakfast and lunch and supper.

7. Use a comma to set off direct discourse:

"It's a total failure," she said.

She said, "It's a total failure."

But do not use a comma for indirect discourse:

> She said that it is a total failure.

> She said it is a total failure.

8. Use a comma to set off "yes" and "no":

Yes, he could take Writing 125 at ten o'clock.

9. Use a comma to set off words of address:

Look, Bill, take Writing 125 at ten o'clock.

10. Use a comma to separate a geographical location within another geographical location:

She was born in Brooklyn, New York, in 1895.

Another way of putting it is to say that a comma is used after each unit of an address, except that a comma is *not* used between the name of the state and the zip code.

11. Use a comma to set off the year from the month or day:

He was born on June 10, 1980.

No comma is needed if you use the form "10 June 1980."

12. Note the position of the comma when used with other punctuation: If a comma is required with parenthetic material, it follows the second parenthesis:

> Because Japan was secure from invasion (even the Mongols were beaten back), its history is unusually self-contained.

The only time a comma may precede a parenthesis is when parentheses surround a digit or letter used to enumerate a series:

> Questions usually fall into one of three categories: (1) true-false, (2) multiple choice, (3) essay.

A comma always goes inside closing quotation marks unless the quotation is followed by a parenthesis:

> "Sayonara," he said.

> "Sayonara" (Japanese for "goodbye"), he said.

The Dash

A dash is made by typing two hyphens without hitting the space bar before, between, or after. It indicates an abrupt break or pause.

1. The material within dashes may be something like parenthetic material (material that is not essential), though by setting it within dashes—an emphatic form of punctuation—the writer gives the material more emphasis than it would get within parentheses:

> The bathroom—that private place—has rarely been the subject of scholarly study.
>
> The Great Wall of China forms a continuous line over 1400 miles long—the distance from New York to Kansas City—running from Peking to the edge of the mountains of Central Asia.
>
> The old try to survive by cutting corners—eating less, giving up small pleasures like tobacco and movies, doing without warm clothes—and pay the price of ill-health and a shortened life-span.
>
> —*Sharon R. Curtin*

Notice that when two dashes are used, if the material within them is deleted the remainder still forms a grammatical sentence.

2. A dash can serve, somewhat like a colon, as a pause before a series. It is more casual than a colon:

> The earliest Shinto holy places were natural objects—trees, boulders, mountains, islands.
>
> Each of the brothers had his distinct comic style—Groucho's double-talk, Chico's artfully stupid malapropisms, Harpo's horseplay.
>
> —*Gerald Mast*

A dash is never used next to a comma, and it is used before a period only to indicate that the sentence is interrupted.

Overuse of the dash—even only a little overuse—gives writing an unpleasantly agitated—even explosive—quality.

Parentheses

Let's begin with a caution: Avoid using parentheses to explain pronouns: "In his speech he (Hamlet) says . . ." If "he" needs to be explained by "Hamlet," omit the "he" and just say "Hamlet."

1. Parentheses subordinate material; what is in parentheses is almost a casual aside, less essential than similar material set off in commas, less vigorously spoken than similar material set off in dashes:

> While guest curator for the Whitney (he has since returned to the Denver Art Museum), Feder assembled a magnificent collection of masks, totems, paintings, clothing, and beadwork.

Another caution: Avoid an abundance of these interruptions, and avoid a long parenthesis within a sentence (you are now reading a simple example of this annoying but common habit of writers who have trouble sticking to the point) because the reader will lose track of the main sentence.

2. Use parentheses to enclose digits or letters in a list that is given in running text:

> The exhibition included: (1) decorative screens, (2) ceramics, (3) ink paintings, (4) kimonos.

3. Do not confuse parentheses with square brackets, which are used around material you add to a quotation. See page 217.

4. For the use of parentheses in documentation, see Chapter 12, "Documentation."

5. Note the position of other punctuation with a parenthesis: The example under rule number 2, of commas preceding parentheses enclosing digits or letters in a list given in running text, is the rare exception to the rule that within a sentence, punctuation other than quotation marks never immediately precedes an opening parenthesis. Notice that in the example under rule number 1, the comma *follows* the closing parenthesis:

> While guest curator for the Whitney (he has since returned to the Denver Art Museum), Feder assembled a magnificent collection of masks, totems, paintings, clothing, and beadwork.

If an entire sentence is in parentheses, put the final punctuation (period, question mark, or exclamation mark) inside the closing parenthesis.

Italics

In typewritten material <u>underlining</u> is the equivalent of *italic* type:

> *This sentence is printed in italic type.*

<u>This sentence is understood to be printed in italic type.</u>

1. Underline or italicize the name of a plane, ship, train, movie, radio or television program, record album, musical work, statue, painting, play, pamphlet, or book. Do not underline or italicize names of sacred works such as the Bible, the Koran, or Acts of the Apostles, or political documents such as the Magna Carta and the Declaration of Independence. Notice that when you write about a newspaper or periodical whose title begins with the article "the," the convention is to give the article in lower case roman letters. You do not italicize it or underline it; it is not treated as part of the title.

2. Use italics only sparingly for emphasis. Sometimes, however, this method of indicating your tone of voice is exactly right:

> In 1911 Jacques Henri Lartigue was not merely as unprejudiced as a child; he *was* a child.
>
> —*John Szarkowski*

3. Use italics for foreign words that have not become a part of the English language:

> Acupuncture aims to affect the *ch'i*, a sort of vital spirit which circulates through the bodily organs.

But:

> He ate a pizza.
>
> She behaved like a prima donna.
>
> Avoid clichés.

4. You may use italics in place of quotation marks to identify a word:

> Honolulu means *safe harbor*.

5. You may also use italics to identify a word or term to which you wish to call special attention:

> Claude Lévi-Strauss tells us that one of the great purposes of art is that of *miniaturization*. He points out that most works of art are miniatures,

being smaller (and therefore more easily understood) than the objects they represent.

Capital Letters

Certain obvious conventions—the use of a capital for the first word in a sentence, for names (of days of the week, holidays, months, people, countries), and for words derived from names (such as pro-French)— need not be discussed here.

1. Titles of works in English are usually given according to the following formula. Use a capital for the first letter of the first word, for the first letter of the last word, and for the first letter of all other words that are not articles, conjunctions, or prepositions:

The Merchant of Venice

A Midsummer Night's Dream

Up and Out

"The Short Happy Life of Francis Macomber"

The Oakland Bee

2. Use a capital for a quoted sentence within a sentence, but not for a quoted phrase (unless it is at the beginning of your sentence) and not for indirect discourse:

He said, "You can even fool some of the people all of the time."

He said you can fool some people "all of the time."

He said that you can even fool some of the people all of the time.

3. Use a capital for a rank or title preceding a proper name or for a title substituting for a proper name:

She said she was Dr. Perez.

He told President Bush that the Vice President was away.

But:

Why would anyone wish to be president?

Washington was the first president.

4. Use a capital when the noun designating a family relationship is used as a substitute for a proper noun:

If Mother is busy, ask Tim.

But:

Because my mother was busy, I asked Tim.

5. Formal geographical locations (but not mere points on the compass) are capitalized:

North America

Southeast Asia

In the Southwest, rain sometimes evaporates before touching the ground.

Is Texas part of the South?

The North has its share of racism.

But:

The wind came from the south.

Texas is bordered on the north by Arkansas, Oklahoma, and New Mexico.

Do *not* capitalize the names of the seasons:

spring, summer, winter, fall

The Hyphen

The hyphen has five uses, all drawing on the etymology of the word *hyphen*, which comes from the Greek for "in one," "together."

1. Use a hyphen to attach certain prefixes to root words. *All-*, *pro-*, *ex-*, and *self-* are the most common of these ("all-powerful," "ex-wife," "pro-labor," "self-made"), but note that even these prefixes are not always followed by a hyphen. If in doubt, check a dictionary. Prefixes before proper names are always followed by a hyphen:

anti-Semite, pro-NATO, un-American

Prefixes ending in *i* are hyphenated before a word beginning with *i*:

anti-intellectual, semi-intelligible

A hyphen is normally used to break up a triple consonant resulting from the addition of a prefix:

ill-lit

2. Use a hyphen to tie compound adjectives into a single visual unit:

out-of-date theory, twenty-three books, a no-smoking area

eighteenth- and nineteenth-century novels

The sea-tossed raft was a common nineteenth-century symbol of the human tragic condition.

But if a compound modifier follows the modified term, it is usually not hyphenated, thus:

The theory was out of date.

3. Use a hyphen to join some compound nouns:

Scholar-teacher, philosopher-poet

4. Use a hyphen to indicate a span of dates or page numbers: 1957–59, pp. 162–68.

The Apostrophe

Use an apostrophe to indicate the possessive, to indicate a contraction, and to form certain unusual plurals.

1. The most common way to indicate the possessive of a singular noun is to add an apostrophe and then an *s:*

A dog's life, a week's work

a mouse's tail, Keats's poems, Marx's doctrines

But some authorities suggest that for a proper noun of more than one syllable that ends in *s* or another sibilant (*-cks, -x, -z*), it is better to add only an apostrophe:

Jesus' parables, Sophocles' plays, Chavez' ideas

When in doubt, say the name aloud and notice if you are adding an *s*. If you are adding an *s* when you say it, add an apostrophe and an *s* when you write it. Our own strong preference, however, is to add an apostrophe and an *s* to all proper nouns:

Jones's book

Kansas's highways

Possessive pronouns, such as *his, hers, its, theirs, ours,* do not take an apostrophe:

his book, its fur

The book is hers, not ours.

The book is theirs.

(*Exception:* indefinite pronouns take an apostrophe, as in "one's hopes" and "others' opinions.")

For plurals ending in *s,* add only an apostrophe to indicate the possessive:

the boys' father, the Smiths' house, the Joneses' car

If the plural does not end in *s,* add an apostrophe and an *s:*

women's clothing, mice's eyes

Don't try to form the possessive of the title of a work (for example, of a play, a book, or a film): Write "the imagery in *The Merchant of Venice*" rather than "*The Merchant of Venice*'s imagery." Using an apostrophe gets you into the problem of whether or not to italicize the *s;* similarly, if you use an apostrophe for a work normally enclosed in quotation marks (for instance, a short story), you can't put the apostrophe and the *s* after the quotation marks, but you can't put it inside either.

2. Use an apostrophe to indicate the omitted letters or numbers in contractions:

She won't.

It's time to go.

the class of '05

3. Until recently an apostrophe was used to make plurals of words that do not usually have a plural, and (this is optional) to make the plurals of digits and letters:

Her speech was full of if's and and's and but's.

Ph.D.'s don't know everything.

Mind your p's and q's. I got two A's and two B's.

He makes his 4's in two ways.

the 1920's

This use of the apostrophe is no longer standard, but it remains acceptable.

Abbreviations

In general, avoid abbreviations except in footnotes and except for certain common ones listed below. And don't use an ampersand (&) unless it appears in material you are quoting, or in a title. Abundant use of abbreviations makes an essay sound like a series of newspaper headlines. Usually, for example, *United States* is better than *U.S.*

1. Abbreviations, with the first letter capitalized, are used before a name:

Dr. Bellini, Ms. Smith, St. Thomas

But: The doctor took her temperature and eighty dollars.

2. Degrees that follow a name are abbreviated:

B.A., D.D.S., M.D., Ph.D.

3. Other acceptable abbreviations include:

A.D., B.C., A.M., P.M., e.g., i.e.

(By the way, *e.g.* means *for example; i.e.* means *that is.* The two ought not to be confused. See pages 280–81 and 284.)

4. The name of an agency or institution (for instance, the Congress of Racial Equality; International Business Machines; Southern Methodist University) may be abbreviated by using the initial letters, capitalized and usually without periods (e.g., CORE), but it is advisable to give the name in full when first mentioning it (not everyone knows that AARP means American Association of Retired Persons, for instance), and to use the abbreviation in subsequent references.

Numbers

1. Write numbers out if you can do so in fewer than three words; otherwise, use figures:

sixteen, seventy-two, ten thousand, one-sixth

10,200; 10,200,000

There are 336 dimples on a golf ball.

But write out round millions and billions, to avoid a string of zeroes:

a hundred and ten million

For large round numbers you can also use a combination of figures and words:

The cockroach is about 250 million years old.

Note, however, that because a figure cannot be capitalized, if a number begins a sentence it should always be written out:

Two hundred and fifty million years ago the cockroach first appeared on earth.

2. Use figures in dates, addresses, decimals, percentages, page numbers, and hours followed by A.M. or P.M.:

February 29, 1900; .06 percent; 6 percent; 8:16 a.m.

But hours unmodified by minutes are usually written out, followed by *o'clock:*

Executions in England regularly took place at eight o'clock.

3. Use an apostrophe to indicate omitted figures:

class of '98

the '90s (but: the nineties)

4. Use a hyphen to indicate a span:

1975–79

10–20

In giving inclusive numbers, give the second number in full for the numbers up through ninety-nine (2–5, 8–11, 28–34). For larger numbers, give only the last two digits of the second number (101–06; 112–14) unless the full number in necessary (198–202).

5. Dates can be given with the month first, followed by numerals, a comma, and the year:

February 10, 1999

or they can be given with the day first, then the month and then the year (without a comma after the day or month):

10 February 1999

6. B.C. follows the year, but A.D. precedes it:

10 B.C.

A.D. 200

The abbreviations B.C. and A.D. are falling out of favor, and are being replaced with B.C.E. ("Before the Common Era") and C.E. ("Common Era"). Both abbreviations follow the year.

7. Roman numerals are less used than formerly. Capital roman numerals were used to indicate a volume number, but volume numbers are now commonly given in arabic numerals. Capital roman numerals still are used, however, for the names of individuals in a series (Elizabeth II) and for the primary divisions of an outline; lowercase roman numerals are used for the pages in the front matter (table of contents, foreword, preface, etc.) of a book. The old custom of citing acts and scenes of a play in roman numerals and lines in arabic numerals (II.iv.17–25) is still preferred by many instructors, but the use of arabic numerals throughout (2.4.17–25) is gaining acceptance.

CHAPTER ELEVEN

USAGE

Some things are said or written and some are not. More precisely, anything can be said or written, but only some things are acceptable to the ears and minds of many readers. "She don't know nothing about it" has been said and will be said again, but many readers who encounter this expression might judge the speaker as a person with nothing of interest to say—and immediately tune out.

Although such a double negative today is not acceptable, it used to be: Chaucer's courteous Knight never spoke no baseness, and Shakespeare's courtly Mercutio, in *Romeo and Juliet*, "will not budge for no man." But things have changed; what was acceptable in the Middle Ages and the Renaissance (for example, emptying chamber pots into the gutter) is not always acceptable now. And some of what was once unacceptable has become acceptable. At the beginning of the twentieth century, grammarians suggested that one cannot use *drive* in speaking of a car; one drives (forces into motion) an ox, or even a person ("He drove her to distraction"), but not a machine. A century of usage, however, has erased all objections.

This chapter presents a list of expressions that, although commonly used, set many teeth on edge. Several decades from now some of these expressions may be as acceptable as "drive a car"; but we are writing for today, and we might as well try to hold today's readers by following today's taste in language.

A Note on Idioms

An idiom (from a Greek word meaning "peculiar") is a fixed group of words, peculiar to a given language. Thus in English we say, "I took a walk," but Germans "make a walk," Spaniards "give a walk," and Japanese "do a walk." (If we think the German, Spanish, and Japanese expressions are odd, we might well ask ourselves where it is that we take a walk to.) If a visitor from Argentina says, in English, that she "gave a walk," she is using *un*idiomatic English, just as anyone who says he knows a poem "at heart" instead of "by heart" is using unidiomatic English.

Probably most unidiomatic expressions use the wrong preposition. Examples:

Unidiomatic	Idiomatic
comply to	comply with
superior with	superior to

Sometimes while we write, or even while we speak, we are unsure of the idiom and we pause to try an alternative—"parallel with?" "parallel to?"—and we don't know which sounds more natural, more idiomatic. At such moments, more often than not, either is acceptable, but if you are in doubt, check a dictionary. (*The American Heritage Dictionary* has notes on usage following the definitions of hundreds of its words.)

In any case, if you are a native speaker of English, when you read your draft you will probably detect unidiomatic expressions such as *superior with*; that is, you will hear something that sounds odd, and so you will change it to something that sounds familiar, idiomatic—here, *superior to*. If any unidiomatic expressions remain in your essay, the trouble may be that an effort to write impressively has led you to use unfamiliar language. A reader who sees such unidiomatic language may sense that you are straining for an effect. Try rewriting the passage in your own voice.

If English is not your first language and you are not yet fluent in it, plan to spend extra time revising and editing your work. Check prepositional phrases with special care. In addition to using a college edition of an English language dictionary, consult reference works designed with the international or bilingual student in mind. One compact book our students find particularly useful is Michael Swan's *Practical English Usage*, published by Oxford University Press. But don't neglect another invaluable resource: students who are native speakers. They will usually be able to tell you whether or not a phrase "sounds right," though they may not know why.

Glossary

a, an Use *a* before words beginning with a consonant ("a book") or with a vowel sounded as a consonant ("a one-way ticket," "a university"). Use *an* before words beginning with a vowel ("an egg") including those beginning with a silent *h* ("an egg," "an hour"). If an initial *h* is pronounced, *a* is normal ("a history course") but if the accent is not on the first syllable, *an* is acceptable, as in "*an* historian."

above Try to avoid writing *for the above reasons, in view of the above,* or *as above.* These expressions sound unpleasantly legalistic. Substitute *for these reasons,* or *therefore,* or some such expression or word.

academics Only two meanings of this noun are widely accepted: (1) "members of an institution of higher learning," and (2) "persons who are academic in background or outlook." Avoid using it to mean "academic subjects," as in "Students should pay attention not only to academics but also to recreation." Revised: "Students should pay attention not only to their courses but also to recreation."

accept, except *Accept* means "to receive with consent." *Except* means "to exclude" or "excluding."

affect, effect *Affect* is usually a verb, meaning (1) "to influence, to produce an effect, to impress," or (2) "to pretend, to put on," as in "He affected an English accent." Psychologists use it as a noun for "feeling," e.g., "The patient experienced no affect." *Effect,* as a verb, means "to bring about" ("The workers effected the rescue in less than an hour"). As a noun, *effect* means "result" ("The effect was negligible").

African American, African-American Both forms are acceptable to denote an American of African ancestry. In recent years these words have been preferred to *black.*

aggravate "To worsen, to increase for the worse," as in "Smoking aggravated the irritation." Although it is widely used to mean "annoy" ("He aggravated me"), many readers are annoyed by such a use.

all ready, already *All ready* means "everything is ready." *Already* means "by this time."

all right, alright The first of these is the preferable spelling; for some readers it is the only acceptable spelling.

all together, altogether *All together* means that members of a group act or are gathered together ("They voted all together"); *altogether* is an adverb meaning "entirely," "wholly" ("This is altogether unnecessary").

allusion, reference, illusion An *allusion* is an implied or indirect reference. "As Lincoln says" is a *reference* to Lincoln, but "As a great man has said," along with a phrase quoted from the Gettysburg Address, constitutes an *allusion* to Lincoln. *Allusion* has nothing to do with *illusion* (a deception). Note the spelling (especially the second *i*) in "disillusioned" (left without illusions, disenchanted).

almost See *most.*

a lot Two words (not *alot*).

among, between See *between.*

amount, number *Amount* refers to bulk or quantity: "A small amount of gas was still in the tank." Use *number,* not *amount,* to refer to separate (countable) units: "He did not know the number of gallons that the tank held." Similarly, "A large number of people heard the lecture" (not "a large amount of people"). And "an amount of money," but "a number of dollars."

analyzation Unacceptable; use *analysis.*

and etc. Because *etc.* is an abbreviation for *et cetera* ("and others"), the *and* in *and etc.* is redundant. (See also the entry on *et cetera.*)

and/or Acceptable, but a legalism and unpleasant-sounding. Often *or* by itself will do, as in "students who know Latin or Italian." When *or* is not enough ("Scripts for the second season of *The Sopranos* were written by Todd Kessler and/or David Chase") it is better to recast ("Scripts for the second season of *The Sopranos* were written by Todd Kessler or David Chase, or both").

ante, anti *Ante* means "before" (*antebellum,* "before the Civil War"); *anti* means "against" (*antivivisectionist*). Hyphenate *anti* before capitals (*anti-Semitism*) and before *i* (*anti-intellectual*).

anxious   Best reserved for uses that suggest anxiety ("He was anxious before the examination"), though some authorities now accept it in the sense of "eager" ("He was anxious to serve the community").

anybody   One word ("Do you know anybody here?"). If two words (*any body*), you mean any corpse ("Several people died in the fire, but the police cannot identify any body").

any more, anymore   *Any more* is used as an adjective: "I don't want any more meat" (here *any more* says something about meat). *Anymore* (one word) is used as an adverb: "I don't eat meat anymore" (here *anymore* says something about eating).

anyone   One word ("Why would anyone think that?"), unless you mean "any one thing," as in "Here are three books; you may take any one." *Anyone* is an indefinite singular pronoun meaning *any person:* "If anyone has a clue, he or she should call the police." In an astounding advertisement, the writer moved from *anyone* (singular) to *their* (third person plural) to *your* (second person): "Anyone who thinks a Yonex racquet has improved their game, please raise your hand."

area of   Like *field of* and *topic of* ("the field of literature," "the topic of politics"), *area of* can usually be deleted. "The area of marketing" equals "marketing."

around   Avoid using *around* in place of *about:* "He wrote it in about three hours." See also *centers on*.

as, like   *As* is a conjunction; use it in forming comparisons, to introduce clauses. (A clause has a subject and a verb.)

> You can learn to write, as you can learn to swim.

> Huck speaks the truth as he sees it.

Like is a preposition; use it to introduce prepositional phrases:

> He looks like me.

> Like Hamlet, Laertes has lost a father.

> She thinks like a lawyer.

A short rule: use *like* when it introduces a noun *not* followed by a verb: "Nothing grabs people like *People.*"

Writers who are fearful of incorrectly using *like* resort to cumbersome evasions: "He eats in the same manner that a pig eats." But there's nothing wrong with "He eats like a pig."

Asian, Oriental   *Asian* as a noun and as an adjective is the preferred word. *Oriental* (from *oriens*, "rising sun," "east") is in disfavor because it implies a Eurocentric view—that is, that things "oriental" are east of the European colonial powers who invented the term. Similarly, **Near East, Middle East,** and **Far East** are terms that are based on a Eurocentric view. No brief substitute has been agreed on for *Near East* and *Middle East*, but *East Asia* is now regarded as preferable to *Far East*.

as of now   Best deleted, or replaced by *now*. Not "As of now I don't smoke" but "Now I don't smoke" or "I don't smoke now" or "I don't smoke."

aspect   Literally, "a view from a particular point," but it has come to mean *topic*, as in "Several aspects should be considered." Try to get a sharper word, for example, "Several problems should be considered," or "Several consequences should be considered."

as such   Often meaningless, as in "Tragedy as such evokes pity."

as to   Usually *about* is preferable. Not "I know nothing as to the charges," but "I know nothing about the charges."

bad, badly   *Bad* used to be only an adjective ("a bad movie"), and *badly* was an adverb ("she sings badly"). In "I felt bad," *bad* describes the subject, not the verb. (Compare "I felt happy," or "I felt good about getting a raise." After verbs of appearing, such as "feel," "look," "seem," "taste," an adjective, not an adverb, is used. If you are in doubt, substitute a word for *bad*, for instance *sad*, and see what you say. Since you would say "I feel sad about his failure," you can say "I feel bad . . . .") But "badly" is acceptable and even preferred by many. Note, however, this distinction: "This meat smells bad" (an adjective describing the meat), and "Because I have a stuffed nose I smell badly" (an adverb describing my ability to smell something).

being   Do not use *being* as a main verb, as in "The trouble being that his reflexes were too slow." The result is a sentence fragment. See pages 247–49.

being that, being as   A sentence such as "Being that she was a stranger . . ." sounds like an awkward translation from the Latin. Use *because*.

beside, besides   *Beside* means "at the side of." Because *besides* can mean either "in addition to" or "other than," it is ambiguous, as in

"Something besides TB caused his death." It is best, then, to use *in addition to* or *other than*, depending on what you mean.

between Only English teachers who have had a course in Middle English are likely to know that between comes from *by twain*. And only English teachers and editors are likely to object to its use (and to call for *among*) when more than two are concerned, as in "among the three of us." Note, too, that even conservative usage accepts *between* in reference to more than two when the items are at the moment paired: "Negotiations *between* Israel and Egypt, Syria, and Lebanon seem stalled." *Between*, a preposition, takes an object ("between you and me"): not "between you and I."

biannually, bimonthly, biweekly Every two years, every two months, every two weeks (*not* twice a year, etc.). Twice a year is *semiannually*; i.e. "half yearly." Because *biannually*, *bimonthly*, and *biweekly* are commonly misunderstood, it is best to avoid them and to say "every two . . ."

Black, black Although one sometimes sees the word capitalized when it refers to race, most publishers use a lowercase letter, making it consistent with *white*, which is never capitalized. See also *African American*.

can, may When schoolchildren asked "Can I leave the room?" their teachers used to correct them thus: "You *can* leave the room if you have legs, but you *may not* leave the room until you receive permission." In short, *can* indicates physical possibility, *may* indicates permission. But because "you may not" and "why mayn't I?" sound not merely polite but stiff, *can* is usually preferred except in formal contexts.

capital, capitol A *capital* is a city that is a center of government. *Capital* can also mean wealth ("It takes capital to start a business"). A *capitol* is a building in which legislators meet. Notice the distinction in the following sentence: "Washington, D.C., is the nation's capital; the capitol ought to have a gold dome."

centers on, centers around Use *centers on*, because *center* refers to a point, not to a movement around.

Chicana, Chicano A Mexican-American (female or male, respectively; the male plural, *Chicanos*, is used for a group consisting of males and females). Although the term sometimes was felt to be derogatory, today it usually implies ethnic pride.

collective nouns   A collective noun, singular in form, names a collection of individuals. Examples: *audience, band, committee, crowd, jury, majority, minority, team.* When you are thinking chiefly of the whole as a unit, use a singular verb (and a singular pronoun, if any): "The majority rules"; "The jury is announcing its verdict." But when you are thinking of the individuals, use a plural verb (and pronoun, if any): "The majority are lawyers"; "The jury are divided and they probably cannot agree." If the plural sounds odd, you can usually rewrite: "The jurors are divided and they probably cannot agree."

compare, contrast   To *compare* is to note likenesses or differences: "Compare a motorcycle with a bicycle." To *contrast* is to emphasize differences.

complement, compliment   *Complement* as a noun means "that which completes"; as a verb, "to fill out, to complete." *Compliment* as a noun is an expression of praise; as a verb it means "to offer praise."

comprise   "To include, contain, consist of": "The university comprises two colleges and a medical school" (not "is comprised of"). Conservative authorities hold that "to be comprised of" is always incorrect, and they reject the form one often hears: "Two colleges and a medical school comprise the university." Here the word should be *compose*, not *comprise.*

concept   Should often be deleted. For "The concept of the sales tax is regressive" write "The sales tax is regressive."

contact   Because it is vague, avoid using *contact* as a verb. *Not* "I contacted him" but "I spoke with him" or "I wrote to him," or whatever.

continual, continuous   Conservative authorities hold that *continuous* means "uninterrupted," as in "It rained continuously for six hours"; *continually* means "repeated often, recurring at short intervals," as in "For a year he continually wrote letters to her."

contrast, compare   See *compare.*

could have, could of   See *of.*

criteria   Plural of *criterion;* hence it is always incorrect to speak of "a criteria," or to say "The criteria is . . ." Correct: "The criterion is simple"; "the criteria are unfair."

data   Plural of *datum.* Although some social scientists speak of "this data," "these data" is preferable: "These data are puzzling." Because the singular, *datum*, is rare and sounds odd, it is best to substitute *fact* or *figure* for *datum*.

different from   Prefer it to *different than*, unless you are convinced that in a specific sentence *different from* sounds terribly wrong, as in "These two books are more different than I had expected." (In this example, "more," not "different," governs "than." But this sentence, though correct, is awkward and therefore it should be revised: "These two books differ more than I had expected.")

dilemma   A situation requiring a choice between equally undesirable alternatives; not every difficulty or plight or predicament is a *dilemma*. Not "Her dilemma was that she had nowhere to go," but "Her dilemma was whether to go out or to stay home: one was frightening, the other was embarrassing." And note the spelling (two *m*'s, no *n*).

disinterested   Though the word is often used to mean "indifferent," "unconcerned," "uninterested," reserve it to mean "impartial": "A judge should be disinterested."

due to   Some people, holding that *due to* cannot modify a verb (as in "He failed due to illness"), tolerate it only when it modifies a noun or pronoun ("His failure was due to illness"). They also insist that it cannot begin a sentence ("Due to illness, he failed"). In fact, however, daily usage accepts both. But because it almost always sounds stiff, try to substitute *because of*, or *through*.

due to the fact that   Wordy for *because*.

each   Although many authorities hold that *each*, as a subject, is singular, even when followed by "them" ("Each of them is satisfactory"), some authorities accept and even favor the plural ("Each of them are satisfactory"). But it is usually better to avoid the awkwardness by substituting *all* for *each*: "All of them are satisfactory." When *each* refers to a plural subject, the verb must be plural: "They each have a book"; "We each are trying." *Each* cannot be made into a possessive; you cannot say "Each's opinion is acceptable."

effect   See *affect*.

e.g.   Abbreviation for *exempli gratia*, Latin "for example." It is thus different from *i.e.* (an abbreviation for *id est*, Latin for "that is"). E.g. (not italicized) introduces an example: "common pets, e.g. cats, dogs,

and birds, have few diseases that can be transmitted to humans."
I.e. (also not italicized) introduces a definition: "Pets, i.e. animals kept
for companionship, cost Americans billions of dollars annually."
Because these two abbreviations of Latin words are often confused, it
may be preferable to avoid them and use their English equivalents.

either . . . or, neither . . . nor If the subjects are singular, use a singular verb: "Either the boy or the girl is lying." If one of the subjects joined
by *or* or *nor* is plural, most grammarians say that the verb agrees with
the nearer subject, thus: "A tree or two shrubs are enough," or "Two
shrubs or a tree is enough." But because the singular verb in the second of these sentences may sound odd, follow the first construction;
that is, put the plural subject nearer to the verb and use a plural verb.
Another point about *either . . . or.* In this construction, "either" serves
as advance notice that two equal possibilities are in the offing. Beware
of putting "either" too soon, as in "Either he is a genius or a lunatic."
Better: "He is either a genius or a lunatic."

enthuse Objectionable to many readers. For "He enthused," say "He
was enthusiastic." Use *enthuse* only in the sense of "to be excessively
enthusiastic," "to gush."

et cetera, etc. Latin for "and other things"; if you mean "and other
people," you need *et al.*, short for *et alii.* Because *etc.* is vague, its use
is usually inadvisable. Not "He studied mathematics, etc." but "He
studied mathematics, history, economics, and French." Or, if the list
is long, cut it by saying something a little more informative than
etc.—for example, "He studied mathematics, history, and other liberal arts subjects." Even *and so forth* or *and so on* is preferable to *etc.*
Confine *etc.* (and most other abbreviations, including *et al.*) to footnotes, and even in footnotes try to avoid it.

Eurocentric language Language focused on Europe—for instance, the
word *Hispanic* when used to refer not to persons from Spain but
persons from Mexico and Central and South America, who may in
fact have little or no Spanish heritage. (The Latin name for Spain was
Hispania.) Similarly, the terms *Near East* and *Far East* represent a
European point of view (near to, and far from Europe), objectionable
to many persons not of European heritage. See *Asian* and *Hispanic.*

everybody, everyone These take a singular verb ("Everybody is here"),
and a pronoun referring to them is usually singular ("Everybody thinks

his problems are suitable topics of conversation"), but use a plural pronoun if the singular would seem unnatural ("Everybody was there, weren't they?"). To avoid the sexism of "Everybody thinks his problems . . . revise to "All people think their problems . . ."

examples, instances See *instances.*

except See *accept.*

exists Often unnecessary and a sign of wordiness. Not "The problem that *exists* here is" but "The problem here is."

expound Usually pretentious for *explain* or *say.* To *expound* is to give a methodical explanation of theological matters.

facet Literally "little face," especially one of the surfaces of a gem. Don't use it (and don't use *aspect* or *factor* either) to mean "part" or "topic." It is most acceptable when, close to its literal meaning, it suggests a new appearance, as when a gem is turned: "Another *facet* appears when we see this law from the taxpayer's point of view."

the fact that Usually wordy. "Because of the fact that boys played female roles in Elizabethan drama" can be reduced to "Because boys played female roles in Elizabethan drama."

factor Strictly speaking, a *factor* helps to produce a result. Although *factor* is often used in the sense of "point" ("Another factor to be studied is . . .), such use is often wordy. "The possibility of plagiarism is a factor that must be considered" simply adds up to "The possibility of plagiarism must be considered." *Factor* is almost never the precise word: "the factors behind Gatsby's actions" are, more precisely, "Gatsby's motives."

famous, notorious See *notorious.*

Far East See *Asian.*

farther, further Some purists claim that *farther* always refers to distance and *further* to time ("The gymnasium is farther than the library"; "Let us think further about this").

fatalistic, pessimistic *Fatalistic* means "characterized by the belief that all events are predetermined and therefore inevitable"; *pessimistic,* "characterized by the belief that the world is evil," or, less gloomily, "expecting the worst."

fewer, less See *less.*

field of See *area of.*

firstly, secondly Acceptable, but it is better to use *first, second.*

former, latter These words are acceptable, but they are often annoying because they force the reader to reread earlier material in order to locate what *the former* and *the latter* refer to. The expressions are legitimately used in order to avoid repeating lengthy terms, but if you are talking about an easily repeated subject—say, Lincoln and Grant—don't hesitate to replace *the former* and *the latter* with their names. The repetition will clarify rather than bore.

good, well *Good* is an adjective ("a good book"). *Well* is usually an adverb ("She writes well"). Standard English does not accept "She writes good." But Standard English requires *good* after verbs of appearing, such as "seems," "looks," "sounds," "tastes": "it looks good," "it sounds good." *Well* can also be an adjective meaning "healthy": "I am well."

graduate, graduate from Use *from* if you name the institution or if you use a substitute word as in "She graduated from high school"; if the institution (or substitute) is not named, *from* is omitted: "She graduated in 1983." The use of the passive ("She was graduated from high school") is acceptable but sounds fussy to many.

he or she, his or her These expressions are awkward, but the implicit male chauvinism in the generic use of the male pronoun ("A citizen should exercise his right to vote") may be more offensive than the awkwardness of *he or she* and *his or her.* Moreover, sometimes the male pronoun, when used for males and females, is ludicrous, as in "The more violence a youngster sees on television, regardless of his age or sex, the more aggressive he is likely to be." Do what you can to avoid the dilemma. Sometimes you can use the plural *their:* "Students are expected to hand in their papers on Monday" (instead of "The student is expected to hand in his or her paper on Monday"). Or eliminate the possessive: "The student must hand in a paper on Monday." See also *man, mankind* on page 287, and "Avoiding Sexist Lanuage," pages 94–96.

Hispanic, Latina, Latino A person who traces his or her origin to a Spanish-speaking country is a *Hispanic.* (Hispania was the Latin name for Spain.) But some people object to the term when applied to persons in the Western Hemisphere, arguing that it overemphasizes the European influence on ethnic identity and neglects the indigenous and black heritages. Many who object to *Hispanic* prefer to call a person of Latin-American descent a *Latina* (the feminine form) or a *Latino* (the masculine form), partly because these words are themselves Latin-American words. (The male plural, *Latinos*, commonly is used for a group consisting of males and females.) But many people object that these words too obscure the unique cultural heritages of, say, Mexican-Americans, Cuban-Americans, and Puerto Ricans.

hopefully   Commonly used to mean "I hope" or "It is hoped" (*"Hopefully*, the rain will stop soon"), but it is best to avoid what some consider a dangling modifier. After all, the rain itself is not hopeful. If you mean "I hope the rain will stop soon," say exactly that. Notice, too, that *hopefully* is often evasive. If the president of the college says, "Hopefully tuition will not rise next year," don't think that you have heard a promise to fight against an increase; you only have heard someone evade making a promise. In short, confine *hopefully* to its adverbial use, meaning "in a hopeful manner": "Hopefully he uttered a prayer."

however   Independent clauses (for instance, "He tried" and "He failed") should not be linked with a *however* preceded by a comma. *In*correct: "He tried, however he failed." What is required is a period ("He tried. However, he failed") or a semicolon before *however* ("He tried; however, he failed).

the idea that   Usually dull and wordy. Not "The idea that we grow old is frightening," but "That we grow old is frightening," or (probably better) "Growing old is frightening."

identify   When used in the psychological sense, "to associate oneself closely with a person or an institution," it is preferable to include a reflexive pronoun, thus: "He identified himself with Hamlet," *not* "He identified with Hamlet."

i.e.   Latin for *id est*, "that is." The English words are preferable to the Latin abbreviation. On the distinction between *i.e.* and *e.g.*, see *e.g.*

immanent, imminent   *Immanent*, "remaining within, intrinsic"; *imminent*, "likely to occur soon, impending."

imply, infer   The writer or speaker *implies* (suggests); the perceiver *infers* (draws a conclusion): "Karl Marx implied that . . . but his modern disciples infer from his writings that . . . ." Although *infer* is widely used for *imply*, preserve the distinction.

incidence, incident   The *incidence* is the extent or frequency of an occurrence: "The incidence of violent crime in Tokyo is very low." The plural, *incidences*, is rarely used: "The incidences of crime and of fire in Tokyo . . . ." An *incident* is one occurrence: "The incident happened yesterday." The plural is *incidents:* "The two incidents happened simultaneously."

individual   Avoid using the word to mean only "person": "He was a generous individual." But it is precise when it implicitly makes a contrast with a group: "In a money-mad society, he was a generous individual"; "Although the faculty did not take a stand on this issue, faculty members as individuals spoke out."

instances   Instead of *in many instances* use *often*. Strictly speaking an *instance* is not an object or incident in itself but one offered as an example. Thus "another instance of his failure to do his duty" (not "In three instances he failed to do his duty").

irregardless   Unacceptable; use *regardless*.

it is   Usually this expression needlessly delays the subject: "It is unlikely that many students will attend the lecture" could just as well be "Few students are likely to attend the lecture."

its, it's   The first is a possessive pronoun ("The flock lost its leader"); the second is a contraction of *it is* ("It's a wise father that knows his child."). You'll have no trouble if you remember that the possessive pronoun *its*, like other possessive pronouns such as *our, his, their*, does *not* use an apostrophe.

kind of   Singular, as in "That kind of movie bothers me." (*Not:* "Those kind of movies bother me.") If, however, you are really talking about more than one kind, use *kinds* and be sure that the demonstrative pronoun and the verb are plural: "Those kinds of movies bother me." Notice also that the phrase is *kind of*, not *kind of a*. Not "What *kind of a* car does she drive?" but "What *kind of* car does she drive?"

Latina, Latino   See *Hispanic*.

latter   See *former*.

lay, lie   *To lay* means "to put, to set, to cause to rest." It takes an object: "May I lay the coats on the table?" The past tense and the participle are *laid:* "I laid the coats on the table"; "I have laid the coats on the table." *To lie* means "to recline," and it does not take an object: "When I am tired I lie down." The past tense is *lay;* the participle is *lain:* "Yesterday I lay down"; "I have lain down hundreds of times without wishing to get up."

lend, loan   The usual verb is *lend:* "Lend me a pen." The past tense and the participle are both *lent. Loan* is a noun: "This isn't a gift, it's a loan." But, curiously, *loan* as a verb is acceptable in past forms: "I loaned him my bicycle." In its present form ("I often loan money") it is used chiefly by bankers.

less, fewer   *Less* (as an adjective) refers to bulk amounts (also called mass nouns): less milk, less money, less time. *Fewer* refers to separate (countable) items: fewer glasses of milk, fewer dollars, fewer hours.

lifestyle, life-style, life style   All three forms are acceptable, but because many readers regard the expression as imprecise, try to find a substitute such as *values.*

like, as   See *as.*

literally   It means "to the letter," "exactly as stated," and "strictly in accord with the primary meaning; not metaphorically." It is not a mere intensive. "He was literally dead" means that he was a corpse; if he was merely exhausted, *literally* won't do. You cannot be "literally stewed" (except by cannibals), "literally tickled pink," or "literally walking on air."

loose, lose   *Loose* is an adjective ("The nail is loose"); *lose* is a verb ("Don't lose the nail").

the majority of   Usually a wordy way of saying *most.* Of course if you mean "a bare majority," say so; otherwise *most* will usually do. Certainly "The majority of the basement is used for a cafeteria" should be changed to "Most of the basement is used for a cafeteria." *Majority* can take either a singular verb or a plural verb. When *majority* refers to a collection—for example, a group acting as a body—the verb is singular, as in "The majority has withdrawn its support from the mayor." But when *majority* refers to members of a group acting as individuals, as in "The majority of voters in this district vote Republican," a plural verb (here, "vote") is usually preferred. If either construction sounds odd, use "most," with a plural verb: "Most voters in this district vote Republican."

man, mankind   The use of these words in reference to males and females sometimes is ludicrous, as in "Man, being a mammal, breast-feeds his young." But even when not ludicrous the practice is sexist, as in "man's brain" and "the greatness of mankind." Consider using such words as *human being, person, humanity, people.* Similarly, for "manmade," *artificial* or *synthetic* may do. See also "Avoiding Sexist Lanuage," pages 94–96.

may, can   See *can.*

me   The right word in such expressions as "between you and me" and "They gave it to John and me." It is the object of verbs and of prepositions. In fact, *me* rather than *I* is the usual form after any verb, including the verb *to be;* "It is me" is nothing to be ashamed of. See the entry on *myself.*

medium, media   *Medium* is singular, *media* is plural: "TV is the medium to which most children are most exposed. Other media include film, radio, and publishing." It follows, then, that *mass media* takes a plural verb: "The mass media exert an enormous influence."

Middle East   See *Asian.*

might of, might have; must of, must have   *Might of* and *must of* are colloquial for *might have* and *must have.* In writing, use the *have* form: "He might have cheated; in fact, he must have cheated."

more   Avoid writing a false (incomplete) comparison such as: "His essay includes several anecdotes, making it more enjoyable." Delete "more" unless there really is a comparison with another essay. On false comparisons see also the entry on *other.*

most, almost   Although it is acceptable in speech to say "most everyone" and "most anybody," it is preferable in writing to use "almost everyone," "almost anybody." But of course: "Most students passed."

myself   *Myself* is often mistakenly used for *I* or *me,* as in "They praised Tony and myself," or "Prof. Chen and myself examined the dead rat." In the first example, *me* is the word to use; after all, if Tony hadn't been there the sentence would say, "They praised me." (No one would say, "They praised myself.") Similarly, in the second example if Prof. Chen were not involved, the sentence would run, "I examined the dead rat," so what is needed here is simply "Prof. Chen and I examined . . . ."

In general, use *myself* only when (1) it refers to the subject of the sentence ("I look out for myself"; "I washed myself") or (2) when it is an intensive: ("I myself saw the break-in"; "I myself have not experienced racism").

nature   You can usually delete *the nature of*, as in "The nature of my contribution is not political but psychological."

Near East   See *Asian.*

needless to say   The reader may well wonder why you go on to say it. Of course this expression is used to let readers know that they are probably familiar with what comes next, but usually *of course* will better serve as this sign.

Negro   Capitalized, whether a noun or an adjective, though *white* is not. In recent years *Negro* has been replaced by *black* or African-American.

neither . . . nor   See *either . . . or.*

nobody, no one, none   *Nobody* and *no one* are singular, requiring a singular verb ("Nobody believes this," "No one knows"); but they can be referred to by a plural pronoun: "Nobody believes this, do they?" "No one knows, do they?" *None*, though it comes from *no one*, almost always requires a plural verb when it refers to people ("Of the ten people present, none are students") and a singular verb when it refers to things ("Of the five assigned books, none is worth reading").

not only . . . but also   Keep in mind these two points: (1) many readers object to the omission of "also" in such a sentence as "She not only brought up two children but practiced law"—it's preferable to write "She not only brought up two children but she also practiced law"— and (2) all readers dislike a faulty parallel, as in "She not only is bringing up two children but practices law." ("Is bringing up" needs to be paralleled with "is also practicing.")

notorious   Widely and unfavorably known; not merely famous, but famous for some discreditable trait or deed.

not . . . un-   Such an expression as "not unfamiliar" is useful only if it conveys something different from the affirmative. Compare the frostiness of "I am not unfamiliar with your methods" with "I am familiar with your methods." If the negative has no evident advantage, use the affirmative.

number, amount   See *amount*.

a number of   Requires a plural verb: "A number of women are presidents of corporations." But when *number* is preceded by *the* it requires a singular verb: "The number of women who are presidents is small." (The plural noun after *number* of course may require a plural verb, as in "women are," but the subject of the sentence is *the number*, which itself remains singular; hence its verb is singular, as in "is small.")

of   Be careful not to use *of* when *have* is required. Not "He might of died in the woods," but "He might have died in the woods." Note that what we often hear as "would've" or "should've" or "must've" or "could've" is "would have" or "should have" or "must have" or "could have," *not* "would of," etc.

off of   Use *off* or *from*: "Take if off the table"; "He jumped from the bridge."

often-times   Use *often* instead.

old-fashioned, old-fashion   Only the first is acceptable.

one   British usage accepts the shift from *one* to *he* in "One begins to die the moment he is born," but American usage prefers "One begins to die the moment one is born." A shift from *one* to *you* ("One begins to die the moment you are born") is unacceptable. As a pronoun, *one* can be useful in impersonal statements such as the sentence about dying, at the beginning of this entry, where it means "a person," but don't use it as a disguise for yourself ("One objects to Smith's argument"). Try to avoid *one*; one *one* usually leads to another, resulting in a sentence that, in James Thurber's words, "sounds like a trombone solo" ("If one takes oneself too seriously, one begins to . . ."). See also *you*.

one of   Takes a plural noun, and if this is followed by a clause, the preferred verb is plural: "one of those students who are," "one of those who feel." Thus, in such a sentence as "One of the coaches who have resigned is now seeking reinstatement," notice that "have" is correct; the antecedent of "who" (the subject of the verb) is "coaches," which is plural. Coaches have resigned, though "one . . . is seeking reinstatement." But in such an expression as "one out of a hundred," the following verb may be singular or plural ("One out of a hundred is," "One out of a hundred are").

only Be careful where you put it. The classic textbook example points out that in the sentence "I hit him in the eye," *only* can be inserted in seven places (beginning in front of "I" and ending after "eye") with at least six different meanings. Try to put it just before the expression it qualifies. Thus, not "Presidential aides are only responsible to one person," but "Presidential aides are responsible to only one person" (or "to one person only").

oral, verbal See *verbal*.

Oriental See *Asian*.

other Often necessary in comparisons. "No American president served as many terms as Franklin Roosevelt" absurdly implies that Roosevelt was not an American president. The sentence should be revised to "No other American president served as many terms as Franklin Roosevelt."

per Usually it sounds needlessly technical ("twice per hour") or disturbingly impersonal ("as per your request"). Preferable: "twice an hour," "according to your request," or "as you requested."

per cent, percent, percentage The first two of these are interchangeable; both mean "per hundred," "out of a hundred," as in "Ninety per cent (or percent) of the students were white." *Per cent* and *percent* are always accompanied by a number (written out, or in figures). It is usually better to write out *per cent* or *percent* than to use a per cent sign (12%), except in technical or statistical papers. *Percentage* means "a proportion or share in relation to the whole," as in "A very large percentage of the student body is white." Many authorities insist that *percentage* is never preceded by a number. Do not use percentage to mean "a few," as in "Only a percentage of students attended the lecture"; a percentage can be as large as 99.99. It is usually said that with *per cent, percent,* and *percentage*, whether the verb is singular or plural depends on the number of the noun that follows the word, thus: "Ninety percent of their books are paperbacks"; "Fifty percent of their library is worthless"; "A large percentage of their books are worthless." But some readers (including the authors of this book) prefer a singular verb after *percentage* unless the resulting sentence is as grotesque as this one: "A large percentage of the students is unmarried." Still, rather than say a "percentage . . . are," we would recast the sentence: "A large percentage of the student body is unmarried," or "Many (or "Most," or whatever) of the students are unmarried."

per se Latin for "by itself." Usually sounds legalistic or pedantic, as in "Meter per se has an effect."

pessimistic See *fatalistic.*

phenomenon, phenomena The plural is *phenomena;* thus, "these phenomena" but "this phenomenon."

plus Unattractive and imprecise as a noun meaning "asset" or "advantage" ("When he applied for the job, his appearance was a plus"), and equally unattractive as a substitute for *moreover* ("The examination was easy, plus I had studied") or as a substitute for *and* ("I studied the introduction plus the first chapter").

politics Preferably singular ("Ethnic politics has been a strong force for a century") but a plural verb is acceptable.

precede, proceed To *precede* is to go before or ahead ("*X* precedes *Y*"). To *proceed* is to go forward ("The spelling lesson proceeded smoothly").

prejudice, prejudiced *Prejudice* is a noun: "It is impossible to live entirely without prejudice." But use the past participle *prejudiced* as an adjective: "They were prejudiced against me from the start."

preventative, preventive Both are acceptable but the second form is the form now used by writers on medicine ("preventive medicine"); *preventative* therefore has come to seem amateurish.

principal, principle *Principal* is (1) an adjective meaning "main," "chief," "most important" ("The principal arguments against IQ testing are three"), and (2) a noun meaning "the chief person" ("Ms. Murphy was the principal of Jefferson High") or "the chief thing" ("She had so much money she could live on the interest and not touch the principal"). *Principle* is always a noun meaning "rule" or "fundamental truth" ("It was against his principles to eat meat").

prior to Pretentious for *before.*

protagonist Literally, the first actor, and, by extension, the chief actor. It is odd, therefore, to speak of "the protagonists" in a single literary work or occurrence. Note also that the prefix is *proto*, "first," not *pro*, "for"; it does *not* mean one who strives for something.

quite Usually a word to delete, along with *definitely, pretty, rather,* and *very. Quite* used to mean "completely" ("I quite understand") but it has come also to mean "to a considerable degree," and so it is ambiguous as well as vague.

quotation, quote Quotation is a noun, quote is a verb. "I will quote Churchill" is fine, but not "these quotes from Churchill." And remember, you may *quote* one of Hamlet's speeches, but Hamlet does not *quote* them; he says them.

rather Avoid use with strong adjectives. "Rather intelligent" makes sense, but "rather tremendous" does not. "Rather brilliant" probably means "bright"; "rather terrifying" probably means "frightening," "rather unique" probably means "unusual." Get the right adjective, not *rather* and the wrong adjective.

the reason . . . is because Usually *because* is enough (not "The reason they fail is because they don't study," but simply "They fail because they don't study"). Similarly, *the reason why* can usually be reduced to *why.* Notice, too, that because *reason* is a noun, it cannot neatly govern a *because* clause: not "The reason for his absence is because he was sick," but "The reason for his absence was illness."

rebut, refute To rebut is to argue against, but not necessarily successfully. If you mean "to disprove," use *disprove* or *refute.*

in regard to, with regard to Often wordy for *about, concerning,* or *on,* and sometimes even these words are unnecessary. Compare: "She knew a great deal in regard to jazz"; "She knew a great deal about jazz." Compare: "Hemingway's story is often misunderstood with regard to Robert Wilson's treatment of Margot Macomber"; "In Hemingway's story, Robert Wilson's treatment of Margot Macomber is often misunderstood."

relate to Usually a vague expression, best avoided, as in "I can relate to Hedda Gabler." Does it mean "respond favorably to," "identify myself with," "interact with" (and how can a reader "interact with" a character in a play?). Use *relate to* only in the sense of "have connection with" (as in "How does your answer relate to my question?"); even in such a sentence a more exact expression is preferable.

repel, repulse Both verbs mean "to drive back," but only *repel* can mean "to cause distaste," "to disgust," as in "His obscenities repelled the audience."

respectfully, respectively *Respectfully* means "with respect, showing respect" ("Japanese students and teachers bow respectfully to
each other"). *Respectively* means "each in turn" ("Professors Arnott,
Bahktian, and Cisneros teach, respectively, chemistry, business, and
biology").

sarcasm Heavy, malicious sneering ("Oh you're really a great friend,
aren't you?" addressed to someone who won't lend the speaker ten
dollars). If the apparent praise, which really communicates dispraise,
is at all clever, conveying, say, a delicate mockery or wryness, it is
irony, not sarcasm.

seem Properly it suggests a suspicion that appearances may be decep-
tive: "He seems honest (but . . .)." Don't say "The book seems to lack
focus" if you believe it does lack focus.

semiannually, semimonthly, semiweekly See *biannually.*

sexist language Language that takes males as the norm. For
example, the use of *he* with reference to females as well as to
males ("When a legislator votes, he takes account of his con-
stituency"), like the use of *man* for all human beings ("Man is
a rational animal"), is now widely perceived as subtly (or not
so subtly) favoring males. See the entries on *he or she; man,
mankind;* and *s/he.*

shall, will, should, would The old principle held that in the first
person *shall* is the future indicative of *to be* and *should* the condi-
tional ("I shall go," "We should like to be asked"); and that *will* and
would are the forms for the second and third persons. When the forms
are reversed ("I will go," "Government of the people . . . shall not perish from the earth"), determination is expressed. But today almost
nobody adheres to these principles. Indeed, *shall* (except in questions)
sounds stilted to many ears.

s/he This relatively new gender-free pronoun ("As soon as the student receives the forms, s/he should fill them out") is sometimes used
in place of *he or she* or *she or he,* which are used to avoid the sexism implied when the male pronoun "he" is used to stand for women
as well as men ("As soon as the student receives the forms, he should
fill them out"). Other, less noticeable and therefore better ways of
avoiding sexist writing are suggested under *he or she.* See also "Avoiding Sexist Language," pages 94–96.

simplistic   Means "falsely simplified by ignoring complications." Do not confuse it with *simplified*, whose meanings include "reduced to essentials" and "clarified."

since, because   Traditional objections to *since*, in the sense of "because," have all but vanished. Note, however, that when *since* is ambiguous and may also refer to time ("Since he joined the navy, she found another boyfriend") it is better to say *because* or *after*, depending on which you mean.

situation   Overused, vague, and often unnecessary. "His situation was that he was unemployed" adds up to "He was unemployed." And "an emergency situation" is probably an emergency.

split infinitives   The infinitive is the verb form that merely names the action, without indicating when or by whom performed ("walk," rather than "walked" or "I walk"). Grammarians, however, developed the idea that the infinitive was "to walk," and they held that one should not separate or split the two words: "to quickly walk." But almost all authorities today accept this usuage. Notice, however, that often the inserted word can be deleted ("to really understand" is "to understand"), and that if many words are inserted between *to* and the verb, the reader may get lost ("to quickly and in the remaining few pages before examining the next question conclude").

stanza   See *verse*.

subjunctive   For the use of the subjunctive with conditions contrary to fact (for instance, "If I were you"), see the entry on *was, were*. The subjunctive is also used in *that* clauses followed by verbs demanding, requesting, or recommending: "She asked that the students be prepared to take a test." But because this last sort of sentence sounds stiff, it is better to use an alternative construction, such as "She asked the students to prepare for a test."

than, then   *Than* is used chiefly in making comparisons ("German is harder than French"), but also after "rather," "other," and "else" ("I'd rather take French than German"; "He thinks of nothing other than sex"). *Then* commonly indicates time ("She took German then, but now she takes French"; "Until then, I'll save you a seat"), but it may also mean "in that case" ("It's agreed, then, that we'll all go"), or "on the other hand" ("Then again, she may find German easy"). The simplest guide: Use *than* after comparisons and after "rather," "other," "else"; otherwise use *then*.

that, which, who   Many pages have been written on these words; opinions differ, but you will offend no one if you observe the following principles. (1) Use *that* in restrictive (that is, limiting) clauses: "The rocking chair that creaks is on the porch." (2) Use *which* in nonrestrictive (in effect, parenthetic) clauses. "The rocking chair, which creaks, is on the porch." (See pages 258–60.) The difference between these two sentences is this: In the first, one rocking chair is singled out from several—the one that creaks; in the second, the fact that the rocking chair creaks is simply tossed in, and is not added for the purpose of identifying the one chair out of several. (3) Use *who* for people, in restrictive and in nonrestrictive clauses: "The women who were playing poker ignored the men"; "The women, who were playing poker, ignored the men." But note that often *that*, *which*, and *who* can be omitted: "The creaky rocking chair is on the porch"; "The women playing poker ignored the men." "The women, playing poker, ignored the men." In general, omit these words if the sentence remains clear.

their, there, they're   The first is a possessive pronoun: "Chaplin and Keaton made their first films before sound tracks were developed." The second, *there*, sometimes refers to a place ("Go there," "Do you live there?"), and sometimes is what is known in grammar as an introductory expletive ("There are no solutions to this problem"). The third, *they're*, is a contraction of "they are" ("They're going to stay for dinner").

this   Often refers vaguely to "what I have been saying." Does it refer to the previous sentence, the previous paragraph, the previous page? Try to modify it by being specific: "This last point"; "This clue gave the police all they needed."

thusly   Unacceptable; *thus* is an adverb and needs no adverbial ending.

till, until   Both are acceptable, but *until* is preferable because *till*—though common in speech—looks literary in print. The following are *not* acceptable: *til, 'til, 'till*.

to, too, two   *To* is toward; *too* is either "also" ("She's a lawyer, too") or "excessively" ("It's too hot"); *two* is one more than one ("Two is company").

topic of   See *area of.*

toward, towards   Both are standard English; *toward* is more common in the United States, *towards* in Great Britain.

type   Often colloquial (and unacceptable in most writing) for *type of,* as in "this type teacher." But *type of* is not especially pleasing either. Better to write "this kind of teacher." And avoid using *type* as a suffix: "essay-type examinations" are essay examinations; "natural-type ice cream" is natural ice cream. Sneaky manufacturers make "Italian-type cheese," implying that their domestic cheese is imported and at the same time protecting themselves against charges of misrepresentation.

unique   The only one of its kind. Someone or something therefore cannot be "rather unique" or "very unique" or "somewhat unique." Instead of saying "rather unique," say *rare,* or *unusual,* or *extraordinary,* or whatever seems to be the best word.

U.S., United States   Generally, *United States* is preferable to *U.S.,* except when used repeatedly as an adjective, in which case, *U.S.* is less cumbersome.

usage   Don't use *usage* where *use* will do, as in "Here Vonnegut completes his usage of dark images." *Usage* properly implies a customary practice that has created a standard: "Usage has eroded the difference between 'shall' and 'will.'"

use of   The use of *use of* is usually unnecessary. "Through the use of setting he conveys a sense of foreboding" may be reduced to "The setting conveys . . ." or "His setting conveys . . ."

utilize, utilization   Often inflated for *use* and *using,* as in "The infirmary has noted that it is sophomores who have most utilized the counseling service." But when one means "find an effective use for," *utilize* may be the best word, as in (here we borrow from *The American Heritage Dictionary*), "The teachers were unable to utilize the new computers," where *use* might wrongly suggest that the teachers could not operate the computers.

verbal   Often used where *oral* would be more exact. *Verbal* simply means "expressed in words," and thus a *verbal agreement* may be either written or spoken. If you mean spoken, call it an *oral agreement.*

verse, stanza A *verse* is a single line of a poem; a *stanza* is a group of lines, commonly bound by a rhyme scheme. But in speaking or writing about songs, usage sanctions *verse* for *stanza*, as in "Second verse, same as the first."

viable A term from physiology, meaning "capable of living" (for example, referring to a fetus at a stage of its development). Now pretentiously used and overused, especially by politicians and journalists, to mean "workable," as in "a viable presidency." Avoid it.

was, were Use the subjunctive form—*were* (rather than *was*)—in expressing a wish ("I wish I were younger") and in "if-clauses" that are contrary to fact ("If I were rich," "If I were you . . .").

we If you mean *I*, say *I*. Not "The first fairy tale we heard" but "the first fairy tale I heard." (But of course *we* is appropriate in some statements: "We have all heard fairy tales"; "If we look closely at the evidence, we can probably agree that . . . .") The rule: Don't use *we* as a disguise for *I*. See pages 107–09.

well See *good.*

well known, widely known Athletes, performers, politicians, and such folk are not really *well known* except perhaps by a few of their friends and their relatives; use *widely known* if you mean they are known (however slightly) to many people.

which Often can be deleted. "Students are required to fill out scholarship applications which are lengthy" can be written "Students are required to fill out lengthy scholarship applications." Another example: "*The Tempest*, which is Shakespeare's last play, was written in 1611"; "*The Tempest*, Shakespeare's last play, was written in 1611," or "Shakespeare wrote his last play, *The Tempest*, in 1611." For the distinction between *which* and *that*, see also the entry on *that.*

while Best used in a temporal sense, meaning "during the time": "While I was speaking, I suddenly realized that I didn't know what I was talking about." While it is not wrong to use *while* in a non-temporal sense, meaning "although" (as at the beginning of this sentence), it is better to use *although* in order to avoid any ambiguity.

Note the ambiguity in: "While he was fond of movies he chiefly saw westerns." Does it mean "Although he was fond of movies," or does it mean "During the time when he was fond of movies"? Another point: Do not use *while* if you mean *and;* "First-year students take English 1-2, while sophomores take English 10-11" (substitute *and* for *while*).

who, whom   Strictly speaking, *who* must be used for subjects, even when they look like objects: "He guessed who would be chosen." (Here *who* is the subject of the clause "who would be chosen.") *Whom* must be used for the objects of a verb, verbal (gerund, participle), or preposition: "Whom did she choose?"; "Whom do you want me to choose?"; "To whom did he show it?" We may feel stuffy in writing "Whom did she choose?" or "Whom are you talking about?" but to use *who* is certain to annoy some reader. Often you can avoid the dilemma by rewriting: "Who was chosen?"; "Who is the topic of conversation?" See also the entry on *that.*

whoever, whomever   The second of these is the objective form. It is often incorrectly used as the subject of a clause. Incorrect: "Open the class to whomever wants to take it." The object of "to" is not "whomever" but is the entire clause—"whoever wants to take it"— and of course "whoever" is the subject of "wants."

who's, whose   The first is a contraction of *who is* ("I'm everybody who's nobody"). The second is a possessive pronoun: "Whose book is it?" "I know whose it is."

will, would   See *shall* and also *would.*

would   "I would think that" is a wordy version of "I think that." (On the mistaken use of *would of* for *would have,* see also the entry on *of.*)

you   In relatively informal writing, *you* is ordinarily preferable to the somewhat stiff *one:* "If you are addicted to cigarettes, you may find it helpful to join Smokenders." (Compare: "If one is addicted to cigarettes, one may . . .") But because the direct address of *you* may sometimes descend into nagging, it is usually better to write: "Cigarette addicts may find it helpful . . ." Certainly a writer (you?) should not assume that the reader is guilty of vices ("You should not molest children") unless the essay is clearly aimed at an audience that admits to these vices, say a pamphlet directed to child molesters who are seeking help. Thus, it is acceptable to say, "If you are a poor speller," but it is not acceptable to say, to the general reader, "You should improve your spelling"; the reader's spelling may not need improvement. And avoid *you* when the word cannot possibly apply to the reader: "A hundred years ago you were faced with many diseases that now have been eradicated." Something like "A hundred years ago people were faced . . ." is preferable.

your, you're   The first is a possessive pronoun ("your book"); the second is a contraction of *you are* ("You're mistaken").

CHAPTER TWELVE

DOCUMENTATION

Documentation

One purpose of documentation is to enable your readers to retrace your steps, to find your source and to read what you read—whether you read it in the library, on the Internet, or in today's newspaper. To make this possible, you must give your readers enough information to locate and identify each source you cite. For printed sources, this information generally includes:

- the author
- the publisher
- the date and place of publication
- a page number

And for electronic sources, this information includes (at minimum):

- the site address
- the date on which you accessed the information.

The way this information is presented varies from discipline to discipline: Sociologists, for example, present the date of publication more prominently than do historians; engineers usually list their sources by number at the end of a research work and in order of their appearance in the text; and literary critics list sources alphabetically by authors' names. In the following pages we discuss in detail two of the most widely used systems of documentation: the Modern Language Association (or MLA) and the American Psychological Association (or APA). At the end of the chapter we provide information on where you can obtain guidance on other systems of documentation.

MLA Format

Citations within the Text   Brief parenthetic citations within the body of the essay are made clear by a list of your sources, entitled Works Cited, appended to the essay. Thus, an item in your list of Works Cited will clarify such a sentence in your essay as

```
According to Angeline Goreau, Aphra Behn in her

novels continually contradicts "the personal

politics she had defended from the outset of her

career as a writer" (252).
```

This citation means that the words inside the quotation marks appear on page 252 of a source written by Goreau, which will be listed in Works Cited. More often than not the parenthetic citation appears at the end of a sentence, as in the example just given, but it can appear elsewhere in the sentence. Its position will depend in part on your ear, and in part on the requirement that you point clearly to the place where your source's idea ends, and your point begins. (In the following example, the idea that follows the parenthetic citation is not Gardiner's, but the writer's own.)

```
Judith Kegan Gardiner, on the other hand,

acknowledges that Behn's work "displays its

conflicts with patriarchal authority" (215),

conflicts that appear most notably in the third

volume of Love Letters.
```

Seven points must be made about these examples:

1. Quotation marks. The closing quotation mark appears after the last word of the quotation, *not* after the parenthetic citation. Since the citation is not part of the quotation, the citation is not included within the quotation marks.

2. Omission of words (ellipsis). If the quoted words are merely a phrase, as in the example above, you do not need to indicate (by three spaced periods) that you are omitting material before or after the quotation. But if the quotation is longer than a phrase, and is not a complete sentence, you must use spaced periods within square brackets to indicate that you are omitting material. (As we note on page 217, not all citation systems require the square brackets, but the MLA now does.) If you omit material from the middle of a sentence, indicate the omission with three spaced periods inside square brackets. If you omit material from the end of the sentence, indicate the omission with three spaced periods within brackets followed by a fourth period, the sentence period. If you omit a whole sentence, the sentence period comes first, followed by by three spaced periods within brackets. If you omit material from the middle of one sentence to the end of another, the sentence period *follows* the three spaced periods inside the brackets. If the ellipsis is followed by a parenthetical citation, the sentence period follows the parenthesis. (For more on ellipses, see page 217.)

3. Addition of words. On occasion, you'll need to add a word or two to a quotation in order to clarify its meaning. If you must make such an addition—and such additions should be kept to a minimum because they're distracting—enclose the word or words in square brackets, *not* parentheses. If the quotation contains a misspelling or other error, transcribe it as it appears in the source, and insert the word "sic" (Latin for "thus," as in "thus the word appears in the source; it's not *my* error") in italics and in square brackets, thus: [*sic*].

4. Punctuation with parenthetic citations. Look again at the two examples given a moment ago. Notice that if you follow a quotation with a parenthetic citation, any necessary period, semicolon, or comma *follows* the parenthetic citation. In the first example (citing page 252 in Goreau), a period follows the citation; in the second (citing page 215 in Gardiner), a comma. In the next example, notice that the comma follows the citation.

```
Johnson insists that "these poems can be inter-

preted as Tory propaganda" (72), but his brief

analysis is not persuasive.
```

If, however, the quotation itself uses a question mark or an exclamation mark, this mark of punctuation appears *within* the closing quotation mark; even so, a period follows the parenthetic citation.

```
Jenkins-Smith is the only one to suggest doubt:

"How can we accept such a superficial reading of

these works?" (178). He therefore rejects the

entire argument.
```

5. Two or more titles by one author. If your list of Works Cited includes more than one work by an author, you will have to give additional information (either in your comment or within the parenthetic citation) in order to indicate *which* of the titles you are referring to. We will go further into this in a moment (on page 305).

6. Long (or "block") quotations. We have been talking about short quotations, which are not set off but are embedded within your own sentences. Long quotations, usually defined as more than three lines of poetry or four lines of prose, are indented ten spaces from the left, as in the example below.

```
Janet Todd explains Behn's reverence for the Stuart

monarchy:

            She was a passionate supporter of both

            Charles II and James II as not simply rulers

            but as sacred majesties, god-kings on earth,

            whose private failings in no way detracted

            from their high office [. . .]. For her,

            royalty was not patriarchal anachronism as

            it would be for liberated women writers a

            hundred years on, but a mystical state. (73)
```

In introducing a long quotation, keep in mind that a reader will have trouble reading a sentence that consists of a lead-in, a long quotation, and then a continuation of your own sentence. It's better to have a short lead-in ("Janet Todd explains Behn's reverence for the Stuart monarchy"), and then set off a long quotation that is a complete sentence or group of sentences and therefore ends with a period. To set off a quotation, begin on a new line, double-space and indent ten spaces (or one inch) from the left margin, and do *not* enclose the quotation within quotation marks. Put a period at the end of the quotation (since the quotation is a complete sentence or group of sentences and is not embedded within a longer sentence of your own), hit the space bar twice, and then, on the same line, give the citation in parentheses. Do *not* put a period after the parenthetic citation that follows a long quotation.

7. Citing a summary or a paraphrase. Even if you don't quote a source directly, but use its point in a paraphrase or a summary, you will give a citation:

```
Goreau notes (89-90) that Behn participated in public

life and in politics not only as a writer: In the

1660s she went to Antwerp as a spy for Charles II.
```

The basic point, then, is that the system of in-text citation gives the documentation parenthetically. Notice that in all but one of the previous examples the author's name is given in the student's text (rather than within the parenthetic citation). But there are several other ways of giving the citation, and we shall now look at them.

Author and Page Number in Parenthetic Citation

```
Heroines who explore their own individuality (with

varying degrees of success and failure) abound in

Chopin's work (Shinn 358).
```

It doesn't matter whether you summarize (as in this example) or quote directly; the parenthetic citation means that your source is page 358 of a work by Shinn, listed in Works Cited, at the end of your essay.

Title and Page Number in Parentheses If, as we mentioned earlier, your list of Works Cited includes two or more titles by an author, you cannot in the text simply give a name and a page reference; the reader would not know to which of the titles you are referring. Let's assume that Works Cited includes two items by Larzer Ziff. In a sentence in your essay you might specify one title, saying something like, "For example, Larzer Ziff, in *The American 1890's*, claims [. . .]." If, however, you do not mention the title in your lead-in, you will have to give the title (in a shortened form) in the parenthetic citation:

```
Larzer Ziff, for example, claims that the novel

"rejected the family as the automatic equivalent

of feminine self-fulfillment" (American 175).
```

Notice in this example that *American* is a short title for Ziff's book *The American 1890's: Life and Times of a Lost Generation*. The full title is given in Works Cited, as is the title of another work by Ziff, but the short title in the parenthetic citation is enough to direct the reader to page 175 of the correct source named in Works Cited.

Notice also that when a short title and a page reference are given in parentheses, a comma is *not* used after the title.

Author, Title, and Page Number in Parentheses We have just seen that if Works Cited includes two or more works by an author, and if in your lead-in you do not specify which work you are at the moment making use of, you will have to give the title as well as the page number in parentheses. Similarly, if for some reason you do not in your lead-in mention the name of the author, you will have to add this bit of information to the parenthetic citation, thus:

```
At least one critic has claimed that the

novel "rejected the family as the automatic

equivalent of feminine self-fulfillment"

(Ziff, American 175).
```

Notice, again, that a comma does *not* separate the title from the page reference; but notice, too, that a comma *does* separate the author's name from the title. (Don't ask us why; ask the Modern Language Association. Or just obey orders.)

A Government Document or a Work of Corporate Authorship   Treat the issuing body as the author. Thus, you will probably write something like this:

> The Commission on Food Control, in <u>Food Resources</u>
>
> <u>Today</u>, concludes that there is no danger (36-37).

A Work by Two or Three Authors   If a work is by *two or three authors*, give their names, either in the parenthetic citation (the first example below) or in a lead-in (the second example):

> Where the two other siblings strive compulsively
>
> either to correct or create problems, the sibling
>
> in the middle passively escapes from her painful
>
> family situation by withdrawing into herself
>
> (Seixas and Youcha 48-49).

or

> Barnet, Bellanca, and Stubbs suggest that the most
>
> efficient way to learn about your library's on-
>
> line resources is to consult a reference librarian
>
> (365).

If there are more than *three authors*, give the last name of the first author, followed by "et al." (an abbreviation for *et alii*, Latin for "and others"), thus:

> Gardner et al. found that . . .

or

> Sometimes even higher levels are found (Gardner et
>
> al. 83).

Parenthetic Citation of an Indirect Source (Citation of Material That Itself Was Quoted or Summarized in Your Source)   Suppose you are reading a book by Jones, and she quotes Smith, and you wish to use Smith's material. Your citation will be to Jones—the source you are using—but of course you cannot attribute Smith's words to Jones. You will have to make it clear that you are quoting not Jones but Smith, and so your parenthetic citation will look like this:

> (qtd. in Jones 84-85)

Parenthetic Citation of Two or More Works

> Some scholars have speculated that Poe died of
>
> rabies, not alcoholism (Walk 44; Hayward 173).

Note that a semicolon, followed by a space, separates the two sources.

A Work in More Than One Volume   This is a bit tricky.

1. If you have used only one volume, in Works Cited you will specify the volume, and so in your parenthetic in-text citation you will need to give only a page number—the very sort of thing illustrated by most of the examples that we have been giving.
2. If you have used more than one volume, your parenthetic citation will have to specify the volume as well as the page, thus:

> Landsdale points out that nitrite combines with
>
> hemoglobin to form a pigment which cannot carry oxy-
>
> gen (2: 370).

The reference is to page 370 of volume 2 of a work by Landsdale.

3. If, however, you are citing not a page but an entire volume—let's say volume 2—your parenthetic citation would be

```
(vol. 2)
```

Or, if you did not name the author in your lead-in, it would be

```
(Landsdale, vol. 2)
```

Notice that

- in citing a volume and page, the volume number, like the page number, is given in arabic (not roman) numerals;
- the volume number is followed by a colon, then a space, then the page number;
- abbreviations such as "vol." and "p." and "pg." are *not* used, except when citing a volume number without a page number, as illustrated in the last two examples.

An Anonymous Work   For an anonymous work, give the title in your lead-in, or give it in a shortened form in your parenthetic citation:

```
Official Guide to Food Standards includes a

statistical table nitrates (362).
```

or

```
A statistical table on nitrites is available

(Official Guide 362).
```

But double-check to make sure that the work is truly anonymous. Some encyclopedias, for example, give the authors' names quietly. If initials follow the article, these are the initials of the author's name. Check the alphabetic list of authors given at the front or back of the encyclopedia.

A Literary Work   You will specify the edition of a literary work in Works Cited—let's say Alvin Kernan's edition of *Othello*, or an edition of

Conrad's *Heart of Darkness* with a preface by Albert Guerard but because classic works of literature are widely available, and your reader may have at hand an edition different from the one that you have read, it is customary to use the following forms.

1. A novel. In parentheses give the page number of the edition you specify in Works Cited, followed by a semicolon, a space, and helpful additional information, thus:

```
(181; ch. 6)
```

or

```
(272; part 1, ch. 7).
```

2. A play. Most instructors want the act, scene, and (if the lines are numbered) the line numbers, rather than a page reference. Thus,

```
(2.4.18-23)
```

refers to lines 18–23 of the fourth scene of the second act.

If you are quoting a few words within a sentence of your own, immediately after closing the brief quotation give the citation (enclosed within parentheses), and, if your sentence ends with the quotation, put the period after the closing parenthesis.

```
That Macbeth fully understands that killing Duncan

is not a manly act but a villainous one is clear

from his words to Lady Macbeth: "I dare do all

that may become a man" (1.7.46). Moreover, even

though he goes on to kill Duncan, he does not go

on to deceive himself into thinking that his act

was noble.
```

If, however, your sentence continues beyond the citation, after the parenthetic citation put whatever punctuation may be necessary (for instance, a comma may be needed), complete your sentence, and end it with a period.

This is clear from his words, "I dare do all that

does become a man" (1.7.46), and he never loses his

awareness of true manliness.

3. A poem. Preferences vary, and you can't go wrong in citing the page, but for a poem longer than, say, a sonnet (fourteen lines), most instructors find it useful if students cite the line numbers, in parentheses, after the quotations. In your first use, preface the numerals with "line" or "lines" (not in quotation marks, of course); in subsequent citations simply give the numerals. For very long poems that are divided into books, such as Homer's *Odyssey*, give the page, a semicolon, a space, the book number, and the line number(s). The following example refers to page 327 of a title listed in Works Cited; it goes on to indicate that the passage occurs in the ninth book of the poem, lines 130–35.

(327; 9.130-35)

Long quotations (more than three lines of poetry) are indented ten spaces. As we explained on page 304, if you give a long quotation, try to give one that can correctly be concluded with a period. After the period, hit the space bar three times, and then, on the same line, give the citation in parentheses.

A Personal Interview   Probably you won't need a parenthetic citation, because you'll say something like

Cyril Jackson, in an interview, said . . .

or

According to Cyril Jackson, . . .

and when your readers turn to Works Cited, they will see that Jackson is listed, along with the date of the interview. But if you do not mention the source's name in the lead-in, you will have to give it in the parentheses, thus:

```
It has been estimated that chemical additives earn

the drug companies well over five hundred million

dollars annually (Jackson).
```

Lectures If you use in your research essay a distinctive phrase, idea, or piece of information from a class lecture or discussion, you'll want to give the speaker credit for it. If you give a signal phrase such as "In a lecture at NYU, Jones said," the parenthetic citation should include only the date of the lecture; if you don't give a signal phrase, then include the speaker's name, followed by a comma, followed by the date. For example:

```
(Cahill, Sept. 20, 2001)
```

(The entry for the lecture on the Works Cited list will contain the title of the lecture—if there is one—and the place it was given.)

Electronic Sources Follow the format for print sources. In some cases, page numbers will be available, in others, paragraphs will be numbered; in still others; no number at all will be given. Use what you have, indicating the author's name or title where necessary, as determined by context. When giving paragraph numbers, use the abbreviation "pars." (Use a comma to separate the abbreviation from the author's name or title.)

```
One lawyer argued that Monica Lewinsky was nowhere

near the White House that day (Hedges, pars. 2-3).
```

A Note on Footnotes in an Essay Using Parenthetic Citations
There are two reasons for using footnotes in an essay that chiefly uses parenthetic citations.

1. In a research paper you will of course draw on many sources, but in other kinds of papers you may be using only one source, and yet within the paper you may often want to specify a reference to a page or (for poetry) a line number, or (for a play) to an act, scene, and line number. In such a case, to append a page headed Work Cited, with a single title,

is silly; it is better to use a single footnote when you first allude to the source. Such a note can run something like this

    ¹All references are to Mary Shelley,

    <u>Frankenstein</u>, afterword by Harold Bloom (New York:

    Signet, 1965).

2. Footnotes can also be used in another way in an essay that documents sources by giving parenthetic citations. If you want to include some material that might seem intrusive in the body of the essay, you may relegate it to a footnote. For example, in a footnote you might translate a quotation given in a foreign language, or in a footnote you might write a paragraph—a sort of mini-essay—in which you offer an amplification of some point. By putting the amplification in a footnote you are signaling to the reader that it is dispensable; it is, so to speak, thrown in as something extra, something relevant but not essential to your argument.

A raised arabic numeral indicates in the body of your text that you are adding a footnote at this point. (The "insert" function of your word-processing program will insert both the raised numeral and the text of your footnote in the appropriate places in your essay; simply click "insert" at the point in the text where you want the footnote to appear, and follow the program's instructions.)

    Joachim Jeremias's <u>The Parables of Jesus</u> is

    probably the best example of this sort of book.¹

Usually the number is put at the end of a sentence, immediately after the period, but put it earlier if clarity requires you to do so.

    Helen Cam¹ as well as many lesser historians

    held this view.

The List of Works Cited   Your parenthetic documentation consists of references that become meaningful when the reader consults a list entitled Works Cited, given at the end of your essay. We give sample entries below, but see also the list of Works Cited at the end of the documented essay reprinted at the end of Chapter 9, "Using Sources" (pages 240–41).

The list of Works Cited continues the pagination of the essay; if the last page of text is 10, then the list begins on page 11. Your last name and the page number will appear in the upper right corner, half an inch from the top of the sheet. Next, type "Works Cited," centered, one inch from the top, then double-space and type the first entry. Here are the governing conventions.

Alphabetic Order

1. Arrange the list alphabetically by author, with the author's last name first.

2. List an anonymous work alphabetically under the first word of the title, or under the second word if the first word is *A, An,* or *The,* or a foreign equivalent.

3. If your list includes two or more works by one author, the work whose title comes earlier in the alphabet precedes the work whose title comes later in the alphabet.

Form on the Page

1. Begin each entry flush with the left margin, but if an entry runs to more than one line, indent five spaces for each succeeding line of the entry.

2. Double-space each entry, and double-space between entries.

From here on, things get complicated. We will begin with

books, then

films, television and radio programs (page 324),

articles in journals and newspapers (pages 324–25), and finally,

electronic sources (pages 326–30).

The forms for books are as follows.

The Author's Name   Note that the last name is given first, but otherwise the name is given as on the title page. Do not substitute initials for names written out-on the title page. (Books by more than one author are treated later in this discussion, pages 316–17.)

If your list includes two or more works by an author, the author's name is not repeated for the second title, but is represented by three hyphens followed by a period and two spaces. When you give two or more works by the same author, the sequence is determined by the alphabetic order of the titles, as in the example below, listing two books by Blassingame, where *Black* precedes *Slave*.

> Bishop, Robert. <u>American Folk Sculpture</u>. New York:
>
> Dutton, 1974.
>
> Blassingame, John W. <u>Black New Orleans, 1860–1880</u>.
>
> Chicago: U of Chicago P, 1973.
>
> ---. <u>The Slave Community: Plantation Life in the</u>
>
> <u>Antebellum South</u>. Rev. ed. New York: Oxford
>
> UP, 1979.
>
> Danto, Arthur. <u>Embodied Meanings</u>. New York:
>
> Farrar, 1994.

We have already discussed the treatment of an anonymous work; in a few moments we will discuss books by more than one author, government documents, and works of corporate authorship.

The Title   Take the title from the title page, not from the cover or the spine, but disregard any unusual typography—for instance, the use of only capital letters, or the use of & for *and*. Italicize or underline the title and subtitle. (The MLA recommends underlining rather than italicizing in texts submitted in courses or for publication because underlining may be more visible to readers.) If you choose to underline the title, use one continuous underline, but do not underline the period that concludes this part of the entry.) Example:

<u>Frankenstein: Or, The Modern Prometheus</u>.

A peculiarity: Italicizing is used to indicate the title of a book, but if a title of a book itself includes the title of a book (for instance, a book about Mary Shelley's *Frankenstein* might include the title of her novel in its own title), the title-within-the-title is neither italicized nor underlined. Thus the title would be given as (if italicized)

The Endurance of Frankenstein.

If it were underlined, it would be

<u>The Endurance of</u> Frankenstein.

Place of Publication, Publisher, and Date For the place of publication, give the name of the city (you can usually find it either on the title page or on the copyright page, which is the reverse of the title page). If several cities are listed, give only the first. If the city is not likely to be widely known, or if it may be confused with another city of the same name (for instance, Cambridge, Massachusetts, and Cambridge, England), add the abbreviated name of the state or country (Cambridge, MA, or Cambridge, Eng.).

The name of the publisher is abbreviated. Usually the first word is enough (Random House becomes Random; Little, Brown and Co. becomes Little), but if the first word is a first name, such as in Alfred A. Knopf, the surname (Knopf) is used instead. University presses are abbreviated thus: Yale UP, U of Chicago P, State U of New York P.

The date of publication of a book is given when known; if no date appears on the book, write but *not* enclosed in quotation marks, "n.d." to indicate "no date."

Here are sample entries, illustrating the points we have covered thus far:

Douglas, Ann. <u>The Feminization of American Culture</u>. New York: Knopf, 1977.

Early, Gerald. <u>One Nation Under a Groove: Motown and American Culture</u>. Hopewell, NJ: Echo, 1995.

Feitlowitz, Marguerite. <u>A Lexicon of Terror:</u>

<u>Argentina and the Legacies of Torture</u>. New

York: Oxford UP, 1998.

Frye, Northrop. <u>Fables of Identity: Studies in</u>

<u>Poetic Mythology</u>. New York: Harcourt, 1963.

---. <u>Fools of Time: Studies in Shakespearian</u>

<u>Tragedy</u>. Toronto: U of Toronto P, 1967.

Kennedy, Paul. <u>Preparing for the Twenty-First</u>

<u>Century</u>. New York: Random, 1993.

Notice that a period follows the author's name, and another period follows the title. If a subtitle is given, as it is for Feitlowitz's book, it is separated from the title by a colon and a space. A colon follows the place of publication, a comma follows the publisher, and a period follows the date.

A Book by More Than One Author   The book is alphabetized under the last name of the first author named on the title page. If there are *two or three authors*, the names of these are given (after the first author's name) in the normal order, *first name first*.

Majors, Richard, and Janet Mancini Billson. <u>Cool</u>

<u>Pose: The Dilemmas of Black Manhood in</u>

<u>America</u>. Lexington, MA: Lexington, 1992.

Notice, again, that although the first author's name is given *last name first*, the second author's name is given in the normal order. Notice, too, that a comma is put after the first name of the first author, separating the authors.

If there are *more than three authors*, give the name of only the first, and then add (but *not* enclosed within quotation marks) "et al." (Latin for "and others").

Belenky, Mary Field, et al. <u>Women's Ways of</u>

 <u>Knowing: The Development of the Self, Voice,</u>

 <u>and Mind</u>. New York: Basic Books, 1986.

Government Documents If the writer is not known, treat the government and the agency as the author. Most federal national documents are issued by the Government Printing Office (abbreviated to GPO) in Washington.

United States Congress. Office of Technology

 Assessment. <u>Computerized Manufacturing</u>

 <u>Automation Employment, Education and the</u>

 <u>Workplace</u>. Washington, DC: GPO, 1984.

Works of Corporate Authorship Begin the citation with the corporate author, even if the same body is also the publisher, as in the first example:

American Psychiatric Association. <u>Psychiatric</u>

 <u>Glossary</u>. Washington: American Psychiatric

 Association, 1984.

Carnegie Council on Policy Studies in Higher

 Education. <u>Giving Youth a Better Chance:</u>

 <u>Options for Education, Work, and Service</u>. San

 Francisco: Jossey, 1980.

A Reprint, for Instance a Paperback Version of an Older Hardback After the title, give the date of original publication (it can usually be found on the copyright page of the reprint you are using), then a period, and then the place, publisher, and date of the edition you are using. The example indicates that Rourke's book was originally published in 1931 and that the student is using the Doubleday reprint of 1953.

> Rourke, Constance. <u>American Humor</u>. 1931. Garden
>
> City, N.Y.: Doubleday, 1953.

A Book in Several Volumes

> Friedel, Frank. <u>Franklin D. Roosevelt</u>. 4 vols.
>
> Boston: Little, 1973.

If you have used more than one volume, in your essay you will (as we explained on page 307) indicate a reference to, say, page 250 of volume 3 thus: (3: 250).

If, however, you have used only one volume of the set—let's say volume 3—in your entry in Works Cited write, after the period following the date, "Vol. 3," as in the next entry:

> Friedel, Frank. <u>Franklin D. Roosevelt</u>. 4 vols.
>
> Boston: Little, 1973. Vol. 3.

In this case, the parenthetic citation will be to the page only, not to the volume and page, since a reader will understand that the page reference must be to this volume. But notice that in Works Cited, even though you say you used only volume 3, you also give the total number of volumes.

One Book with a Separate Title in a Set of Volumes

Sometimes a set of volumes with a title makes use also of a separate title for each book in the set. If you are listing such a book, use the following form:

> Churchill, Winston. <u>The Age of Revolution</u>. Vol. 3
>
> of <u>A History of the English-Speaking Peoples</u>.
>
> New York: Dodd, 1957.

A Book with an Author and an Editor

> Churchill, Winston, and Franklin D. Roosevelt.
>
> <u>The Complete Correspondence</u>. 3 vols. Ed.

Warren F. Kimball. Princeton, NJ: Princeton

UP, 1985.

Shakespeare, William. <u>The Sonnets</u>. Ed. William

Burto. New York: NAL, 1965.

If you are making use of the editor's introduction or other
editorial material, rather than of the author's work, list the book
under the name of the editor, rather than of the author, following
the form we give in a moment for "An Introduction, Foreword, or
Afterword."

A Revised Edition of a Book

Hall, James. <u>Dictionary of Subjects and Symbols in</u>

<u>Art</u>. 2nd ed. New York: Harper, 1979.

A Translated Book

Allende, Isabel. <u>The Stories of Eva Luna</u>. Trans.

Margaret Sayens Peden. New York: Atheneum,

1991.

But if you are discussing the translation itself, as opposed to the book,
list the work under the translator's name. Thus

MacAdam, Alfred, trans. <u>Family Portrait with</u>

<u>Fidel: A Memoir</u>. By Carlos Franqui. New York:

Random, 1984.

An Introduction, Foreword, or Afterword

Wolff, Cynthia Griffin. Introduction. <u>The House Of</u>

<u>Mirth</u>. By Edith Wharton. New York: Penguin,

1985. vii-xxvi.

Usually a book with an introduction or some such comparable material is listed under the name of the author of the book (here Wharton), rather than under the name of the writer of the introduction (here Wolff), but if you are referring to the apparatus rather than to the book itself, use the form just given. The words Introduction, Preface, Foreword, and Afterword are neither enclosed within quotation marks nor underlined.

A Book with an Editor but No Author   Anthologies of literature fit this description, but here we have in mind a book of essays written by various people but collected by an editor (or editors), whose name appears on the collection.

Baldick, Chris. <u>The Oxford Book of Gothic Tales</u>.

New York: Oxford UP, 1993.

A Work in a Volume of Works by One Author   The following entry indicates that a short work by Susan Sontag—an essay called "The Aesthetics of Science"—appears in a book by Sontag entitled *Styles of Radical Will*. Notice that the inclusive page numbers of the short work are cited—not merely page numbers that you may happen to refer to, but the page numbers of the entire piece.

Sontag, Susan. "The Aesthetics of Science." In

<u>Styles of Radical Will</u>. New York: Farrar,

1969. 3-34.

A Work in an Anthology—That Is, in a Collection of Works by Several Authors   There are several possibilities here. Let's assume, for a start, that you have made use of one work in an anthology. In Works Cited, begin with the author (last name first) and title of the work you are citing, not with the name of the anthologist or the title of the anthology. Here is an entry for Coleridge's poem "Kubla Khan," found on pages 501–03 in the second volume of a two-volume anthology edited by David Damrosch and several others.

Coleridge, Samuel Taylor. "Kubla Khan." <u>The</u>

<u>Longman Anthology of British Literature</u>. Ed.

```
David Damrosch et al. 2 vols. New York:

Longman, 1999. 2: 501-03.
```

Now let's assume that during the course of your essay you refer to several works, rather than to only one work in this anthology. You can, of course, list each work in the form just given. Or you can have an entry in Works Cited for Damrosch's anthology, under Damrosch's name, and then in each entry for a work in the anthology you can eliminate some of the data by simply referring to Damrosch, thus:

```
Coleridge, Samuel Taylor. "Kubla Khan." Damrosch

2: 501-03.
```

Again, this requires that you also list Damrosch's volume, thus:

```
Damrosch, David, et al., eds. The Longman

Anthology of British Literature. 2 vols. New

York: Longman, 1999.
```

The advantage of listing the anthology separately is that if you are using a dozen works from the anthology, you can shorten the dozen entries in Works Cited merely by adding one entry, that of the anthology itself. Notice, of course, that in the body of the essay you would still refer to Coleridge and to your other eleven authors, not to the editor of the anthology—but the entries in Works Cited will guide the reader to the book you have used.

A Book Review

```
Vendler, Helen. Rev. of Essays on Style. Ed. Roger

Fowler. Essays in Criticism 16 (1966):

457-63.
```

If the review has a title, give it between the period following the reviewer's name and "Rev."

If a review is anonymous, list it under the first word of the title, or under the second word if the first word is *A*, *An*, or *The*. If an anonymous review has no title, begin the entry with "Rev. of" and then give the title of the work reviewed; alphabetize the entry under the title of the work reviewed.

An Article or Essay—Not a Reprint—in a Collection   A book may consist of a collection (edited by one or more persons) of new essays by several authors. Here is a reference to one essay in such a book. (The essay, by Smith, occupies pages 178–94 in a collection edited by Lubiano.)

```
Smith, David Lionel. "What Is Black Culture?" The

    House That Race Built. Ed. Wahneema Lubiano.

    New York: Vintage, 1998. 178-94.
```

An Article or Essay Reprinted in a Collection   The previous example (Smith's essay in Lubiano's collection) was for an essay written for a collection. But some collections reprint earlier material, for example essays from journals, or chapters from books. The following example cites an essay that was originally printed in a book called *The Cinema of Alfred Hitchcock*. This essay has been reprinted in a later collection of essays on Hitchcock, edited by Arthur J. LaValley, and it was LaValley's collection that the student used.

```
Bogdanovich, Peter. "Interviews with Alfred

    Hitchcock." The Cinema of Alfred Hitchcock.

    New York: Museum of Modern Art, 1963. 15-18.

    Rpt. in Focus on Hitchcock. Ed. Albert J.

    LaValley. Englewood Cliffs, NJ: Prentice,

    1972. 28-31.
```

The student has read Bogdanovich's essay or chapter, but not in Bogdanovich's book, where it occupied pages 15–18. The student actually read the essay on pages 28–31 in a collection of writings on Hitchcock, edited by LaValley. Details of the original publication—title, date, page numbers, and so forth—were found in LaValley's collection. Almost all editors will include this information, either on the copyright page or at the foot of the reprinted essay, but sometimes they do not give the original page numbers. In such a case, you need not give the original numbers in the entry.

Notice that the entry begins with the author and the title of the work you are citing (here, Bogdanovich's interviews), not with the name of the editor of the collection or the title of the collection. In the following example, the student used an essay by Arthur Sewell; the essay was originally on pages 53–56 in a book by Sewell entitled *Character and Society in Shakespeare*, but the student encountered the piece on pages 36–38 in a collection of essays, edited by Leonard Dean, on Shakespeare's *Julius Caesar*. Here is how the entry should run:

```
Sewell, Arthur. "The Moral Dilemma in Tragedy:

    Brutus." Character and Society in

    Shakespeare. Oxford: Clarendon, 1951. 53-56.

    Rpt. in Twentieth Century Interpretations of

    Julius Caesar. Ed. Leonard F. Dean. Englewood

    Cliffs, NJ: Prentice, 1968. 36 38.
```

An Encyclopedia or Other Alphabetically Arranged Reference Work

The publisher, place of publication, volume number, and page number do *not* have to be given. For such works, list only the edition (if it is given) and the date.

For a *signed* article, begin with the author's last name. (If the article is signed with initials, check the volume for a list of abbreviations—it is usually near the front, but it may be at the rear—which will say what the initials stand for, and use the following form.)

```
Messer, Thomas. "Picasso." Encyclopedia Americana.

    1998 ed.
```

For an *unsigned article*, begin with the title of the article.

"Automation." <u>The Business Reference Book.</u> 1977 ed.

"Picasso, Pablo (Ruiz y)." <u>Encyclopaedia</u>

   <u>Britannica: Macropaedia.</u> 1985 ed.

A Film   Begin with the director's name (last name first), followed by "dir." Next give the title of the film, underlined, then a period, two spaces, the name of the studio, the date, and a period.

Spielberg, Steven, dir. <u>Saving Private Ryan.</u>

   Paramount, 1998.

A Television or Radio Program

<u>Sixty Minutes</u>. CBS. 31 Jan. 2001.

An Article in a Scholarly Journal   The title of the article is enclosed within quotation marks, and the title of the journal is underlined to indicate italics.

Some journals are paginated consecutively—the pagination of the second issue begins where the first issue leaves off; but other journals begin each issue with page 1. The forms of the citations differ slightly. First, an article in a *journal that is paginated consecutively:*

Jacobus, Mary. "Tess's Purity." <u>Essays in</u>

   <u>Criticism 26</u> (1976): 318-38.

Jacobus's article occupies pages 318–38 of volume 26, which was published in 1976. (Note that the volume number is followed by a space, and then by the year, in parentheses, and then by a colon, a space, and the page numbers of the entire article.) Because the journal is paginated consecutively, the issue number does *not* need to be specified.

For a *journal that begins each issue with page 1* (there will be four page 1's each year if such a journal is a quarterly), the issue number must be given. After the volume number, type a period and (without hitting the space bar) the issue number, as in the next example.

```
Spillers, Hortense J. "Martin Luther King and the

    Style of the Black Sermon." The Black Scholar

    3.1 (1971): 14-27.
```

Spillers's article appeared in the first issue of volume 3 of *The Black Scholar.*

An Article in a Weekly, Biweekly, or Monthly Publication   The date and page numbers are given, but volume numbers and issue numbers are usually omitted for these publications. The following example is for an article in a weekly publication:

```
McCabe, Bernard. "Taking Dickens Seriously."

    Commonwealth 14 May 1965: 245-46.
```

An Article in a Newspaper   Because a newspaper usually consists of several sections, a section number or a capital letter may precede the page number. The example indicates that an article begins on page 1 of section 1 and is continued on a later page.

```
Bennet, James. "Judge Cites Possible Breaches of

    Ethics Guidelines by Starr." New York Times 8

    Aug. 1998. Sec. 1: 1;.
```

An Interview   The citation gives the name of the person you interviewed, the form of the interview ("personal," "telephone," "e-mail"), and the date.

```
Curley, Michael. Personal interview. 3 Jul. 2000.
```

A Lecture   In addition to the date of the lecture and the name of the speaker, the citation should include the title of the presentation (if there is one) and the place it was given. If there is no title, use a descriptive word or phrase such as "class lecture," but do not use quotation marks. If the lecture was sponsored by a particular organization or group, give that information before the date.

Cahill, Patricia A. Class lecture on <u>Othello</u>.

Emory Univ. 20 Sept. 1999.

McNamara, Eileen. "Truth and Ethics in Writing."

The Writers Writing for a Living Lecture.

Wellesley College Writing Program, Wellesley,

MA. 10 Feb. 1999.

Portable Database Sources Material obtained from a portable database, such as a CD-ROM, magnetic tape, or diskette, is treated like print material, but with one important difference: You must specify the physical form of the source. This information comes after the underlined title of the source, and before the city of publication.

<u>Database of African-American Poetry, 1760–1900</u>.

CD-ROM. Alexandria, VA: Chadwyck-Healy, 1995.

Gates, Henry Louis, and Kwame Anthony Appiah, eds.

<u>Encarta Africana</u>. CD-ROM. Redmond, WA:

Microsoft, 1999.

If the database is periodically published and updated, then some additional information is required. You must include the original date of publication of the material you're using, as well as the date of publication for the database. And if the source of the information is not also the distributor (the MLA publishes the CD-ROM version of the MLA International Bibliography, for example, but SilverPlatter distributes it), you must include the distributor (or vendor's) name as well.

Odygaard, Floyd D. P. "California's Collodion

Artist: The Images of William Dunniway."

<u>Military Images</u> 1995 16.5: 14–19. <u>America:</u>

<u>History and Life on Disc</u>. CD-ROM. ABC-Clio.

Winter 1997–98.

On-line Sources On-line sources are treated like books and articles, with four major (and many minor) exceptions:

- The **Internet address** of the source is given in angle brackets at the end of the entry.

- The **date accessed**—the date on which *you* found the source—is included in the citation.

- **Page numbers** are included in the citation *only* if the source is paginated. (This is often the case with full-text on-line versions of books and journal articles, in which case the pagination follows that of the print source.)

- Sometime paragraphs are numbered; the citation gives **paragraph numbers** when the sources provides them.

The basic format for an on-line source follows that of a print source. You give, in the following order,

- author,
- title,
- publication information (including date of original publication, if applicable), and
- page or paragraph numbers if available.

Then you give additional information—as much as is applicable and available—in the following order.

- name of database, project, periodical, or site (underlined),
- number of volume, issue, or version,
- date of posting,
- name of site sponsor (if applicable),
- date *you* consulted the material, and
- electronic address (or URL) in angle brackets.

Again, keep in mind that one purpose of documentation is to enable your readers to retrace your steps. It may also be useful to keep in mind that like the Internet itself, guidelines for citing electronic sources are continually evolving. Our guidelines are based on the format given in "MLA Style" [20 May 1999] <http://www.mla.org/main stl.htm#sources>.

Here are some examples.

1. A Novel

Jewett, Sarah Orne. <u>The Country of the Pointed

Firs. 1910</u>. Bartleby Archive. Columbia U. 3

June 1999. <http://www.cc.columbia.edu/

acis/bartleby/jewett>.

2. Journal Article

Fluck, Winfried. "'The American Romance' and the

Changing Functions of the Imaginary." <u>New

Literary History</u> 27.3 (1996): 415–57. <u>Project

Muse</u>. JHU. 1 May 1998. <http://muse:jhu.edu:80/

journals/new_literary_history/v27/27.3fluck.html>.

3. Magazine Article (from a Print Source)

Murphy, K. "Do Food Additives Subtract from

Health?" <u>Business Week</u> 6 May 1996: 140.

<u>Lexis-Nexis</u>. 12 May 1998.

4. Magazine Article (No Print Source)

Green, Laura. "Sexual Harassment Law: Relax

and Try to Enjoy It." <u>Salon.</u> 3 March 1998.

14 Aug. 1998. <http://www.salon1999.com/

mwt/feature/1998/03/cov_03featurea.html>.

5. Article in a Reference Work

"Chopin, Kate." <u>Britannica Online</u>. Vers 98.1.1.

June 1998. Encyclopaedia Britannica. 14 Aug.

1998. <http://www.eb.com:180/cgi-

bin/g?DocF=micro/125/57.html>.

Reuben, Paul P. "Chapter 6: 1890-1910: Kate Chopin

(1851-1904)." <u>PAL: Perspectives in American</u>

<u>Literature--A Research and Reference Guide</u>.

20 March 1998. <http://www.csustan.edu/

english/reuben/pal/chap6/chopin.html>.

6. Personal Website

Mendelsson, Jonathan. Homepage. 8 Jan. 1999.

<http://www.mit.edu/~jrmendel/index.html>.

7. E-mail

Maphet, Mercedes. "Re: Kate Chopin Diaries."

E-mail to author. 4 May 1998

8. Posting to a Discussion List

Searls, Damion. "Re: Fiction Inspired by Woolf."

VWOOLF@lists.acs.ohio-state.edu. On-line

posting. 30 Oct. 1998.

Although we have covered the most common sources, it is entirely possible that you will come across a source that does not fit any of the categories that we have discussed. For several hundred pages of explanation of these matters, covering the proper way to cite all sorts of troublesome and unbelievable (but real) sources, see Joseph Gibaldi, *MLA Handbook for Writers of Research Papers*, 5th ed. (New York: Modern Language Association of America, 1999). Numerous Websites also provide additional information about and discussion of documenting on-line sources. The research skills you've developed will enable you to locate and evaluate these sites, but to get you started, here are two useful citations.

```
Harnack, Andrew, and Gene Kleppinger. "Beyond the

    MLA Handbook: Documenting Electronic Sources

    on the Internet." 25 Nov. 1996. 15 July 2001.

    <http://english.ttu.edu/kairos/1.2/inbox/mla_

    archive.html#citing_sites>.

Walker, Janice R. MLA-Style Citations of

    Electronic Source." Ver. 1.3, Rev. Jan. 1999.

    15 July 2001. <http://www.cas.usf.edu/

    english/walker/mla.html>.
```

Note: On page 227–41 we reprint a student's research essay in MLA format.

APA Format

The MLA style is used chiefly by writers in the humanities. Writers in the social sciences and in business, education, and psychology commonly use a style developed by the American Psychological Association. In the following pages we give the chief principles of the APA style, but for full details the reader should consult the fifth edition (2001) of *Publication Manual of the American Psychological Association.*

An Overview of the APA Format   A paper using the format prescribed by the American Psychological Association will contain brief parenthetical citations within the text and will end with a page headed "References," which lists all of the author's sources. This list of sources begins on a separate page, continuing the pagination of the last page of the essay itself. Thus, if the text of the essay ends on page 8, the first page of references is page 9.

Here are some general guidelines for formatting both the citations within the text and the list of references at the end of the essay.

Citations within the Text   The APA style emphasizes the date of publication; the date appears not only in the list of references at the end of the paper but also in the paper itself, when you give a brief parenthetic citation of a source that you have quoted or summarized or in any other way used. Here is an example:

```
Statistics for church attendance are highly

unreliable (Catherton, 1991, p. 17).
```

Note that unlike the MLA, the APA uses commas to separate elements inside the parenthetic citation, and that a "p." precedes the page number. The parenthetic citation may appear at the end of the sentence, or after the clause that contains the references, or after the author's name—whichever placement makes things clearest for the reader. In the example below, the date of publication appears immediately after the author's name; the page reference is given at the end of the sentence:

```
According to Catherton (1991), statistics for

church attendance are highly unreliable (p. 17).
```

The title of Catherton's book or article will be given in your list entitled References. By turning to the list, the reader will learn in what publication Catherton made this point.

A Summary of an Entire Work

```
Catherton (1991) concluded the opposite.
```

Or

```
Similar views are easily found (Catherton, 1991;

Brinnin and Abse, 1992).
```

A Reference to a Page or Pages

```
Catherton (1991, p. 107) argues that "church

attendance is increasing but religious faith is

decreasing."
```

A Reference to an Author Represented by More Than One Work Published in a Given Year in the References
As we explain in discussing the form of the material in References, if you list two or more works that an author published in the same year, the works are listed in alphabetic order, by the first letter of the title. The first work is labeled *a*, the second *b*, and so on. Here is a reference to the second work that Catherton published in 1997:

```
Boston is "a typical large Northern city" so far

as church attendance goes (Catherton, 1997b).
```

The List of References

Form on the Page

1. Begin each entry flush with the left margin, but if an entry runs to more than one line, indent five spaces for each succeeding line of the entry.
2. Double-space each entry, and double-space between entries.

Alphabetic Order

1. Arrange the list **alphabetically by author.**

2. Give the **author's last name first,** then the initial *only* of the first and of the middle name (if any).

3. If there is more than one author, name all of the authors, again inverting the name (last name first) and giving only initials for first and middle names. (But do not invert the editor's name when the entry begins with the name of an author who has written an article in an edited book. See the example below, page 335, illustrating "A Work in a Collection of Essays.") When there are two or more authors, use an ampersand (&) before the name of the last author. When there are more than six authors, the seventh and all additional authors are indicated with "et al." Here is an example of an article in the seventh volume of a journal called *Journal of Experimental Social Psychology:*

> Berscheid, E., Hatfield, E., & Bohrnotott, C.
>
> (1971). Physical attractiveness and dating
>
> choice: A test of the matching hypothesis.
>
> *Journal of Experimental Social Psychology* 7,
>
> 173–89.

4. If there is more than one work by an author, list the works in the order of publication, the earliest first.

If two works by an author were published in the same year, give them in alphabetic order by the first letter of the title, disregarding *A*, *An*, or *The*, and their foreign equivalents. Designate the first work as "a," the second as "b." Repeat the author's name at the start of each entry.

If the author of a work or works is also the co-author of other works listed, list the single-author entries first, arranged by date. Following these, list the multiple-author entries, in a sequence determined alphabetically by the second author's name. Thus, in the example below, notice that the works Bem wrote unassisted are listed first, arranged by date, and when two works appear in the same year they are arranged alphabetically by title. These single-author works are followed by the multiple-author works, with the work written with Lenney preceding the work written with Martyna and Watson.

> Bem, S. L. (1974). The measurement of
>
> psychological androgyny. *Journal of*
>
> *Consulting and Clinical Psychology, 42,*
>
> 155–62.

Bem, S. L. (1981a). The BSRI and gender schema theory: A reply to Spence and Helmreich. *Psychological Review, 88,* 369-71.

Bem, S. L. (1981b). Gender schema theory: A cognitive account of sex typing. *Psychological Review, 88,* 354-64.

Bem, S. L., & Lenney, E. (1976). Sex-typing and the avoidance of cross-sex behavior. *Journal of Personality and Social Psychology, 33,* 48-54.

Bem, S. L., Martyna, W., & Watson, C. (1976). Sex-typing and androgyny: Further exploration of the expressive domain. *Journal of Personality and Social Psychology, 34,* 1016-23.

Form of Title

1. In references to books, capitalize only the first letter of the first word of the title (and of the subtitle, if any) and capitalize proper nouns. Italicize the complete title and type a period after it.

2. In references to articles in periodicals or in edited books, capitalize only the first letter of the first word of the article's title (and subtitle, if any), and all proper nouns. Do not put the title within quotation marks. Type a period after the title of the article. For the title of the journal, and the volume and page numbers, see the next instruction.

3. In references to periodicals, capitalize all important words, as you would usually do. (Note that the rule for the titles of periodicals differs from the rule for books and articles.) Give the volume number in arabic numerals, and underline it. Do *not* use *vol.* before the number, and do not use *p.* or *pg.* before the page numbers.

Sample References

A Book by One Author

> Money, J. (1980). *Love and love sickness: The science of sex, gender difference and pair-bonding*. Baltimore: Johns Hopkins Press.

A Book by More than One Author

> Spence, J. T., & Helmreich, R. L. (1978). *Masculinity and femininity*. Austin: University of Texas Press.

A Collection of Essays

> Bundy, W. P. (Ed.). (1985). *The nuclear controversy*. New York: New American Library.

A Work in a Collection of Essays

> Rogers, B. (1985). The Atlantic alliance. In W. P. Bundy (Ed.). *The nuclear controversy* (pp. 41–52). New York: New American Library.

Government Documents If the writer is not known, treat the government and the agency as the author. Most federal documents are issued by the Government Printing Office in Washington.

> United States Congress. Office of Technology Assessment (1984). *Computerized manufacturing automation: Employment, education, and the workplace*. Washington, DC: U.S. Government Printing Office.

An Article in a Journal That Paginates Each Issue Separately

> Swinton, E. (1993, Winter). New wine in old casks:
>
> Sino-Japanese and Russo-Japanese war prints.
>
> *Asian Art*, 27-49.

The publication is issued four times a year, each issue containing a page 27. It is necessary, therefore, to tell the reader that this article appears in the winter issue.

An Article in a Journal with Continuous Pagination

> Herdt, G. (1991). Representations of homosexuality.
>
> *Journal of the History of Sexuality, 1,*
>
> 481-504.

An Article from a Monthly or Weekly Magazine

> Corliss, R. (1993, March 8). Bill Murray in the
>
> driver's seat. *Time*, p. 67.

An Article in a Newspaper

> Perry, T. (1993, 16 February). Election to give
>
> Latinos new political clout in San Diego.
>
> *Los Angeles Times*, sec. A, p. 3.

(*Note:* If no author is given, simply begin with the article title, followed by the date in parentheses.)

A Book Review

> Bayme, S. (1993). Tradition or modernity? [Review
>
> of Neil Gillman, *Sacred fragments: Recovering*
>
> *theology for the modern Jew.*] *Judaism, 42,*
>
> 106-13.

Bayme is the reviewer, not the author of the book. The book under review is called *Sacred fragments: Recovering theology for the modern Jew*, but the review, published in volume 42 of a journal called *Judaism*, had its own title, "Tradition or Modernity?"

Electronic Sources   References to electronic sources generally follow the format for printed sources. Include

- the author,
- the year of publication (in parentheses),
- the title (and edition, if applicable),

then give the retrieval statement, which includes

- the date retrieved, and
- the name and/or the address of the source. (Note that the period does *not* come at the end of an Internet address.)

The examples below follow guidelines set forth by *The Publication Manual of the American Psychological Association*, fifth edition (2001).

1. A Professional or Government Site

> Edlefsen, M. & Brewer, M. S. (no date).
>
>> Nitrates/nitrites. Retrieved May 6, 1998,
>>
>> from The National Food Safety Database:
>>
>> http://www.foodsafety.org/il/il089.htm
>
> National Cancer Institute (1996, June). *NCI fact*
>
>> *sheet*. Food additives. Retrieved May 4, 1998,
>>
>> from http://nisc8a.upenn.edu/pdg_html/6/
>>
>> eng/600037.html

2. An Encyclopedia Article

> Muckraker (journ.). (1994–1998). In *Britannica*
>
>> *Online*. Retrieved January 2, 1999, from

http://www.eb.com:180cgibin/g?DocF=index/mu/
ckr.html

3. A Newspaper Article

Legator, M., & Daniel, A. (1995). Reproductive
systems can be harmed by toxic exposure.
Galveston County Daily News. Retrieved May 6,
1998, from http://www.utmb.edu/toxics/
newsp.htm#canen

Warrick, P. (1994, June 8). A frank discussion.
Los Angeles Times, E1. Retrieved May 6, 1998,
from Lexis-Nexis.

4. A Journal Article

Tollefson, C. (1995, May 29). Stability preserved;
preservatives; food additives '95. *Chemical
Marketing Reporter* 247(22) SR28. Retrieved
May 6, 1998, from Lexis-Nexis.

5. A Book

Riis, J. (1890). *How the other half lives*. New
York: Charles Scribner's Sons [Electronic
Version]. David Phillips. Retrieved September
14, 1998, from http://www.cis.edu/amstud/
inforev/riis/ch#3/html

A Note on Other Systems of Documentation

The MLA style is commonly used in the humanities, and the APA style is commonly used in the social sciences, but many other disciplines use their own styles. What follows is a list of handbooks that give the systems used in some other disciplines.

Biology

Council of Biology Editors, Style Manual Committee. *Scientific Style and Format: CBE Style Manual for Authors, Editors, and Publishers in the Biological Sciences.* 6th ed. New York: Cambridge University Press, 1994.

Chemistry

American Chemical Society. *ACS Style Guide: A Manual for Authors and Editors.* 2nd ed. Washington, DC: American Chemical Society, 1997.

Geology

U.S. Geological Survey. *Suggestions to Authors of the Reports of the United States Geological Survey.* 8th ed. Washington, DC: GPO, Department of the Interior, 1997.

Law

The Bluebook: A Uniform System of Citation. 16th ed. Cambridge, MA: Harvard Law Review Association, 1996.

Mathematics

American Mathematical Society. *A Manual for Authors of Mathematical Papers.* 8th ed. Providence, RI: American Mathematical Society, 1990.

Medicine

American Medical Association. *Manual of Style.* 9th ed. Acton, MA: Publishing Sciences Group, 1997.

Physics

American Institute of Physics. *Style Manual for Guidance in the Preparation of Papers.* 4th ed. New York: American Institute of Physics, 1990.

A Sample Research Essay In APA Format

In Chapter 9, "Using Sources," we reprint a research essay in MLA format on pages 227–41. In the following research essay, a student, Jacob Alexander, uses the APA form of in-text citations, which are clarified by a list headed "References." Our annotations in the margins of the essay point to noteworthy features of Alexander's use of sources and of the system of citation.

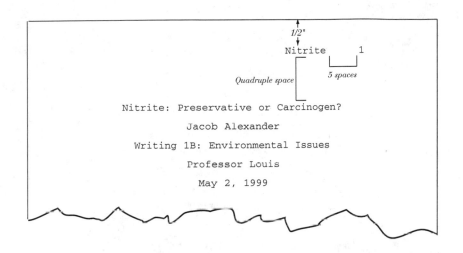

1/2"

Nitrite   1

5 spaces

Quadruple space

Nitrite: Preservative or Carcinogen?

Jacob Alexander

Writing 1B: Environmental Issues

Professor Louis

May 2, 1999

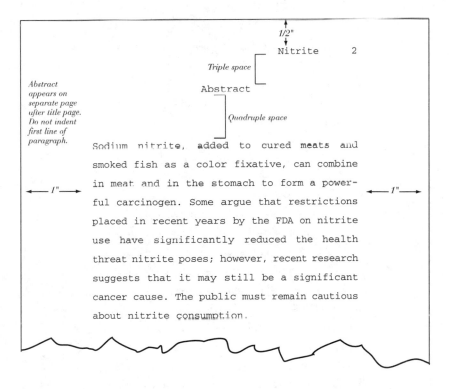

1/2"

Nitrite   2

Triple space

Abstract appears on separate page after title page. Do not indent first line of paragraph.

Abstract

Quadruple space

◄— *1"* —►

Sodium nitrite, added to cured meats and smoked fish as a color fixative, can combine in meat and in the stomach to form a powerful carcinogen. Some argue that restrictions placed in recent years by the FDA on nitrite use have significantly reduced the health threat nitrite poses; however, recent research suggests that it may still be a significant cancer cause. The public must remain cautious about nitrite consumption.

◄— *1"* —►

Page number and short form of title appear on every page

Nitrite: Preservative or Carcinogen?

According to Julie Miller Jones, a professor of food and nutrition and the author of <u>Food Safety,</u> "average Americans eat their weight in food additives every year" (cited in Murphy, 1996, p. 140). There are approximately fifteen thousand additives currently in use (National Cancer Institute Fact Sheet [NCI], 1996); many of them are known to be dangerous. Of these, nitrites may be among the most hazardous of all. In this country, ham, bacon, corned beef, salami, bologna, lox, and other cold cuts and smoked fish almost invariably contain sodium nitrite. In fact, one-third of the federally inspected meat and fish we consume--more than seven billion pounds of it every year--contains this chemical (Jacobson, 1987, p. 169).

Just how dangerous are nitrites, and why-- if they really <u>are</u> dangerous--does the food industry still use them? Both questions are difficult to answer. Some experts say that nitrites protect consumers from botulism, a deadly disease that can be caused by spoiled food, and that "the benefits of nitrite additives outweigh the risks" (Edlefsen & Brewer, no date). Others argue that the dangers nitrites once posed have been significantly reduced--even eliminated--by restrictions placed on their use by the Food and Drug Administration. Nevertheless, the evidence has long suggested that nitrites are linked to stomach cancer; recent research has

An indirect reference. Alexander consulted Murphy, who quotes Jones.

Citation gives author because Jacobson is not named in the text. Note format: author, date of publication, and page number preceded by a "p."

Nitrite   4

linked nitrites to leukemia and brain tumors as well (Warrick, 1994; Legator & Daniel, 1995).

Perhaps the only certain conclusions one can reach are that the effects of nitrite on the human body are still to some degree uncertain-- and that to protect themselves, consumers must be cautious and informed.

That nitrite is a poison has been clear for almost three decades. In 1974, Jacqueline Verrett, who worked for the FDA for fifteen years, and Jean Carper reported on several instances of people poisoned by accidental overdoses of nitrites in cured meats:

> In Buffalo, New York, six persons were hospitalized with "cardiovascular collapse" after they ate blood sausage which contained excessive amounts of nitrites . . . In New Jersey, two persons died and many others were critically poisoned after eating fish illegally loaded with nitrites. In New Orleans, ten youngsters between the ages of one and a half and five became seriously ill . . . after eating wieners or bologna overnitrited by a local meat-processing firm; one wiener that was obtained later from the plant was found to contain a whopping 6,570 parts per million. In Florida, a three-year-old boy died after eating hot dogs with three times greater nitrite concentration than the government allows. (pp. 138-39)

Nitrite   5

The chemical has the unusual and difficult-to-replace quality of keeping meat a fresh-looking pink throughout the cooking, curing, and storage process (Assembly of Life Science, 1982, p. 3). The nitrous acid from the nitrite combines with the hemoglobin in the blood of the meat, fixing its red color so that the meat does not turn the tired brown or gray natural to cured meats.

Unfortunately, it does much the same thing in humans. Although most of the nitrite passes through the body unchanged, a small amount is released into the bloodstream. This combines with the hemoglobin in the blood to form a pigment called methemoglobin, which cannot carry oxygen. If enough oxygen is incapacitated, a person dies. The allowable amount of nitrite in a quarter pound of meat has the potential to incapacitate between 1.4 and 5.7 percent of the hemoglobin in an average-sized adult (Verrett & Carper, 1974, pp. 138-39). One of the problems with nitrite poisoning is that infants under a year, because of the quantity and makeup of their blood, are especially susceptible to it.

If the consumer of nitrite isn't acutely poisoned (and granted, such poisonings are rare), his or her blood soon returns to normal and this particular danger passes: the chemical, however, has long-term effects, as research conducted in the 1970's clearly established. Nitrite can cause headaches in people who are especially sensitive to it, an upsetting symptom

Nitrite   6

considering that in rats who ate it regularly
for a period of time it has produced lasting
"epileptic like" changes in the brain--
abnormalities which showed up when the rats
were fed only a little more than an American
fond of cured meats might eat (Wellford, 1973,
p. 173). Experiments with chickens, cattle,
sheep, and rats have shown that nitrite, when
administered for several days, inhibits the
ability of the liver to store vitamin A and
carotene (Hunter, 1972, p. 90). And finally,
Nobel laureate Joshua Lederberg points out that,
in microorganisms, nitrite enters the DNA.
"If it does the same thing in humans," he says,
"it will cause mutant genes." Geneticist Bruce
Ames adds, "If out of one million people, one
person's genes are mutant, that's a serious
problem . . . . If we're filling ourselves now
with mutant genes, they're going to be around
for generations" (cited in Zwerdling, 1971,
pp. 34-35).

   By far the most alarming characteristic of
nitrite, however, is that in test tubes, in
meats themselves, in animal stomachs, and in
human stomachs--wherever a mildly acidic
solution is present--it can combine with amines
to form nitrosamines. And nitrosamines are
carcinogens. Even the food industry and the
agencies responsible for allowing the use of
nitrite in foods admit that nitrosamines cause
cancer. Edlefsen and Brewer, writing recently
for the National Food Safety Database, note that

Nitrite   7

An on-line source. (The authors and title are named in the sentence; the source has no date or page numbers.)

"over 90 percent of the more than 300 known nitrosamines in foods have been shown to cause cancer in laboratory animals." They continue: "No case of human cancer has been shown to result from exposure to nitrosamines," but they acknowledge that "indirect evidence indicates that humans would be susceptible" (no date).

It is important to note that nitrite alone, when fed to rats on an otherwise controlled diet, does not induce cancer. It must first combine with amines to form nitrosamines. Considering, however, that the human stomach has the kind of acidic solution in which amines and nitrites readily combine, and considering as well that amines are present in beer, wine, cereals, tea, fish, cigarette smoke, and a long list of drugs including antihistamines, tranquilizers, and even oral contraceptives, it is hardly surprising to find that nitrosamaines have been found in human stomachs.

When animals are fed amines in combination with nitrite, they developed cancer with a statistical consistency that is frightening, even to scientists. Verrett and Carper report that after feeding animals 250 parts per million (ppm) of nitrites and amines, William Lijinsky, a scientist at Oak Ridge National Laboratory,

> found malignant tumors in 100 percent of the test animals within six months . . . . "Unheard of," he says . . . . "You'd usually expect to find 50 percent at the most. And the cancers are all over

Nitrite   8

the place--in the brain, lung, pancreas,

stomach liver, adrenals, intestines. We

open up the animals and they are a

bloody mess." [He] believes that

nitrosamines, because of their incredi-

ble versatility in inciting cancer, may

be the key to an explanation for the

mass production of cancer in seemingly

dissimilar populations. In other words,

nitrosamines may be a common factor in

cancer that has been haunting us all

these years. (1974, p. 136)

Verrett and Carper (1974, pp. 43-46) list

still more damning evidence. Nitrosamines have

caused cancer in rats, hamsters, mice, guinea

pigs, dogs, and monkeys. It has been proven

that nitrosamines of over a hundred kinds cause

cancer. Nitrosamines have been shown to pass

through the placenta from the mother to cause

cancer in the offspring. Even the lowest levels

of nitrosamines ever tested have produced can-

cer in animals. When animals are fed nitrite

and amines separately over a period of time,

they develop cancers of the same kind and at

the same frequency as animals fed the corre-

sponding nitrosamines already formed.

To address these problems (and in response

to intense public concern), in 1978, the FDA

ruled that a reducing agent, such as ascorbic

This on-line source did not provide a date of publication. acid, must be added to products containing

nitrite; the reducing agent inhibits the forma-

tion of nitrosamines (Edlefsen & Brewer, no

Nitrite   9

date). And in the last two decades, at least,
the furor over nitrite seems as a consequence
to have abated. In fact, a 1997 article published by the International Food Information
Council Foundation (a group primarily sponsored
by the food industry, according to information
provided by its Website), celebrates nitrite as
a "naturally-derived" substance that, according
to the American Academy of Science, has never
been found to cause cancer. On the contrary,
the anonymous author states, nitrite does many
good things for consumers; it may even help to
fight cancer: "it safeguards cured meats against
the most deadly foodborne bacterium known to
man" and helps with "promoting blood clotting,
healing wounds and burns and boosting immune
function to kill tumor cells."

Other experts are less certain that reducing agents have entirely solved the nitrosamine
problem. The <u>Consumer's Dictionary of Food</u>
<u>Additives</u> notes that one common agent, sodium
ascorbate, which is added to the brine in which
bacon is cured, "offers only a partial barrier
because ascorbate is soluble in fatty tissues"
(Winter, 1994, p. 282). But in the wake of several studies it is unclear that "inhibiting"
the formation of nitrosamines actually makes
nitrites safe to consume.

The Los Angeles Times reports that one of
these studies, conducted by John Peters, an
epidemiologist at USC, found that "children who
eat more than 12 hot dogs per month have nine

*No citation
is given here
because all
information
is included
in the
sentence
itself.*

times the normal risk of developing childood

leukemia" (Warrick, 1994). Interestingly, the

study was focused not on nitrites, but rather on

electromagnetic fields. "'Dietary exposure to

processed or cured meats was part of a little

side questionnaire to our study on electro)

(magnetic fields," Peters said. "We were as

surprised as anyone by the hot dogs findings.

An indirect
reference.

. . . It was the biggest risk for anything we saw

in the study--about four times the risk for

EMF's" (cited in Warrick, 1994).

    In another of these recent studies, hot

dogs were linked to brain tumors: researchers

found that "children born to mothers who ate at

least one hot dog per week while pregnant have

Authors are
named in the
sentence and
the on-line
sources isn't
paginated.
Only
publication
date is cited.

twice the risk of developing brain tumors, as do

children whose fathers ate too many hot dogs

before conception" (Warrick, 1994). Dr. M.

Legator and Amanda Daniel comment that "these

studies confirm thirty years worth

of scientific research on the cancer causing

properties of preserved meats and fish" (1995).

    The question, then, is why nitrite

continues to be used in so much of the meat

Americans consume. Although nitrite adds a small

amount to flavor, it is used primarily for

cosmetic purposes. Food producers are of course

also quick to point out that nitrite keeps

people safe from botulinum in cured meats, an

argument to which the public may be particularly

susceptible because of a number of recent and

serious food scares. Nevertheless, some evidence

Nitrite   11

suggests that the protection nitrite offers is
both unnecessary and ineffective.

Michael Jacobson explains the preservative
action of nitrite:

> Nitrite makes botulinum spores sensitive
> to heat. When foods are treated with
> nitrite and then heated, any botulinum
> spores that may be present are killed. In
> the absence of nitrite, spores can be
> inactivated only at temperatures that
> ruin the meat products . . . . Nitrite's
> preservative action is particularly
> important in foods that are not cooked
> after they leave the factory, such as
> ham, because these offer an oxygen-free
> environment, the kind in which botulinum
> can grow. The toxin does not pose a
> danger in foods that are always well
> cooked, such as bacon, because the toxin
> would be destroyed in cooking.
>
> Laboratory studies demonstrate
> clearly that nitrite can kill botulinum,
> but whether it actually does in
> commercially processed meat has been
> called into question. Frequently, the
> levels used may be too low to do
> anything but contribute to the color.
> (1987, p. 165)

Bratwurst and breakfast sausage are manufac-
tured now without nitrite because they don't
need to be colored pink; bacon is always cooked
thoroughly enough to kill off any botulinum

Nitrite   12

spores present. Certainly there are other ways
of dealing with botulism. High or low temperature prevents botulism. What nitrite undoubt-
edly does lower, however, is the level of care
and sanitation necessary in handling meat.

Clearly, the use of nitrite adds immeasur-
ably to the profit-making potential of the meat
industry, but why does the federal government
allow this health hazard in our food? In the
first place, nitrite and nitrate have been used
for so long that it is hard for lawmakers to get
past their instinctive reaction, "But that's the
way we've always done it." Indeed, the Romans
used saltpeter, a nitrate, to keep meat and, as
early as 1899, scientists discovered that the
nitrate breaks down into nitrite and that it is
the nitrite which actually preserves the red
color in meats (Jacobson, 1987, pp. 164-65).
Thus, by the time the U.S. Department of Agri-
culture and the Food and Drug Administration got
into the business of regulating food, they
tended to accept nitrite and nitrate as givens.

A second reason for the inadequacy of
regulation is that government mechanisms for
protecting the consumer are full of curious
loopholes. In 1958 Congress passed the Food
Additive Amendment, including the Delaney
Clause, which clearly states that additives
should be banned if they induce cancer in laboratory animals. Unfortunately, however, the
amendment does not apply to additives that were
in use before it was passed, so, since nitrite

*Note that a
reference to a
single page is
preceded by
"p." and that
a reference to
two or more
pages is
preceded by
"pp."*

Nitrite   13

and nitrate had already been in use for a long
time, they were automatically included on the
list of chemicals "Generally Recognized as
Safe." To complicate matters further, nitrite
in meat is regulated by the USDA, while
nitrite in fish is under the jurisdiction of
the FDA. And these agencies generally leave it
to industry--the profit-maker--to establish
whether or not an additive is safe. The final
irony in this list of governmental errors is
that the FDA depends heavily, for "independent" research and advice, on the food commit-
tees of the National Academy of Sciences,
which Daniel Zwerdling claims are "like a
Who's Who of the food and chemical industry"
(1971, p. 34). (This, of course, is the organization cited in the anonymous web posting
quoted above, the organization that holds that
"nitrite levels in cured meat have not been
linked to the development of human cancers.")

Because the author is named in the sentence, the citation gives only the date and page number.

Clearly, consumers need to be informed;
clearly, it is unwise to count on government
agencies for protection against the dangers food
additives may pose. Some experts continue to
argue that nitrite is safe enough; Edelfson and
Brewer, for example, cite a 1992 study by J. M.
Jones that suggests that drinking beer exposes a
consumer to more nitrite than does eating
bacon—and that new car interiors are a significant source of nitrite as well.[1] Others recom-

An explanatory footnote.

[1]Presumably the exposure here results from contact, not ingestion.

Nitrite   14

mend caution. One expert advises: "If you must
eat nitrite-laced meats, include a food or
drink high in vitamin C at the same time--for
example, orange juice, grapefruit juice, cran-
berry juice, or lettuce" (Winter, 1994, p.
282). And, in fact, a study by a committee
organized by the National Academy of Science
strongly implies (Assembly, 1982, p. 12) that
the government should develop a safe alternative to nitrites.

In the meantime, the chemical additive
industry doesn't seem very worried that alternatives, such as biopreservatives, will pose a
threat to its profits. An industry publication, "Chemical Marketing Reporter," recently
reassured its readers by announcing that
"around 82.5 million pounds of preservatives,
valued at $133 million, were consumed in the
US in 1991." The report also stated that
"though the trend toward phasing out controversial preservatives like sulfites, nitrates
and nitrites continues, natural substitutes
remain expensive and often less than effective, making biopreservatives a distant
threat" (Tollefson, 1995).

References begin on new page   Nitrite   15

References

Assembly of Life Science. (1982). <u>Alternatives to</u>

Second and subsequent lines of entries are indented five spaces

<u>the current use of nitrite in food</u>.

Washington, DC: National Academy Press.

Edlefsen, M. & Brewer, M. S. (no date). <u>The</u>

<u>national food safety database</u>.

Nitrates/Nitrites. Retrieved May 6, 1998,

from http://www.foodsafety.org/il/il089.htm

A book. Capitalize only the first word in book and article titles.

Hunter, B. T. (1972). <u>Fact/book on food additives</u>

<u>and your health</u>. New Canaan, CT.: Keats.

International Food Information Council

Foundation. (1997). Nitrite: keeping food

safe. <u>Food Insight</u>. Retrieved July 15, 2001,

from http://ific.org/proactive/newsroom/

release.vtml?id=18036

Jacobson, M. F. (1987). <u>Eater's digest</u>.

Washington, DC: Center for Science in the

Public Interest.

An on-line version of printed newspaper article. Capitalize all important words in newspaper and periodical titles.

Legator, M. & Daniel, A. (1995). Reproductive

systems can be harmed by toxic exposure.

<u>Galveston County Daily News</u>. Retrieved May

6, 1998, from http://www.utmb.edu/toxics/

newsp.htm#canen

Murphy, K. (1996, May 6). Do food

additives subtract from health?

<u>Business Week</u>, p. 140. Retrieved July

30, 1998, from Lexis-Nexis.

National Cancer Institute (1996, June).

<u>NCI fact sheet</u>. Food additives.

Retrieved May 4, 1998, from

An on-line version of printed magazine article. Note that the year precedes the month and date in the parentheses following the author.

Nitrite   16

http://nisc8a.upenn.edu/pdghtml/6/eng/

600037.html

Tollefson, C. (1995, May 29). Stability

preserved; preservatives; food

additives '95. <u>Chemical Marketing</u>

<u>Reporter 247</u>(22) SR28. Retrieved

May 6, 1998, from Lexis-Nexis.

Verrett, J., & Carper, J. (1974). <u>Eating may</u>

<u>be hazardous to your health</u>. New York:

Simon and Schuster.

Warrick, P. (1994, June 8). A frank

discussion. <u>Los Angeles Times</u>,

E1. Retrieved May 6, 1998, from

Lexis-Nexis.

Welford, H. (1973). <u>Sowing the wind: a</u>

<u>report from Ralph Nader's Center for</u>

<u>Study of Responsible Law on food</u>

<u>safety and the chemical harvest</u>. New

York: Bantam.

Winter, R. (1994). <u>A consumer's dictionary</u>

<u>of food additives</u> (Updated 4th ed.).

New York. Crown.

Zwerdling, D. (1971, June). Food pollution.

<u>Ramparts, 9</u>(11), 31-37, 53-54.

A book by two authors. Note use of ampersand between authors' names.

Use "p." or "pp." when citing books or newspapers, but not periodicals. Ramparts is a periodical.

CHAPTER THIRTEEN

MANUSCRIPT PREPARATION

I love being a writer. What I can't stand is the
paperwork.

—*Peter De Vries*

Basic Manuscript Form

When you submit a piece of writing to your instructor or to anyone else,
make sure it looks good. You want to convey the impression that you care
about what you've written, that you've invested yourself and your time
in it, that the details matter to you.

Much of what follows is ordinary academic procedure. Unless your
instructor specifies something different, you can adopt these principles
as a guide.

1. Print your essay on 8½-by-11-inch paper of good weight. Use
fresh, plain white paper; don't use the reverse sides of an old draft or lab
report; avoid fancy or colored paper.

**2. Make sure that the printer has enough ink and that the print
is dark and clear.** One sure way to irritate your instructor is to turn
in an essay with nearly invisible print.

3. Do not use a fancy font. Unless your instructor specifies something else, stick to Times or Courier. And use a reasonable point size:
Generally a twelve-point font will do.

4. Print your essay on one side of the paper only. If for some reason you have occasion to submit a handwritten copy, use lined paper and write on every other line in black or dark blue ink.

5. Set the line spacing at "double." The essay (even the heading—see item 6 below) should be double-spaced—not single-spaced, not triple-spaced.

6. In the upper left-hand corner, one inch from the top, put your name, your instructor's name, the course number, and the date. Put your last name before the page number (in the upper right-hand corner) of each subsequent page, so the instructor can easily reassemble your essay if somehow a page gets detached and mixed with other papers.

7. Titles. Use this form for your title: Hit the "enter" (or "return") key *once* after the date and then center the title of your essay. We give instructions for punctuating titles in Chapter 10, but we'll reiterate the most important points here. Capitalize the first letter of the first and last words of your title, the first word after a semicolon or colon if you use either one, and the first letter of all the other words except articles, conjunctions, and prepositions, thus:

```
Two Kinds of Symbols in To Kill a Mockingbird
```

Notice that your own title is neither underlined nor enclosed in quotation marks. (If, as here, your title includes material that would normally be italicized or in quotation marks, that material continues to be so written.) If the title runs more than one line, double-space between the lines.

8. Begin the essay just below the title. (Again, you'll hit "enter" or "return" only once.) If your instructor prefers a title page, begin the essay on the next page and number it 1. The title page is not numbered.

9. Margins. Except for page numbers, which should appear one-half inch from the top of the page, leave a one-inch margin at top, bottom, and sides of text.

10. Number the pages consecutively, using arabic numerals in the upper right-hand corner, half an inch from the top. Do not put a period or a hyphen after the numeral, and do not precede the numeral with "page" or "p." (Again, if you give the title on a separate sheet, the page that follows it is page 1. Do not number the title page.)

11. Paragraphs. Indent the first word of each paragraph five spaces from the left margin.

12. Proofreading. Check for typographical errors, and check spelling. Use your word processor's spell-check program—but don't rely on it exclusively. This program will flag words that are not in its dictionary and offer suggestions for correcting mistakes. (A misspelled word is of course not in the dictionary and thus flagged.) But a word flagged is not necessarily misspelled; it may simply not be in the program's dictionary. Proper names, for example, regularly get flagged. Keep in mind also that most programs cannot distinguish between homophones (*to, too, two; there, their; alter, altar*), nor can they tell you that you should have written *accept* instead of *except.*

13. Print a copy of your essay for yourself and keep it until the original has been returned. It is a good idea to keep notes and drafts too. They may prove helpful if you are asked to revise a page, substantiate a point, or supply a source you omitted.

14. Fasten the pages of your paper with a paper clip in the upper left-hand corner. Stiff binders are unnecessary; indeed, they are a nuisance to the instructor, adding bulk and making it awkward to write annotations.

Double space

1"

Your Name

Your Instructor's Name — *Font is Courier*

Writing 127

April 1, 2001

— *Capitalize main words in title*

Formatting Your Essays: The Right

Way to Do It

Center title

Print your essay on 8-1/2-by-11-inch paper of good weight, and make sure that the printer has enough ink and that the print is dark and clear. Do not use a fancy font. Unless your instructor specifies something else, stick to Times or Courier. And use a reasonable point size: generally a 12-point font will do. The essay (even the heading) should be double-spaced--not single-spaced, not triple-spaced--and it should be printed on one side of the paper only.

5 spaces, or tab

⟵ 1" ⟶

In the upper left-hand corner, one inch from the top, put your name, your instructor's name, the course number, and the date, all on separate lines. Put your last name before the page number (in the upper right-hand corner) of each subsequent page, so the instructor can easily reassemble your essay if somehow a page gets detached and mixed with other papers. Hit the "enter" (or "return") key <u>once</u> after the date and then center the title of your essay. Capitalize the first letter of the first and last words of your title, the first word after a semicolon or colon if you use either one, and

1"

↑
1/2"
↓

Your name 2

the first letter of all the other words except
articles, conjunctions, and prepositions.
Notice that your own title is neither underlined nor enclosed in quotation marks. If the
title runs more than one line, double-space
between the lines. Begin the essay just below
the title. (Again, you'll hit "enter" or
"return" only once.) If your instructor prefers
a title page, begin the essay on the next page
and number it 1.

Except for page numbers, which should
appear one-half inch from the top of the page,
leave a one-inch margin at top, bottom, and
sides of text. Number the pages consecutively,
using arabic numerals in the upper right-hand
corner, half an inch from the top. Do not put a
period or a hyphen after the numeral, and do not
precede the numeral with "page" or "p."

Indent the first word of each paragraph
five spaces from the left margin.

Fasten the pages of your paper with a
paper clip in the upper left-hand corner. Stiff
binders are unnecessary; indeed, they are a nuisance because they add bulk and make essays
difficult to annotate. Spell-check your essay
and proofread it carefully; make a copy for
yourself, and then turn the essay in.

Using Quotations (and Punctuating Quotations Correctly)

If you are writing about a text, or about an interview, quotations from your material or subject are indispensable. They not only let your readers know what you are talking about, they give your readers the material you are responding to, thus letting them share your responses. But quote sparingly and quote briefly. Use quotations as evidence, not as padding. If the exact wording of the original is crucial, or especially effective, quote it directly, but if it is not, don't bore the reader with material that can be effectively reduced either by summarizing or by cutting. And make sure, by a comment before or after a quotation, that your reader understands why you find the quotation relevant. Don't count on a quotation to make your point for you.

Here are some additional matters to keep in mind, especially as you revise.

1. Identify the speaker or writer of the quotation. Usually this identification precedes the quoted material (e.g., "Smith says, . . .") in accordance with the principle of letting readers know where they are going. But occasionally it may follow the quotation, especially if the name will provide a meaningful surprise. For example, in a discussion of a proposed tax reform, you might quote a remark hostile to it and then reveal that the author of the proposal was also the author of the remark.

2. When you introduce a quotation, consider using verbs other than "says." Depending on the context—that is, on the substance of the quotation and its place in your essay—it might be more accurate to say "Smith argues," "adds," "contends," "points out," "admits," or "comments." Or, again with just the right verb, you might introduce the quotation with a transitional phrase: "In another context Smith had observed that . . ." or "To clarify this point Smith refers to . . ." or "In an apparent contradiction Smith suggests . . ." But avoid such inflated words as "opines," "avers," and "is of the opinion that." The point is not to add "elegant variation" (see page 118) to your introduction of someone else's words, but accuracy and grace. A verb often used *in*accurately is "feels." Ralph Linton does not "feel" that "the term *primitive art* has come to be used with at least three distinct meanings." He "points out," "writes," "observes," or "says" so.

3. Distinguish between short and long quotations and treat each appropriately.

Enclose *short quotations,* four (or fewer) lines of typing, within quotation marks:

> Anne Lindbergh calls the harrowing period of the kid-
> napping and murder of her first child the "hour of
> lead." "Flying," she wrote, "was freedom and beauty
> and escape from crowds."

Set off *long quotations* (more than four lines of typing). Do *not* enclose them within quotation marks. To set off a quotation, begin a new line, indent ten spaces from the left margin, and type the quotation double-spaced:

> The last paragraphs of <u>Five Years of My Life</u>
> contain Dreyfus's words when he was finally freed:
>> The Government of the Republic gives me
>> back my liberty. It is nothing to me
>> without honor. Beginning with today, I
>> shall unremittingly strive for the
>> reparation of the frightful judicial error
>> of which I am still the victim. I want all
>> France to know by a final judgment that I
>> am innocent.
> But he was never to receive that judgment.

Note that long quotations are usually introduced by a sentence ending with a colon (as in the above example) or by an introductory phrase, such as "Dreyfus wrote."

4. Don't try to introduce a long quotation into the middle of one of your own sentences. It is too difficult for the reader to come out of the quotation and to pick up your thread. Instead, introduce the quotation, as we did above, set the quotation off, and then begin a new sentence of your own.

5. An embedded quotation (that is, a quotation embedded into a sentence of your own) must fit grammatically into the sentence of which it is a part. For example, suppose you want to use Othello's line "I have done the state some service."

Incorrect

```
Near the end of the play Othello says that he "have
done the state some service."
```

Correct

```
Near the end of the play Othello says that he has
"done the state some service."
```

Correct

```
Near the end of the play, Othello says, "I have done
the state some service."
```

6. Quote exactly. Check your quotation for accuracy at least twice. If you need to edit a quotation—for example, in order to embed it grammatically, or to inform your reader of a relevant point—observe the following rules:

To add or to substitute words, enclose the words in square brackets—not parentheses.

```
"In the summer of 1816 we [Mary Wollstonecraft and
Percy Bysshe Shelley] visited Switzerland and became
the neighbors of Lord Byron."
```

```
Trotsky became aware that "Stalin would not hesitate
a moment to organize an attempt on [his] life."
```

Indicate the omission of material with ellipses (three periods, with a space between periods and before and after each period).

```
The New York Times called it "the most intensive man-
hunt . . . in the country's history" (3 March 1932).
```

If your sentence ends with the omission of the last part of the original sentence, use four periods: one immediately after the last word quoted, and three (spaced) to indicate the omission.

```
The manual says, "If your sentence ends with the
omission of the last part of the original sentence,
use four spaced periods . . ."
```

Notice that if you begin the quotation with the beginning of a sentence (in the example we have just given "If your" is the beginning of a quoted sentence), you do *not* indicate that material preceded the words you are quoting. Similarly, if you end your quotation with the end of the quoted sentence, you give only a single period, not an ellipsis, although of course the material from which you are quoting may have gone on for many more sentences. But if you begin quoting from the middle of a sentence, or end quoting before you reach the end of a sentence in your source, it is customary to indicate the omissions. But even such omissions need not be indicated when the quoted material is obviously incomplete—when, for instance, it is a word or phrase. Note: the MLA requires square brackets around ellipses when words are omitted from quoted material; for more on the MLA guidelines, see pages 302-03.

7. Use punctuation accurately. There are three important rules to observe:

Commas and periods go inside the quotation marks.

```
"The land," Nick Thompson observes, "looks after us."
```

Semicolons and colons go outside quotation marks.

```
He turned and said, "Learn the names of all these
places"; it sounded like an order.
```

Question marks, exclamation points, and dashes go inside if they are part of the quotation, outside if they are your own.

```
Amanda ironically says to her daughter, "How old are
you, Laura?"
```

(The question mark is part of the quotation and therefore goes inside the quotation marks.)

8. Use single quotation marks for a quotation within a quotation.

```
The student told the interviewer, "I ran back to the
dorm and I called my boyfriend and I said, 'Listen,
this is just incredible,' and I told him all
about it."
```

9. Enclose titles of short works in quotation marks. Short works include: chapters in books, short stories, essays, short poems, songs, lectures, speeches, and unpublished works (even if long).

Underline, or use italic type, for titles of long works. (Underlining indicates *italic* type, used in print and available on computers but ordinarily not available on typewriters.) Underline (or italicize) titles of published book-length works: novels, plays, periodicals, collections of essays, anthologies, pamphlets, textbooks, and long poems (such as *Paradise Lost*). Underline (or italicize) also titles of films, compact discs, television programs, ballets, operas, works of art, and the names of planes, ships, and trains.

Exception: Titles of sacred works (for example, the New Testament, the Hebrew Bible, Genesis, Acts, the Gospels, the Koran) are neither underlined nor enclosed within quotation marks. To cite a book of the Bible with chapter and verse, give the name of the book, then a space, then an arabic numeral for the chapter, a period, and an arabic numeral (*not* preceded by a space) for the verse, thus: Exodus 20.14–15. Standard abbreviations for the books of the Bible (for example, Chron.) are permissible in footnotes and in parenthetic citations within the text.

10. Use quotation marks to identify a word or term to which you wish to call special attention. (But italics, indicated by underlining, may be used instead of quotation marks.)

```
By "comedy" I mean not only a funny play, but any
play that ends happily.
```

11. Do not use quotation marks to enclose slang or a term that you fear is too casual; use the term or don't use it, but don't apologize by putting it in quotation marks, as in these examples.

Incorrect
```
Because of "red tape" it took three years.
```

Incorrect
```
At last I was able to "put in my two cents."
```

In both of these sentences the writers are signaling their uneasiness; in neither is there any cause for uneasiness.

12. Do not use quotation marks to convey sarcasm, as in the following sentence:

```
These "politicians" are nothing but thieves.
```

Sarcasm, usually a poor form of argument, is best avoided. But of course there are borderline cases when you may want to convey your dissatisfaction with a word used by others.

```
African sculpture has a long continuous tradition,
but this tradition has been jeopardized by the intro-
duction of "civilization" to Africa.
```

Perhaps the quotation marks here are acceptable, because the writer's distaste has not yet become a sneer and because she is, in effect, quoting. But it is probably better to change "civilization" to "western culture," omitting the quotation marks.

13. Do not enclose the title of your own essay in quotation marks, and do not underline or italicize it.

Corrections in the Final Copy

Extensive revisions should have been made in your drafts, but minor last-minute revisions may be made on the finished copy. Proofreading may catch some typographical errors, and you may notice some small weaknesses. You can make corrections with the following proofreader's symbols. If you did not find an error in each triangle, look again.

1. *Changes* in wording may be made by crossing through words and rewriting just above them, either on the typewriter or by hand in pen:

```
When I first moved to the United States at the age
            no
of nine, I had few doubts as to my identity.
```

2. *Additions* should be made above the line, with a caret (^) below the line at the appropriate place:

```
When I first moved to the United States at the
         of
age nine, I had no doubts as to my identity.
    ^
```

3. *Transpositions* of letters may be made thus:

```
When I frist moved to the United States at the age

of nine, I had no doubts as to my identity.
```

4. *Deletions* are indicated by a horizontal line through the word or words to be deleted. Delete a single letter by drawing a vertical or diagonal line through it.

```
When I first moved to the United States at at the age

of nine, I had no doubts as to my identity.
```

5. *Separation* of words accidentally run together is indicated by a vertical line, *closure* by a curved line connecting the things to be closed up.

```
When I first moved to the United States at the age of

nine, I had no dou bts as to my identity.
```

6. *Paragraphing* may be indicated by the paragraph symbol before the word that is to begin the new paragraph.

```
When I first moved to the United States at the age

of nine, I had no doubts as to my identity. ¶Within a

year, however, . . .
```

Last Words

A rich patron once gave money to the painter Chu Ta, asking him to paint a picture of a fish. Three years later, when he still had not received the painting, the patron went to Chu Ta's house to ask why the picture was not done. Chu Ta did not answer, but dipped a brush in ink and with a few strokes drew a splendid fish. "If it is so easy," asked the patron, "why didn't you give me the picture three years ago?" Again Chu Ta did not answer. Instead, he opened the door of a large cabinet. Thousands of pictures of fish tumbled out.

Credits

Index

Additional Titles of Interest

Note to Instructors: Any of these Penguin-Putnam, Inc., titles can be packaged with this book at a special discount. Contact your local Allyn & Bacon/Longman sales representative for details on how to create a Penguin-Putnam, Inc., Value Package.

Albee, *Three Tall Women*

Alger, *Ragged Dick and Struggling Upward*

Allison, *Bastard Out of Carolina*

Augustine, *The Confessions of St. Augustine*

Austen, *Persuasion*

Austen, *Pride and Prejudice*

Austen, *Sense and Sensibility*

Azuela, *The Underdogs*

Behn, *Oroonoko, the Rover and Other Works*

Bellamy, *Looking Backward*

Bellow, *The Adventures of Augie March*

Bloom, *Shakespeare: The Invention of the Human*

Bowring, *The Diary of Lady Murasaki*

Boyle, *Tortilla Curtain*

C. Bronte, *Jane Eyre*

E. Bronte, *Wuthering Heights*

M. Cather, *My Antonia*

W. Cather, *O Pioneers!*

Cervantes, *Don Quixote*

Chaucer, *Canterbury Tales*

Chopin, *The Awakening*

Conde, *Segu*

Conrad, *Nostromo*

Dante, *The Divine Comedy, Volume 1: Inferno*

Defoe, *Robinson Crusoe*

DeLillo, *White Noise*

Dickens, *Great Expectations*

Dickens, *Hard Times*

Dos Passos, *Three Soldiers*

Douglass, *Narrative of the Life of Frederick Douglass*

Du Bois, *The Souls of Black Folk*

Franklin, *Benjamin Franklin: The Autobiography & Other Writings*

Gantz, *Early Irish Myths & Sagas*

Golding, *Lord of the Flies*

Grahame, *The Wind in the Willows*

Guthrie, *Bound For Glory*

Hansberry, *A Raisin in the Sun*

Hardy, *Jude the Obscure*

Hawthorne, *The Scarlet Letter*

Homer, *The Iliad*

Homer, *The Odyssey*

Hulme, *The Bone People*

Karr, *The Liar's Club*

Kerouac, *On the Road*

Kesey, *One Flew over the Cuckoo's Nest*

S. King, *Misery*

M.L. King Jr., *Why We Can't Wait*

Lavin, *In a Cafe*

Lewis, *Babbit*

Machiavelli, *The Prince*

Markandaya, *Nectar in a Sieve*

Marquez, *Love in the Time of Cholera*

Marx, *The Communist Manifesto*

Mcbride, *The Color of Water*

McGinniss, *Selling of the President*

Miller, *Death of a Salesman*

Moliere, *Tartuffe and Other Plays*

Morrison, *Beloved*

Morrison, *Sula*

Morrison, *The Bluest Eyes*

Orwell, *1984*

Plato, *The Republic*

Plato, *The Last Days of Socrates*

Raybon, *My First White Friend*

Rose, *Lives on the Boundary*

Rose, *Possible Lives*

Rushdie, *Midnight's Children*

Sanders, *The Epic of Gilgamesh*

Shakespeare, *Four Great Comedies*

Shakespeare, *Four Great Tragedies*

Shakespeare, *Four Histories*

Shakespeare, *Hamlet*

Shakespeare, *King Lear*

Shakespeare, *MacBeth*

Shakespeare, *The Merchant of Venice*

Shakespeare, *Othello*

Shakespeare, *The Taming of the Shrew*

Shakespeare, *Twelfth Night*

Shelley, *Frankenstein*

Silko, *Ceremony*

Sinclair, *The Jungle*

Slocum, *Sailing Alone Around the World*

Solzhenitsyn, *One Day in the Life of Ivan Denisovich*

Sophocles, *Three Theban Plays*

Spence, *Death of Woman Wang*

Steinbeck, *The Grapes of Wrath*

Steinbeck, *Of Mice and Men*

Steinbeck, *The Pearl*

Stevenson, *Dr. Jekyll and Mr. Hyde*

Stowe, *Uncle Tom's Cabin*

Swift, *Gulliver's Travels*

Twain, *The Adventures of Huckleberry Fin*

Voltaire, *Candide, Zadig & Selected Stories*

Wharton, *Ethan Frome*

Williams, *Eyes on the Prize*

Wilson, *Fences*

Wilson, *Joe Turner's Come and Gone*

Woolf, *Jacob's Room*